The
Hundred
Million Dollar
Lunch

STERLING QUINLAN

The Hundred Million Dollar Lunch

J. PHILIP O'HARA, INC. CHICAGO

J. Philip O'Hara, Inc. 20 East Huron, Chicago 60611.
Published simultaneously in Canada by Van Nostrand
Reinhold Ltd., Scarborough, Ontario.

LC Number: 73–20838
ISBN: 0–87955–310–3
First Printing: D

for David, Terry and Tom

Contents

Preface

This book represents a blend of the new and the old journalism. Quotations from the twenty-five-year-old record are accurate and taken verbatim. Elsewhere, where quotations are needed to reflect the attitude of principals, I have used the freer form of the new journalism to portray as accurately as I can the truth about persons and situations. Likewise, I have taken the liberty of expressing thoughts and reflections of principal characters during moments of crisis and stress. Chapter seven, for instance, is entirely my own hypothesis of how that fateful meeting went (commissioners are notoriously shy about disclosing how their momentuous deliberations are carried out). Chapter seven was written after extensive interviews and discussions with principals. In terms of substance, I believe it to be accurate. It will be interesting to see if any of the principals have comments to make on chapter seven.

This book could not have been written without the generous cooperation of many individuals. I won't attempt to name them. They include some commissioners who were involved, and some who were not; ex-chairmen of the FCC who were involved, and who were not; numerous FCC staff personnel; legal counsel for both sides; principals of both sides; editors and reporters for industry trade magazines; college professors and broadcast executives; and average citizens of Boston whom I called on the phone at random. The list of those who deserve the author's gratitude extends into the hundreds. *They know who they are.* To all, my profound thanks.

While it is hoped that this book will be "must" reading for future broadcasters and communication lawyers, I have eliminated the usual procedure of peppering every page with footnotes, believing that this not only would serve the cause of tedium, but might slow the reader to a permanent halt.

There is one interesting by-product of this book that I think is worth mentioning. In addition to many private, off-the-record interviews, there were many that were on the record—more explicitly, on tape.

These tapes, some thirty hours of them, are being donated to Boston University where they will be codified, shortened to some reasonable length, and made available to students of that school who may wish to take a vicarious journey with me through the difficult, but rewarding, task of writing this book. In addition, all pertinent working notes and the original manuscript will reside in that school's library.

Chicago, February 1974

Prologue

How do you lose a VHF television license in the nation's fifth largest television market, Boston? How do you eliminate one of that city's four major newspapers, the Boston *Herald Traveler?*

How do you blow one hundred million dollars? Two thousand jobs? Sixty million in stockholders profits?

It isn't easy. That much can be said for certain.

It takes lots of luck, most of it bad.

It takes seventeen years of legal wrangling and two million dollars (at least) in legal expenses.

It takes a pixilated course by one of the six major regulatory bodies of the federal government, the Federal Communications Commission. It also takes the cooperation of the U.S. Court of Appeals and the Supreme Court of the United States.

Not to mention the friendly assistance of the Department of Justice and the Federal Bureau of Investigation.

If you mix all these ingredients and shake well, being sure to add plenty of juicy issues, including the one of ex parte contact between a principal and a former chairman of the FCC—an issue which, like Hamlet's ghost, simply would not go away—and if you season well with spices of innuendo and slander, cook just right (timing always being important), and if you fight valiantly, even desperately, then lo! presto! You can bring it off! You, too, can experience the heartbreak and loss incurred by a flick of a switch at three o'clock in the morning on March 19, 1972. You, too, can witness the death of a television station. A loss that involved:

- The longest regulatory case in the history of the United States.
- One hundred million dollars.
- Loss of a 125-year-old newspaper, reducing the number of sources of news and opinion in Boston from four to three, and eliminating the only Republican voice in heavily Democratic Boston.
- Several hundred petitions, briefs, filings and appearances at the FCC, the U.S. Court of Appeals and the Supreme Court.
- Fifty million words spoken; thirty million words written.
- One hundred and three thousand pages, reaching three stories high, and weighing 1,100 pounds.
- Four million dollars expense to all parties. One million expense to U.S. taxpayers.
- Reducing the value of some seven hundred television licenses in the United States by at least 10 percent, and in some cases as much as 40 percent.
- Directly influencing and helping to start a wave of "claim-jumping" of television licenses by minority groups, disaffected dissidents and outright opportunists.

Yes. All this can be done, and has been done in the famous Boston case involving the loss of WHDH-TV and the *Herald Traveler*.

You, too, can lose a television station. But it takes lots of hard work, many years of valiant struggle, and as was said at the beginning: lots of luck—most of it bad.

And it takes the most expensive lunch in history!

PART I

1947–1969

1

The
Whorehouse
Era

The story could begin almost anywhere—in 1947 when WHDH, Inc. first filed its application; or, in 1954 when Colonel James D. Cunningham began his comparative hearing after a seven-year delay caused by the FCC moratorium on granting further TV licenses; or, it could begin in 1956 when Hearing Examiner Cunningham ruled for Greater Boston Television Corp., *not* WHDH; or, it could begin in April of 1957 when the Commission *overruled* Cunningham and awarded Channel 5 in Boston to WHDH.

It matters not where you begin this *incredible* case which spans twenty-five years. Wherever one begins, one finds the course totally consistent: that is, totally zigzag, loaded with inconsistencies and replete with ironies.

Doughty old Colonel Cunningham was shocked at the Commission's reversal of his decision in favor of Greater Boston. He had ruled out WHDH, Inc. almost entirely on the grounds of diversification, because it was owned by the Boston Herald Traveler Corporation, publisher of two of Boston's six daily papers. Giving it the Channel, he said, would be to concentrate in the same hands no fewer than five "instrumentalities for the dissemination of news and views within the same area." In addition, the record showed, the Herald Traveler Corporation, a few years earlier, had violated the Sherman Antitrust Act when it permitted combinations of advertising in its newspaper and on its radio station. "There is a policy of mutual promotion," Cunningham said, "between the two papers and station WHDH, its primary purpose being to promote the *Herald* and *Traveler* papers."

Of all places one could begin, perhaps the best place is on a warm spring day in April of 1958 when a certain newsmaking committee of Congress was having another of its field days, pouring out the gossipy kind of charges, allegations and innuendo that were, indeed, making front pages that year in most of the nation's metropolitan newspapers.

This was called the House Subcommittee on Legislative Oversight. Its target was the major regulatory agencies of the U.S. government in Ike's administration. And it was spawned by none less than Speaker of the House, Sam Rayburn.

Its particular, most favored, and most vulnerable target was the Federal Communications Commission—the same Commission that, months before, had finessed Colonel Cunningham by giving Channel 5 to the *Herald Traveler* instead of Cunningham's choice, Greater Boston Telecasters. For this, and many other reasons, the subcommittee had good reason to zero in on the FCC.

As one famous lawyer, and former chairman of the Commission, put it: "Let's face it. This was the 'Whorehouse Era' of the Commission. When matters were *arranged*, not adjudicated."

And, as a current commissioner recently expressed it: "This was the era when the Commission lost its virginity, and liked it so much, it turned pro!"

An exaggeration; nevertheless, it conveys the present attitude toward those in high places on the Commission at the time. It was a bizarre, unsavory era marked by quiz program scandals; payola at many levels; freewheeling trips; gifts; double, and sometimes triple, expense accounts; and ex parte contacts.

The Commission has become relatively chaste again. Staffers who remember, feel expiated, and are willing to talk freely, and with some humor, about the period. There is only *one* commissioner remaining from that era. He is Robert E. Lee and he came through the scandals unscathed. Disagreed with, yes. Propositioned, certainly. But his record remained unblemished along with that of a number of other men of calibre such as commissioners: Cox, Bartley, Hyde, Craven, Ford, Cross and others.

"It was like a race track up here," one of them said. "Guys running up and down the hall, barging into offices trying to find another arm to twist." The commissioners and bureau chiefs were often bemused, vexed and sometimes outraged by the swirling forces of political conflict (almost frontier style); by brazen attempts at ex parte communication; and blatant "offers." But the good ones managed to stay clean, perhaps because of some quirk of nature, or character, that would have made them lousy "accommodators."

Others were not so fortunate.

WHDH-TV wasted no time going on the air, once it got the Commission's okay. Eight months after getting the green light on April 24, 1957, Channel 5 signed on with the call letters: WHDH-TV; owned and operated by the Boston Herald Traveler Corporation. There was only one desperate, last-chance appeal hanging over their heads—this being the final appeal by the three losers; Greater Boston Television, Inc., Massachusetts Bay Telecasters, Inc. and Allen B. DuMont to be filed with District of Columbia, U.S. Circuit Court of Appeals. No one gave the appeals the slightest chance of succeeding.

Early in 1958, however, after WHDH-TV had already signed on the air, the Legislative Oversight Committee began functioning. After an abortive start against the Civil Aeronautics Bureau, Chief Counsel Bernard Schwartz began striking paydirt. Schwartz was a brilliant, but ineffectual-looking man, an academician with five degrees, two of which were doctorates. Oren Harris and the eleven committee members of both parties had picked him because they thought he was "safe." Schwartz quickly proved to be far from "safe."

He hit the FCC where it was most vulnerable: Richard Mack. Mack was a commissioner, unfortunately. He was a political hack from Miami, a heavy drinker, a lightweight thinker, and a lackey of a slick lawyer and political fixer named Thurman A. Whiteside. In far shorter time than the subcommittee could figure out a way to get rid of troublemaker Schwartz, the academician had nailed Commissioner Richard Mack to the cross. Evidence was developed to prove that Mack had been working long and hard to put Channel 10, Miami, in the hands of National Airlines. His close friend, Whiteside, was on retainer for the airline, so the logical first thing Whiteside did was to get Mack to "pledge" his vote in the stormy comparative hearing involving Channel 10. In return, Thurman Whiteside showed proper appreciation. He gave Mack: 1) $2,650; 2) one-sixth interest in a Miami insurance firm that sold some twenty thousand dollars worth of insurance to the winner of Channel 10 (you guessed it, National Airlines)— and from this stock Mack received ten thousand dollars; 3) all the stock in a loan company which netted him several more thousands; 4) other gifts, "advances" and payments too numerous to mention, including the assumption of a mortgage on a building.

It was during this hearing that an inadvertent reference to Boston was made. From no less an authority than the often-fed, ex-chairman of the FCC, George C. McConnaughey. The date was April 2, 1958. McConnaughey was being asked questions about ex parte attempts on the part of individuals in the Miami Channel 10 case. Committee counsel asked if he remembered ever having had offers of lunch from Robert B. Choate of the Herald Traveler Corporation in Boston.

McConnaughey admitted that he had. "Mr. Choate asked to have lunch with me."

"Did you?"

"As a matter of fact, I did."

"What was the purpose of that lunch?"

"As I recall, Mr. Choate merely wanted to meet me."

"About what?"

"Nothing much, really. We met and talked about various things. He did not say anything about his application except to say that his group had an application pending, and that they were very capable people and he just wanted to tell me that. That's all."

That was enough. The item got only modest coverage in the nation's press except in the *Boston Globe* which gave it heavy play. The lack of national coverage was understandable, for Boston wasn't the target of Bernard Schwartz and his investigating staff. Not yet. He had Boston on his calendar for later, along with sixteen other television cases that smacked of scandal. However, Schwartz was mousetrapped and fired before he could go that far. So, for the present, Richard Mack was the subcommittee's prime target. John Doerfer would come later.

On July 31, a hot, humid day in 1958, the U.S. Court of Appeals acted. It took cognizance of those chance remarks made by McConnaughey in the legislative oversight hearings three months earlier. It did more than that. It dropped a bombshell on WHDH-TV by remanding the *entire* proceedings to the FCC with instructions to look into the matter. The court said, in effect: we want an evidentiary hearing into these allegations of ex parte contacts with Commissioner McConnaughey and/or others on the Commission, or staff. All parties are entitled to participate. And for good measure, we will permit the attorney general to participate as amicus curae, "friend of the court." It also means that the long arm of the Department of Justice—the FBI—is entitled to take an interest in the proceedings if asked.

The Commission, with John Doerfer as chairman, did a fast shuffle. It took only a scant six months to react. On December 4, 1958 it did what it had no other choice but do: ordered the Boston record reopened and invited all parties to help the Commission decide if there had, indeed, been more hanky-panky than usual. The issues to be decided were: 1) Should any member of the Commission, who voted in favor of WHDH, have disqualified himself? 2) Did anyone try to influence the Commission? 3) Did anyone at *any* level know, aid, abet, secure or ratify any hanky-panky? 4) Was the grant of WHDH-TV over Greater Boston TV void *ab initio,* "at the start"; or was the grant voidable, and should action be taken to set it aside? Also, were any of the other applicants beyond the pale of the kind of scrupulous rules of conduct that were supposed to apply—the lack of which had helped create the Legislative Oversight Subcommittee in the first place.

All parties showed up. WHDH-TV reluctantly. Greater Boston and Massachusetts Bay Telecasters had no choice since they were parties to the original hearing. The *Boston Globe* newspaper, which was not a party, but which had filed a blockbuster of a petition in a desperate effort to head off the *Herald Traveler,* was permitted to participate on Issue 1 of the four issues to be heard by Special Hearing Examiner Horace Stern. Issue 1 dealt with the matter of whether any commissioner, or commissioners, should have disqualified himself in the original vote favoring WHDH; the vote that was cast by Chairman McConnaughey, and Commissioners Lee, Mack and Doerfer.

From the beginning, it became clear that Chairman McConnaughey was going to be the star witness of the eight-day drama in the cold, stark Commission hearing room. Now he was *Ex-*Chairman McConnaughey, for he had resigned somewhat unexpectedly eighteen months before, and was back in his home state of Ohio doing a thriving law business.

The other star witness was the imperious, proud president of the Herald Traveler Corporation and president of WHDH, Inc., Mr. Robert B. Choate. A member of one of Boston's famous families which had founded Choate School, and who was known by his close friends as "Beanie."

At the hearing all the major participants were conspicuous for their rather poor memories and conflicting testimony. Yes, they admitted, there had been a couple of luncheons between McConnaughey and Choate.

"I remember only one," said McConnaughey. "At the Statler or Mayflower Hotel. I can't remember which."

"No, it was two luncheons," corrected Choate. "The first one was in late '54, or was it '55? Our mutual friend, Charley Mills was with us."

"I don't remember the first luncheon," said McConnaughey.

Choate refreshed McConnaughey's memory. "The first one was at the Raleigh or Willard Hotel. I don't remember which. Our second luncheon wasn't at the Mayflower. It was at the Statler. And it occurred about April of 1956. Charley Mills was with us that time, too."

"Anyone else?" asked Examiner Stern.

"Yes sir. Tom Joyce."

"Who is he?"

"Thomas M. Joyce, a lawyer for our company. But he wasn't present in any legal capacity."

"I shouldn't think so," Stern commented.

After the dates and locations were finally established, Stern got into the more important matter of who said what to whom.

Neither Choate nor McConnaughey could remember much of what was said.

"He was obviously trying to size me up," explained McConnaughey. "And, letting me size him up. Everyone tries to impress the chairman of the FCC."

"Mutual friend," Charles F. Mills had a somewhat better memory. The first meeting, he said, was indeed at the Raleigh, and the conversation was general . . . of a social nature. He did recall that Choate asked about FCC procedures; how long Colonel Cunningham would take to reach his decision; and what would the procedure be afterwards.

Regarding the second meeting (which Mills again thoughtfully arranged), Mills recalled that he heard Choate say something about Cunningham having already reached his decision, and that it was negative against the *Herald Traveler;* so now, what was the procedure to follow? Could the matter be reviewed, and if so, by whom?

Choate and McConnaughey remembered nothing about this, prompting Mills to add quickly that, well, he wasn't really *that* interested in the conversation; he had just come along for a friendly meal and wasn't that interested in what was being said.

Examiner Horace Stern found nothing wrong with this. Judges, he said, were frequently consulted on procedural matters. Such conversations were distinctly not of an ex parte nature.

Choate, Mills and Joyce remembered much more about the second luncheon. That was the time, they said, that they brought with them an amendment to a bill they wanted to get passed. A very important bill to newspapers everywhere in America.

"We called it the Dempsey Amendment to the Harris-Beamer bills," explained Choate. "Senator Jack Kennedy introduced it for us to the House Subcommittee and he likes it. If you read it we think you'll like it, too."

The Harris-Beamer bills threatened to hurt newspapers in the "diversification" issue which was raging then, as it has ever since, in the Commission's list of criteria for deciding comparative contests for TV licenses. There were some "myopic" souls within the Commission (as there are still) who felt that a concentration of media in the hands of a few was not necessarily in the "public interest, convenience or necessity." The newspaper industry was vocally fighting the Harris-Beamer bills. The American Newspaper Publishers Association was lobbying effectively to have the bills killed. Robert B. Choate naturally wanted to do his part.

Ex-Chairman McConnaughey, however, turned a deaf ear. "I can't discuss that," he said curtly.

So the amendment wasn't discussed. They talked social chitchat and went their separate ways. One thing they had to admit about the chairman; he was an inexpensive date at lunch. He ate sparingly but drank good scotch. He was a skinny little man, weighing not more than 110 pounds, with a waffled, craggy, prune-wrinkled face and a wiry, short frame that made him look like the number one gnome in Santa's mafia. He was considered a staunch and loyal friend of AT&T, having procured for them several sizeable rate increases during his term.

Some time after this second lunch, Choate admitted that he had invited McConnaughey to go with him to a Washington gridiron dinner, but that the chairman had turned him down.

As the hearing continued it became clear that McConnaughey, and perhaps others, were indeed busy in those hectic days. Emissaries emerged frequently from Boston to plead their respective causes.

Dr. Allen B. DuMont hosted McConnaughey at the Raleigh Hotel. He too, as McConnaughey put it, "was trying to make a good impression on me because I was chairman; giving me to understand that he was a good fellow and a responsible citizen."

Forrester A. Clark, director and vice president of Massachusetts Bay Telecasters was also extremely busy during this period. He frankly admitted that he visited Henry Cabot Lodge, Senator Saltonstall, Sinclair Weeks, Robert Cutler, Leonard Hall, Representatives Bates and Curtis, urging them to take note of the furious political activity surrounding the Boston fight for Channel 5.

"All we ask is that you remain neutral," he pleaded.

Robert Cutler showed one of Clark's memos to Sherman Adams who promptly called Rosel Hyde and assured him that neither Ike, nor the White House, had any interest in, or intentions of interfering in, the Boston TV struggle.

Clark left no doors unopened. In February of 1956 he, too, had McConnaughey to lunch, privately, in his rooms at the Mayflower Hotel and told him how worried his people were about getting a fair deal. He pointed out the non-partisan makeup of his group, which included such distinguished stockholders as Arthur Fiedler, Dominick DiMaggio and John P. Marquand. He urged McConnaughey to read the Massachuetts Bay brief.

Examiner Stern later commented rather wryly that Clark probably shouldn't have done that. That came close to ex parte conduct. "He may have stepped somewhat out of bounds in the presentation he made to McConnaughey on the merits of his associates," said Stern, in what can only be regarded as a masterpiece of understatement.

The *Boston Globe*, however, was even *more* energetic in its efforts to dissuade anyone and everyone from awarding a powerful VHF TV license to a competitor. To them, this was tantamount to putting them out of business.

Even before the Commission reversed Colonel Cunningham's decision, *Globe* executives heard rumblings that this was likely to happen (few secrets are kept in Washington). So, Messrs. William Davis Taylor, president of the *Globe* and publisher of the paper, and John S. Taylor, vice-president, treasurer and director, rushed to the ramparts in the nation's capital to put on a blitzkreig protest before Senators Saltonstall and John Kennedy; Congressmen Martin and McCormack; Max Rabb; Senators Payne and Bridges; Sinclair Weeks; and Vice President Nixon's secretary. They phoned Sherman Adams and wrote to President Eisenhower telling them of the evils of newspaper ownership of a VHF station in Boston, and what it would do to the *Globe*. Sherman Adams, then wearing the fine vicuna coat Bernard Goldfine had given him (although the world did not know that as yet), assured the Taylors that there was really nothing he could do. The White House simply did not make a practice of interfering with its regulatory agencies.

Ike's special counsel, Gerald D. Morgan, replied in the same vein.

Undeterred, because they had no application pending and were not in danger of being considered ex parte, the Taylors cabbed it over to the grim post office mausoleum where the FCC occupied several floors, and before the sun set on the next day, they had seen all seven of the commissioners: McConnaughey, Bartley, Lee, Craven, Mack, Doerfer and Hyde.

When this brought no results, or so it seemed, Messrs. Taylor and Taylor filed their blockbuster petition with the Commission a few weeks before McConnaughey and his quorum of Doerfer, Lee and Mack had reversed Cunningham.

Scarcely a month after Cunningham had been overruled, the *Globe* filed its lengthy petition with supporting affidavits giving three reasons why the *Herald Traveler* should never be permitted to own a TV station in Boston. They raised the spectre of antitrust:

1) The *Herald Traveler* was using its AM station in a manner that gave it unfair competitive advantage over the *Globe;* hence it was reasonable to assume that it would use a TV station in the same manner. 2) It had uttered threats about driving the *Globe* out of business. 3) It had attempted to upset loan agreements of the *Globe* made for the purpose of erecting a new plant—all this in order to force a merger between the two companies, thereby eliminating the *Globe's* competition.

The general counsel for the FCC, upon receiving copies of these strong complaints, became fearful that this possibly involved a violation of the Sherman Antitrust Act in the communications field. So he sent copies to the antitrust division of the Department of Justice. In no time at all the FBI was scurrying around, tapping phones of Choate and all of his first level executives, in one of its common "special" investigations.

After this there was some communication between McConnaughey and then chief of the antitrust division, Victor R. Hansen, about the status of the *Globe's* complaint—exchanges which, the *Globe* claimed, should have been made part of the record and that all parties, including themselves, should have been notified. Therefore, for these, and several other ambiguous reasons, the *Globe* pleaded that, in accordance with Issue 1 of the ex parte hearing, Chairman McConnaughey should have disqualified himself from voting in the Boston decision.

Examiner Horace Stern did not see it that way. After hearing all the testimony, he found *no* reason why McConnaughey should have disqualified himself. He further found no evidence of real, nitty gritty ex parte conduct between McConnaughey and Choate; or McConnaughey and any of the others of the frantic "persuaders" who were continually badgering him. Horace Stern, later, was to hear four other similar cases involving ex parte conduct in comparative hearings and he found *all* of them guilty in one degree or another. In this case, however, he ruled: *No one* was guilty of indiscretion, impropriety, misconduct or illegality.

The award of Channel 5 to the *Herald Traveler* remained pristine and deserving. The license was neither void *ab initio,* nor "voidable" because of the facts presented.

On September 23, 1959 he released his decision. Now everyone could go home. Robert B. Choate could go back to Boston and worry about the fight with the *Boston Globe.* McConnaughey could return to his law practice in Ohio. Greater Boston TV and Massachusetts Bay could pay their legal bills and chalk this one up to experience. And the busy Taylors, William and John, could go back to the *Boston Globe* and prepare for some stiff competition.

As far as everyone was concerned the case was closed. Certainly in some quarters there were sighs of relief. That "goddam Legislative Oversight Committee" had shaken the bushes quite enough. It was time to get back to normal and make some money.

There was, though, one darkling cloud on the horizon, which none of the parties knew about. In July of that year, after Horace Stern had closed his record in the special hearing, but before he released his decision, the attorney general none other than William P. Rogers, later of President Nixon's cabinet, but now trusty amicus curiae, filed a certain brief for the United States with the Federal Communications Commission.

It was a brief that was to cause the general counsel of the Commission to shudder, not to mention Chairman John Doerfer and his six nervous colleagues.

2

Attorney General: No! Newton Minow Agrees

The attorney general's brief for the United States wasted no time getting to the point. Under a section called "conclusions of law," it stated:

"The facts of record suggest that Robert Choate, president of WHDH, went beyond the 'recognized and public processes of adjudication' on behalf of his application:

"First, as Choate testified, after the necessity for a comparative hearing became clear, 'I got Senator Saltonstall to write the then chairman of the Commission.' Choate's purpose in writing Senator Saltonstall was to have him question the 'impartiality' of the Commission's treatment of newspaper applicants because the Commission, 'had, in fact . . . decided . . . ten out of twelve comparative newspaper cases against the newspaper on the diversification . . . factor.' Though *The Boston Post* had filed an application on April 6, 1954, Choate's letter of June 1954, to Senator Saltonstall stated simply, 'As you know, we are an applicant for Channel 5' and bluntly asked the senator to 'put the Commission on record' on this issue. Choate's letter was calculated to result, as in fact it did, in a senatorial letter unbeknownst, as far as the record shows, to any other applicant, and certainly not included in the comparative hearing record. . .

"Second, as Mr. Mills best recollects, Choate sought a luncheon meeting with McConnaughey, shortly after the latter's appointment. Choate's purpose, as McConnaughey concluded, was to 'make a good impression, to put (his) best foot forward and let me know what responsible, capable people they were.'

"By Choate's second luncheon with McConnaughey, however, Choate's purpose had become more concrete. The examiner's decision against WHDH on diversification grounds, had come down. Appeal was pending before the Commission. So it was that Choate took with him, to give to McConnaughey, a comprehensive memorandum prepared by Choate's lawyer, arguing reasons why 'the criterion of diversification as it is applied by the Commission has no place in the Commission's decisional process.' That memorandum, in practical coverage, stated every argument WHDH deemed worthy of advancing against the examiner's holding on the diversification issue. It was that memorandum, in Choate's words, that sketches 'a fair and accurate picture of the purpose of the meeting.' And this 'purpose' becomes crucial since, as Choate put it, 'I certainly was scared that I might lose' the award on diversification grounds.

"This context compels the conclusion that Choate, as WHDH's president, '. . . attempted to influence' the Commission with respect to the proceedings in a 'manner' beyond the 'recognized and public processes of adjudication.' WHDH sought senatorial aid, and tried via off-the-record meetings with McConnaughey, to 'influence' the Commission on a prime issue in the proceeding. And even McConnaughey, who in his own words, 'kept an open door' and 'would talk to anybody . . . ,' felt it necessary, as Choate put it, to 'turn me off.' "

Next the attorney general turned his talents to the matter of Forrester Clark and his ex parte efforts on behalf of Massachusetts Bay Telecasters:

"Much the same goes for Forrester Clark's efforts on behalf of MBT. At his private luncheon with McConnaughey, Clark did not limit himself to an oblique plea for fairness and a decision of the case on its merits apart from political pressures (a type of plea which should be made openly, if at all, and not in private conversation). Instead, Mr. Clark devoted some time to a discussion of the positive qualifications of MBT to secure a television license and operate in the public interest.

"Both WHDH and MBT, then, sought 'to influence' the Commission's consideration of this matter in a 'manner' at odds with the 'recognized and public processes of adjudication.' Off-the-record efforts on key issues—either character or diversification—cannot be deemed in accord with such 'processes.'

"Both WHDH and MBT should be disqualified. The time honored rule is that 'From the moment that . . . (an applicant) ceases to depend upon the justice of his case and seeks discriminatory and favored treatment . . . (he) is fortunate if he loses no more than the rights he seeks to obtain.' These two applicants ceased 'to depend upon the merits of' their cases and sought 'discriminatory and favored treatment' by attempting to influence the Commission in a manner other than 'the recognized and public processes of adjudication.' "

With that, the brief ended with the stark conclusion, "Thus, the public interest compels the disqualification of WHDH and MBT. Both 'attempted to influence' a commissioner in a 'manner' at odds with the 'recognized and public processes of adjudication.' Accordingly, the award of Boston Channel 5 to WHDH must be set aside as 'void *ab initio.*' And this comparative proceeding should be reopened."

The brief was "respectfully submitted" by William P. Rogers.

The inner sanctum at the Commission felt the shock waves rolling over them. Not in years had they received such a strong filing on behalf of the people of the United States. It was made that much more forceful because it was so at odds with Special Hearing Examiner Horace Stern's benign conclusions which totally vindicated Robert Choate, and only mildly slapped Massachusetts Bay on the wrist for the activities of Forrester Clark. It was almost as if the Department of Justice, and Examiner Stern, had heard two entirely different cases!

And of course the action put the Commission squarely in the middle—especially new Chairman John C. Doerfer. And the middle was a position Doerfer did not relish, for he was *already* in the middle as a result of the disclosure of some of his "peccadilloes" by energetic Bernard Schwartz and his ubiquitous Legislative Oversight Committee. These disclosures became so juicy that Chairman Doerfer was relieved of *any* responsibility for recommending a decision on the Boston case. President Eisenhower, before he left office in the final year of his term in 1960, requested Doerfer's resignation, which was promptly given.

As soon as John F. Kennedy took office he appointed Newton N. Minow as chairman of the FCC. Minow had no ties with the industry. He was a fast-rising, brilliant young lawyer from Chicago and the president had instructed him, along with others of the regulatory commissions, to get in there and do what they were supposed to do; *Regulate! Activate!*

As Minow later said, "It didn't take a genius to size things up." He was, to put it mildly, disenchanted. The scandal surrounding John Doerfer had not been as bad as that involving Richard Mack; but it seemed worse because he had the eminent position of chairman of the Commission.

Chairman Doerfer's problem was that he liked to take trips. An affable fellow who wanted to be liked (and was), Doerfer traveled to many cities as the guest of this broadcasting company or that; when he returned home he would receive in the mail a check from the particular host broadcasting company covering his expenses; but in addition, Doerfer always put in his *own* expense account which the government paid. In one situation, on a swing to the West Coast, as a guest of two broadcast companies and the National Association of Broadcasters, Chairman Doerfer was paid *three times* for the same expenses. Doerfer came up with details of "honorariums" covering twelve trips, amounting to two thousand dollars. He also admitted to a long, restful week on George Storer's yacht on a trip from Miami to Bimini. Some people thought this a bit odd, in view of the fact that the Storer Broadcast group had a case pending before the FCC.

An ironic twist to the Doerfer hearing is the fact that, as a result of it, Bernard Schwartz was fired as chief counsel of the Legislative Oversight Committee. He had been too diligent in his job. Disclosure of Doerfer's "peccadilloes" made the Committee members, and other congressmen, decidedly nervous. They, too, were making trips at government expense (just as they are doing today); and they, too, were accepting "honorariums," either outright, or in the form of campaign contributions. Oren Harris, chairman of the House Committee on Interstate and Foreign Commerce (of which legislative oversight was a subcommittee), had refreshed himself with a long trip from the North Pole to the South Pole. But that was nothing compared to the daring he flashed when he cut himself in for 25 percent of a radio station in Eldorado, Arkansas; a station that was seeking authority for more power from the FCC so it could, in turn, arrange better financing. He paid only five hundred dollars in cash for his 25 percent interest in KRBB and signed a promissory note for $4500. As soon as Harris got his piece of the station, the Commission approved the increase in power; immediately after that, a bank extended a line of credit for $400,000 and RCA added its own line of credit for equipment in the amount of $200,000.

Somehow, this story got "leaked" to the press. Some say Bernard Schwartz did it. No matter. The heat in the daily press was so intense that Congressman Harris, chairman of the most powerful committee in Congress, had to sell his interest in KRBB.

But Schwartz' days were numbered. Even doughty old Sam Rayburn, who spawned the Legislative Oversight Committee, grew restive. What was this committee up to, he wanted to know? Was it trying to be one of those "runaway committees"? And why was it "fly specking" all this expense account nonsense?

Bernard Schwartz was fired from the Legislative Oversight Committee by a seven-to-four vote a few days after the Doerfer hearings concluded. Morgan Moulder, chairman of the committee, was so incensed that he resigned also. But before he left, Schwartz led the committee onto the trail of the famous Sherman Adams—Bernard Goldfine influence-peddling scandal, not to mention numerous other TV cases that were in various stages of on-going investigation. He had by now a list of seventeen TV cases that were worthy of being looked into. Six of them seemed particularly kinky, involving comparative hearings. Some sixty TV cases had been decided in the last few years in the closing phase of the initial "grab" for valuable VHF franchises. There was a disturbing (to Schwartz) inconsistency on the part of the Commission in its decisions; often it seemed to favor concentration of ownership and control. And for those naïve enough to think that politics was not a factor, Schwartz had evidence that at least eight outspokenly Republican papers had won TV licenses and ten Democratic papers had been denied. No Republican paper *lost* a comparative TV hearing except in cases where there were two powerful Republican interests. Then, of course, one of them had to lose. No important paper, according to Schwartz, that had supported Adlai Stevenson, had *ever* won a comparative TV case.

Nevertheless, the faucet turned on by Bernard Schwartz could not easily be shut off. The furor created by the Legislative Oversight Committee was so great that, after his forced resignation, the committee could not be folded, or abandoned. The press, and the nation, were too interested. So, Oren Harris did the only astute political thing he could do: He *assumed* the chairmanship himself! After all, why turn away from a good press? Hang in there and keep a good thing going!

This, then, was the state of affairs at the Commission in 1961 when Newton Minow succeeded Frederick Ford as chairman. One can only imagine his astonishment when he learned that his colleagues, despite the attorney general's strong brief, had voted to let WHDH-TV *retain* Boston's Channel 5! It did, however, ask the court of appeals to remand the case back to them. It asked that all parties be required to file new briefs and to appear again at a new oral hearing to state their qualifications. It scheduled such a hearing for October 16, 1961. While the Commission disagreed with Horace Stern, it did not go as far as Newton Minow would have gone. The Commission said that *both* the *Herald Traveler* and Massachusetts Bay had "sinned" by attempting to influence the Commission. But nevertheless, these activities did not represent "absolute" disqualification.

Minow would have opted for sterner measures, but he was certain that, when it came to the re-hearing, their actions would be more stringent. In the meantime, his disenchantment had been mounting. In April of 1961 he exorcised himself of some of his indignation by delivering his famous, stinging, "vast wasteland" rebuke to broadcasters at their annual establishment convention in Washington.

Only three parties moved forward in the new hearing. Allen B. DuMont dismissed its application for the obvious reason that it was woefully weak on the aspect of local ownership. The key elements among determinative criteria, without any precise mathematical formula as to weight, or priority, were:

- Local ownership
- Integration of ownership and management
- Past performance
- Broadcast experience
- Proposed programming and policies
- Diversification of control of media of mass communications

A year after the new hearing, giving plenty of time for the deliberative process, four of Chairman Minow's colleagues gave him a gift he found indeed hard to digest: Commissioners Hyde, Lee, Ford and Cross voted to grant WHDH-TV's license! But they did it in a strange way: they voted to grant the license for a *four-month period only!* This gave slight comfort to the *Herald Traveler*, for it gave them only a slightly better hold on the tenuous grip they already had, which was no license at all; merely a special temporary authority to broadcast from day to day. But, in the view of some industry lawyers, at least it was a *valid* license. Some FCC parliamentarians said that, having survived these two fierce onslaughts by the Commission, they now would hold the channel forever. As one of them put it, "The Commission spanks, but never hurts."

Newton Minow's indignation turned to downright disgust. Matters had not improved noticeably in the scandal-ridden broadcast industry. The Legislative Oversight Committee, with Oren Harris in charge, was still going full blast. Richard Mack had long since resigned and was involved in a federal conspiracy suit along with his buddy, Thurman Whiteside. That trial ended in a hung jury, but the careers of both men were ruined beyond repair. Whiteside later committed suicide and Mack died penniless of acute alcoholism. Charles Van Doren confessed that he had been cheating in the quiz program *Twenty-One*. Evidence of other payola was uncovered, both on the air with disc jockeys and with other quiz programs, as well as behind the scenes in the TV license scramble. Evidence of off-record efforts to influence Commission votes had now been uncovered in at least six more TV cases. Trafficking in valuable franchises continued merrily on its way. It was a sad, grim time, as Minow remembers it, and his disgust clearly showed when he wrote his bitter dissent.

"I do not agree that the Commission serves the public interest with another award of Channel 5 in Boston to WHDH even though limiting the award to four months may serve some salutory purposes.

"In my view, there is serious question whether an award to any one of the present applicants can be said to be in the public interest.

"But in any event, there is no justification on this record for preferring WHDH, an applicant who has engaged in ex parte attempts to influence the Commission's decisional process over Greater Boston, the only present applicant who has not."

The majority vote in favor of a grant to WHDH-TV for a four-month period was based, as in the original decision in 1957, on the station's greater broadcast experience. And, in effect, the majority said, there was a demerit plague on all three applicants: Massachusetts Bay, for the activities of Forrester Clark; WHDH-TV, for Mr. Choate's activities; and in the case of Greater Boston, they revived a matter that had been aired extensively in the 1957 hearing concerning one, Michael Henry. Mr. Henry was to be the general manager of the station if its group won, but he committed the error of giving "false testimony" in connection with an episode in his past; an episode involving his having been disbarred from the practice of law in a southern state.

Mr. Minow wrote, "I would not deny the applications of Greater Boston and Massachusetts Bay. Neither would I grant the application of WHDH. I would reopen the record now to new or amended applications, and while they are being considered on an expedited basis, permit WHDH to continue broadcasting only as an interim trustee."

Calling attention to the profits WHDH-TV had made in its five years of broadcasting on merely a special temporary authority with no specified tenure of license, Minow wryly pointed out that, in 1961, the revenues of the three Boston commercial TV stations totaled slightly over twenty-one million, with gross profits before taxes of $9,650,000. Or, in terms of depreciated captial, "profits of 337 percent."

Minow went on to say, "While it has found 'no evidence of any ex parte contacts of any kind on the part of Greater Boston,' it now makes the critical finding that 'false testimony' by Greater Boston's proposed general manager, Mr. Henry, is equivalent to the misconduct of WHDH and Massachusetts Bay.

"Thus, one of the underlying premises of the majority's decision is that we are faced with three applicants who are all seriously lacking in character."

The chairman then took the majority to task for concluding that, since all three applicants were besmirched rather equally, the decision had to be made on "conventional criteria." In his opinion, Mr. Choate's "much greater importance" to WHDH required that the demerit assessed against WHDH be correspondingly greater.

"Clearly," he wrote, "Mr. Choate's demerit goes to the heart of the entire WHDH application, just because he himself is so important a figure in the application. Just as clearly, the same cannot be said of Mr. Henry and Greater Boston.

"In sum, the majority of opinion avoids any meaningful consideration of the misconduct found in the 1960 decision—and disregards it in reassessing the 1957 comparison."

Then Minow struck hard at the diversification issue. "The *Herald Traveler* papers accept advertising only upon a combined-rate basis, and time on WHDH has been sold in combination with space in the *Herald* and *Traveler*. WHDH enjoys special privileges in obtaining advertising and the printing of its logs in the *Herald Traveler* papers, and the newspapers enjoy reciprocal advantages through promotional announcements carried over the radio stations (AM and FM) without charge. Station personnel have been instructed to identify WHDH at station breaks as the *Herald Traveler* station, and news broadcasts are identified as 'Herald News' and 'Traveler News.' Mr. Choate testified 'that there is a policy of mutual promotion between the newspapers and the radio station, and that the programming of the television station will be adapted to the best possible promotion of the *Herald Traveler* where it is feasible to do so.' "

Minow then chided Commissioner Rosel Hyde for concluding, as far back as 1957, that the "public interest, convenience and necessity would be served best by selecting an applicant which would offer a higher degree of diversification."

Why talk about that, Minow asked. "Today's decision must be grounded on today's record" . . . and the record of WHDH "is seriously diminished by the conduct of Mr. Choate."

"For all of these reasons," Newton Minow concluded, "I am persuaded that the public interest is not well served by the action the Commission takes today. . . . So far as I am concerned, the existing temporary licensee will not enjoy a preferred position in any (further) proceeding."

Two commissioners absented themselves from this particular decision. They were Commissioners Robert Bartley and T.A.M. Craven. And two of the four commissioners who voted for the four-month renewal felt concerned enough about their vote to file statements to "explain" their position.

Commissioner Frederick W. Ford said, "It was with great reluctance that I originally disagreed with Judge Stern's initial decision in this case, in which he found 'not a shred of credible evidence' indicating culpable misconduct by Robert Choate of WHDH . . . Accordingly, I approved the Commission's decision of July 14, 1960, and the subsequent recommendation that the case be remanded."

Now Mr. Ford went on to explain that he had had a distinct change of heart. "I cannot conceive of an applicant of Mr. Choate's age, background and experience believing that two lunches and an invitation to a large banquet would establish a personal relationship with a commissioner which would influence his vote. As Judge Stern concluded, there is no evidence that this was the case, and it would take considerably more than the isolated contacts found in this record to support such an inference."

His conclusion: "I must conclude on a comparative basis that the conduct of Mr. Choate does not affect adversely the conclusion of the Commission in its 1957 decision that the grant of the application of WHDH would best serve the public interest, convenience and necessity."

Commissioner John S. Cross' concurring statement had some candor and a trace of wit. "I concur in the decision of the majority to award a four-month license to WHDH. I do so, however, mainly to finalize this case which has been pending for so long.

"By concurring in the majority opinion, I am admittedly making a Hobson's choice in favor of the least undesirable of the three demerited applicants . . . Moreover, it finalizes this long-standing proceeding."

To which many said, "Amen!" The Boston case was getting to be a thorn in everyone's side. The case simply would not go away; nor would it lend itself to a solution everyone could agree upon. But insiders claimed that the worst was now over for the Herald Traveler Corporation. There would be some waning, phasing-out flak, particularly to appease the likes of Newton Minow. There were even some words in the decision about starting an entire new proceeding for Channel 5. But insiders did not take this kind of talk seriously. WHDH-TV had weathered the storm and they should be grateful to get out with a whole skin.

Robert "Beanie" Choate was not grateful, however. He still nursed a deep and abiding anger at having his name and honor tarnished by all this nonsense. At one point he had grown so infuriated that he had charged down to Washington and barged in, unannounced, on the head of the Justice Department, demanding: "Indict me or exonerate me!"

The poor fellow behind the desk hadn't the slightest idea who Choate was, or what he was talking about.

Choate returned home to concentrate on supervising the station's application for a renewal of license which it had been told to file within a month.

And at the Commission, another zigzag was being prepared.

3

Longest Hearing on Record

The *Herald Traveler* wasted no time filing its renewal application —the first one in five years of operation. The station's four-month license period was to expire January 26, 1963; the renewal application was filed October 25, 1962.

The renewal, however, was never granted. Instead, in return for its promptness, WHDH-TV was hit with a lightning bolt; *New applicants were invited by the FCC to file applications in competition with WHDH-TV in what is called a comparative hearing!* This was the third such life-or-death contest for the embattled incumbent. The FCC indeed was embarked on a new zigzag course.

One year later, in October of 1963, after the inevitable appeals, and a generous "convenience period" for other applicants to prepare their filings, the Commission designated two new applicants with two of the old: WHDH-TV, of course; and Greater Boston TV Inc., which now called itself Greater Boston II.

Massachusetts Bay Telecasters decided it had had enough. The zealous efforts of Forrester Clark had given his group a substantial demerit. They no longer had the heart to continue the costly and seemingly interminable fight.

The two new applicants were: Charles River Civic Television

Inc., named after the Charles River in Boston; and Boston Broadcasters Incorporated.

Later that year, before the hearing could begin a cataclysmic event occurred; *Robert Choate died!*

The event, for the *Herald Traveler,* was remarkably fortuitous. Certainly now, with the proud, haughty, imperious Boston Brahmin out of the way, the issue of Choate's ex parte conduct would, they were convinced, be moot and irrelevant.

Poor Choate had fallen upon evil times after the ex parte affair. For one thing, he had lost his job as chief executive officer of the *Herald Traveler.* He was kicked upstairs as a result of some corporate hijinks that, later, were to receive considerable attention at the hearing. In the fall of 1963, Robert "Beanie" Choate became embroiled in a bitter policy dispute that, had it gone his way, might have *saved* the station. The *Herald* and *Traveler* newspapers (morning and evening) were losing money at a rate that had begun to alarm certain substantial stockholders who called this to Choate's attention. Choate conceded that it might indeed be sensible to sell off the papers if the proper price could be gotten. Word of his possible action leaked out. His number two man, George Akerson, solicited and obtained the support of other major stockholder groups who had sufficient votes to defeat Choate's course of action. He was immediately kicked upstairs to the post of chairman of the board, where he could repent for his sins.

In retrospect, the irony of this action—one of the dozens of ironies in the Boston case—was the fact that, had the Herald Traveler Corporation followed Choate's recommendation and divested itself of the papers, the all important diversification issue, that of multi-media ownership, would have been *removed* from the case. And it was this very issue that the Commission leaned so heavily on in its decision six years later!

Poor Choate could not seem to do anything right. Or, as someone observed, "Even when 'Beanie' was right, he was wrong."

Shortly after that, the old gentleman's health began to fail. Before he could become familiar with his new office in the back of the television station, he underwent an operation for detached retina of the eye. Then he took a vacation in Arizona to recover his strength. However, his health worsened. Four days before Christmas of 1963, Robert B. Choate breathed his last, a victim of a brain tumor. His few close friends knew that "Beanie" died of a broken heart. His dignity had been demeaned; his honor besmirched. His proud family name had been held up to ridicule without "just cause." For the fact of the matter was, Robert Choate had never been convicted of *anything*. He had *not* been indicted. He had been, his friends said, victimized by rumor and innuendo; slander and malice. When the body was lowered into the grave, his associates went through the mourning rituals; made all the proper condolences to his bitter widow; and secretly breathed a sigh of relief over the fact that the old gentleman's death now eliminated the haunting phantom issue of ex parte conduct. Now it no longer mattered *what* had been said at those two McConnaughey luncheons in Washington. Now it would cease to be an issue at the comparative hearing which all four applicants were so rigorously preparing for.

Indeed, WHDH-TV was not in the least perturbed when the court of appeals, which held jurisdiction of the case all this while, told the Commission to add the Choate matter as an issue. To wit: What effect, if any, did Choate's death have on WHDH-TV's standing?

And so, on June 27, 1964, the longest continuous hearing in American regulatory history began in the largest hearing room of the Commission in its drab quarters in the Post Office Building of Washington D.C.

It began under Hearing Examiner Herbert Sharfman who undoubtedly wondered why this dubious honor had befallen him. Hadn't he already done his bit by handling two other onerous cases, the Miami Channel 10 case and the Edward H. Lamb case? He wished his friend and colleague, Examiner David Kraushaar, who originally had been assigned the case, had not disqualified himself on a minor technicality.

Herb Sharfman was a mild-mannered, gentle intellectual, one of the best examiners in Commission history; a master of judicial prose whose decisions were already being read in law classes. But lately he was beginning to have doubts about the system. Wasn't there a better way than to go through these long, protracted hearings, followed by an extensive period required to write the decision, then an even longer period for oral argument before the Commission, followel by an even longer wait for the seven commissioners to vote; and after that usually came an appeal to the District of Columbia Circuit Court of Appeals. Who benefited in the end except the lawyers? Not that he begrudged counsel their fees. They were brilliant and hard working; they pretended to believe in the system also, although one sometimes overheard their cynical laughter at luncheon tables and in informal conversations. Lawyers knew they had a good thing and they zealously worked to keep the system as it was. Herb had written an article recently asking questions about the system; but he hadn't had the initiative, or was it courage, to submit the article. One day soon, he kept telling himself, he *would* submit it. The nagging question kept recurring: would that hurt his career? Open him to criticism. He had had plenty of that. Cautious, perhaps was a better word. Yes, one had to be circumspect in this hearing game. Assiduously, he had built a reputation as one of the best in the business. He knew that students and lawyers who practiced before the Commission read his decisions carefully. That was gratifying, to a degree. Yet, sometimes he felt nagging doubts and a certain sense of guilt about the meaningfulness of his work; especially now, as he faced a long, involved notoriety-filled hearing with four eager principals and four tough law firms; with issues that would be worried like a dog worries a bone. The character assassination! God, it was awful to hear the charges and counter charges. What had he said about that in his article?

"Since the stakes are high, FCC cases are strenuously litigated. Counsel miss few points and pull fewer punches. It is probable that an FCC comparative hearing is a better forum for hearing of one's forgotten peccadilloes than a political campaign."

Lawyers who practiced before the Commission were cruel and uncompromising. They would go to any lengths to find character defects in unsuspecting witnesses. He looked now at Benito Gaguine, the tough little Frenchman, who formerly had worked at the Commission. Now there was a bantam rooster. Indefatigable. He never gave up. An angry terrier. Benny represented Boston Broadcasters, a group he had not heard much about; except that they supposedly came loaded with "stars"; their pockets were lined with gold; and they had a list of academicians that was formidable.

WHDH-TV, of course, would stand on its record. And, why not, Sharfman thought. It had managed to survive for five long years, knowing that it was in trouble from the very first day on the air. Certainly WHDH-TV must have conscientiously built a record of which it was proud. And certainly, William Dempsey, their lawyer, would attempt to get the Choate ex parte matter stipulated out of contention. Sharfman saw nothing wrong with that. One couldn't help feeling sorry for Choate. Especially since his falling out with his own people last year. Herb thought about cruel events he had been forced to witness, be a part of, and adjudicate, in past hearings. In his heart he guessed he had always been something of a softie in terms of the human condition. Looking at Bill Dempsey now, and comparing him with Gaguine, he shuddered a little. Both were equally good, but with widely differing styles. Bill Dempsey was soft-spoken, understated, with a mind like a steel trap. He could shift gears several times in the midst of a single sentence. He would be a worthy match for diminutive Benito. Dempsey was a handsome, gray-haired fellow who was a qualified mathematician in addition to his skills as a lawyer.

Harry Plotkin, of course, he also knew well. Harry came from Harvard Law School and had spent several distinguished years on the Commission. He was as brilliant, in his way, as Dempsey and Gaguine were in theirs. Harry's thoughts came tumbling out so rapidly the court reporter sometimes could not keep up with them. Sharfman smiled as he recalled an incident when a reporter asked if Plotkin could speak slower. Irritated by the interruption in his trend of thought, he snapped back: "No, I can't!" Harry represented the second of the two new applicants, Charles River Civic TV: another gilt-edged applicant; well prepared; well rehearsed; well financed; and rumored to have, as a member of its group, one of the famous Cabot clan of Boston. Now, thought Sharfman, if BBI comes up with a member of the Lodge family, the setting will be complete!

J. Joseph Maloney, Jr., representing Greater Boston II, was a lawyer he did not know much about. Maloney was not a Washington lawyer, but a partner in a Boston firm. He would spend his time commuting between Washington and Boston. He wondered if Maloney was a bit out of his element. This was a special kind of jungle, this FCC arena. Nevertheless, Maloney had impressed him during the prehearing conference. He was a sanguine fellow, somewhat brash, befitting his Gaelic nature. Joe Maloney laughed a lot, perhaps because he was so confident. Greater Boston had almost won the license initially. In the original hearing, James Cunningham had found for Greater Boston, but then had been reversed by the Commission which gave the license to the *Herald Traveler*. Herb Sharfman felt a twinge as he wondered if the same thing would happen to him. Greater Boston had hung in all this time, at Lord knows how much expense! Now it had reorganized itself into Greater Boston II retaining most of its former principals, but washing out Michael Henry, the proposed general manager, who had earned his cause a demerit because he had been found "lacking in candor" in not revealing the fact that he once had been disbarred as a lawyer. Poor fellow, Herb mused. Where was Henry now? It was this kind of thing he disliked intensely about these hearings. He hoped there would be a minimum of character assassination this time around; but he doubted if his hope would come true.

While Sharfman was sizing up various counsel and initial witnesses, the others were sizing him up as well. All but Maloney knew him, either by virtue of the fact that they had appeared before him in previous hearings, or had known him during their own careers at the Commission.

Yet they didn't *really* know Herb Sharfman. No one really knew the man. He was an admitted loner. Nobody knew that he read Proust: or that he also read everything from "labels on catsup bottles to magazines like *Sports Illustrated*." He spoke and read seven languages. He liked television. He was an extrovert. He shot a good game of pool and played tournament-quality table tennis. In his youth he had almost upset the great Coleman Clark. Still, no one really *knew* him. Was he liked? Sharfman neither knew, nor cared. How can you like a man you don't really know? But, certainly, everyone admired and respected him. Lawyers studied his decisions because they were marvels of lucid logic and rhetoric sometimes so brilliant that readers marveled at them. A Sharfman decision was a pleasure to read because of its syntax; its phrase making; its literary allusions. But Sharfman in action was something else. He grinned a lot, but that was a facade. He spoke in a high-pitched voice that, incongruously, sounded a little like that of the great comedian, Ed Wynn. He was always equable, always under control. He often gave attorneys and witnesses the idea that they had made an impression on him. The "book" on Sharfman was that he was "a pretty slick article." "One falls into the trap of thinking that he has Sharfman figured out," one lawyer explained, "which is the first mistake you make. And you make that mistake rather early in the game. Later, after you are wiser, and perhaps sadder, you come to realize that neither you, nor anyone else, really has Herb Sharfman figured out."

Smiling at his "clan," as he called them, Hearing Examiner Sharfman took a deep, judicious breath and put on his best judicial manner: "Gentlemen," he began, "as was agreed upon in the pre-hearing conferences, we shall begin with each applicant in the order of docket number. WHDH-TV, first. Greater Boston II, second. Charles River, third. Boston Broadcasters will be fourth. Therefore we shall open with Mr. William Dempsey, of the firm of Dempsey and Koplovitz, representing WHDH-TV. Mr. Dempsey, I have not seen you in action for some time. It will be a pleasure to hear you again. You may proceed."

Bill Dempsey put in his case for WHDH-TV in his characteristic splendid fashion. What was that old saw, thought Sharfman, about a good lawyer being unable to make a good case if it was not in the wood; but a poor lawyer could *hurt* a good case. Here there were two positive factors at work. Dempsey was a great lawyer. And he had a good case to put in. WHDH-TV had a fine station, no question about that, in terms of the standards of commercial VHF stations at the time. It had an excellent news operation; the first in Boston to have an hour early-evening news show. It had an excellent, nightly series called *Dateline Boston*; an ample staff; good facilities; two helicopters for news and special-events coverage; four radio-equipped cruise cars; a standby generator; large studios; and sufficient quota of public service. The station did not editorialize, but that was no great sin in those days. Editorializing was commended by the Commission, but not really insisted on. Many of the large stations were cautious about this new freedom to editorialize. Paranoid perhaps about the trouble they could get into if they did, and not too worried about the fact that they didn't, even though the Commission encouraged it. Certainly WHDH-TV met well the important criteria of: broadcast experience; past broadcast record; proposed programing policies and programing staff and technical facilities. Only in diversification was the station weak—as it always had been due to its ownership by the *Herald Traveler*, which, with its two daily newspapers, its AM and FM radio stations, had something of a communication stranglehold on the Boston area. But then, Sharfman remembered, the Commission had explicitly stated that "lack of diversification" had *never* been considered to be "totally disqualifying."

So, on the clear-cut issues, like "experience," "programing and past record," WHDH-TV seemed to Sharfman to be exemplary. But there were other issues to be considered in the criteria check-off list that a hearing examiner must consider. Criteria that remained troublesome, pervasively vague, and undefined—criteria he had written about in his article. How about that article, he thought. Should he go ahead and submit it to, perhaps *Harpers,* or *Atlantic Monthly*? Chances are they wouldn't accept it. But, wasn't that a copout on his part? Shouldn't he at least *submit* it? He had labored long and hard over it. Like the paragraph that went;

". . . *the winner may be not the one who gives the most direct assurance of furnishing the best program service, but the one who has the preferred combination of mystical attributes subsumed under the following rubrics: local ownership; participation in civic activity; integration of ownership and management; diversity of business interests; broadcast experience; past broadcast record; proposed program policies and programing, including preparation for operation; proposed staff and technical facilities; diversity of the ownership of the media of mass communication; and character. Far from being merely the means by which the Commission tests the focal promise, they have acquired a kind of metonymical importance in themselves. The criteria have evolved and attained a sanctified status in Commission decisions . . . astonishingly, a good program service, the desideratum, is only one of the criteria, apparently of equal standing with the others."*

Joe Maloney next put in the case for GBII. Sharfman was somewhat puzzled. His seemed like a rather truncated case. They flattered WHDH-TV by imitation. They had no ascertainment surveys. GBII would be happy, it said, to take over WHDH-TV's facilities, staff (all but the general manager) and continue the same kind of excellent service presently rendered by WHDH-TV. To be sure, GBII had purged, sanitized itself of Michael Henry, the fellow who had brought a demerit to GBI. But, generally, the case seemed weak. Joe Maloney, however, was the picture of effusive, genial confidence as he repeated much of what he had told Cunningham years before.

Maloney, however, felt he had reasons for being confident. He had heard rumors to the effect that, this time around, it was going to be curtains for WHDH-TV. Newton Minow had resigned as chairman, but the new chairman, E. W. Henry, was said to share the same stiff regulatory attitude of his predecessor. The message was that the hearing would merely be a device by which the slate could be "rubbed clean." Whichever career-minded hearing examiner got this "plum," he would certainly "read the signs." After a long, judicious hearing, he would rule for one of the *other* applicants. And how, Maloney thought, could that "other" be any other than GBII, which had *won* the original hearing under Cunningham? Therefore GBII would not have to "phony up" its case with a lot of extravagant claims and promises.

Charles River, the third applicant to put in its case, and the first of the two new applicants, was a cat of a different stripe. Sure enough, it *did* have a Cabot: Thomas D. Cabot; urbane; sophisticated; a millionaire industrialist with interests in many parts of the world; a bona fide member of the illustrious Boston Cabots. Not only that, but Charles River had *two* Cabots! The second was Judge Charles C. Cabot, a distant cousin of Thomas Cabot, and a distinguished jurist. He was associate justice of the Superior Court of Massachusetts.

Charles River came up with an angle that was unique even to Herb Sharfman who thought he had heard of every angle. Charles River presented itself as a *nonprofit foundation!All* of its profits would be turned over to charity! Wow, thought Sharfman. Inspiration had seized *someone*. Harry Plotkin seemed bursting with pride as he explained the complex eleemosynary formula which spoke eloquently of the altruism of the Charles River stockholders.

Finally, came Benito Gaguine; irrepressible Benny, street smart Benny, former aide to Commissioner Rosel Hyde. Gaguine unleashed, on behalf of BBI, the wildest set of proposals Sharfman had ever heard. And anyone else, for that matter.

BBI comprised some thirty illustrious academicians and professional men who promised the stars, the sky, the moon and even the stratosphere. Sharfman sat in disbelief as he listened to Benny rattle off a set of program proposals and policies that included:

- Twenty-four-hour broadcast day, five days a week.
- 36.3 percent of its 160.5 hour per week schedule would be local, live!
- 25 percent of its ownership would go to key employees with no one owning more than 7 percent.
- Profits would be *minimized!*
- Less commercials than the NAB code allowed.
- Extremely high integration of ownership into the station's daily operation.
- No paid political or religious advertising. Candidates would be given free time.

And much, much more. Benny positively beamed as he placed his case on the record with an air of sanctity that ill befits him. With proper robes and the ennobling grace of years, Benito could have passed for the sanguine *Il Papa John!* Sitting next to him was his smiling acolyte: Nathan David, former Commission lawyer, who was said to have been the architect of BBI's "paper perfect" proposal.

Sharfman reflected on another paragraph in his unsubmitted article, one dealing with the subject of "ownership."

"Local ownership of a proposed station, whether individually or, if a corporation, by resident stockholders, is a competitive advantage. The Commission's justification has a certain a priori appeal. Like other criteria, however, it has never, so far as I know, been put to any systematic test. There are no statistics on whether locally-owned stations are run better 'in the interest of the community' than absentee-owned stations. . . . The last thing many small towns need, one might say, is local ownership reflecting merely the tastes of resident pooh bahs and nabobs. With outside control may come fresh breezes blowing away the accumulated smugness of the years."

Was that heresy, Sharfman wondered? He didn't think so. It was merely rhetorical reflection. At one thousand dollars per day, these bright attorneys might shudder at reading his mind (or the article); but maybe others would be interested. Applicants, for instance, who spent millions in these exercises in futility. And taxpayers who, in a sense, footed the bill for these interminable, unsatisfying and frustrating hearings.

Sharfman also pondered the paragraph dealing with "integration of ownership and management". Benny wouldn't like that one at all, he decided. Neither would Charles River. *"This,"* he had written, *"is the most esoteric of the major criteria. . ."* It ended with, *"It seemed to me that the Commission's rationalization makes as much sense as a pronouncement that the corner grocery —100 percent-owner-operated—is more 'efficient' solely because of that fact than a chain store."*

At any rate, the hearing wasn't dull, Sharfman mused as the weeks rolled on. Tedium and boredom were usually pandemic in

this business; but not this time. The Lamb hearing had put him in
the hospital for fifteen days. He wondered if this one would do the
same. The Miami hearing had almost put him in the hospital.
When the Commission overruled him afterwards—after he had
ruled for Katzentine and WKAT—he had truly felt like getting
sick. Never in his wildest dreams had he thought he would be
overruled on that one. What was the percentage of hearing rever-
sals these days, he wondered. Someone said it was almost two to
one, but he didn't think it was that bad. More like one reversal out
of three. Joe Maloney of GBII was a delightful guy, he told himself,
as he heard Maloney reply to an opposing counsel who cried out:
"That's unfair!" after some remark by Maloney.

"I'm never unfair," Maloney replied. "When I cross-examine
I'm always fair—and underhanded."

Which brought a round of laughter. Even Sharfman joined in.

Gaguine remained continually aggressive; always fighting delays. "Every day this hearing goes on, WHDH-TV makes ten thousand dollars!" protested Gaguine. And, as the days wore on, he increased the figure until it reached $22,000 per day! This was
understandable, if not entirely relevant, thought Sharfman. Yet
Benny spent more time cross-examining witnesses than anyone
else.

They were into gut issues now; the cruel part. God help anyone
who had a "character deficiency" in an FCC hearing. All three
opposing counsel ganged up on WHDH-TV. A transfer of control
issue was introduced. When Akerson took over from Choate, the
station had not notified the Commission on the proper forms. Then
there were some instances of improper logging; lack of editorializing; accusations of the station being used improperly in matters of
joint promotion, and selling combinations of advertising in both
the papers and the radio and television stations. Another issue
claimed was the "usurpation" of control by George Akerson with
the help of shrewd, thickly-accented Henry Garfinkle, the newspaper and magazine distributor, who owned 15.4 percent of *Herald Traveler* stock. The "October Putsch," Benny Gaguine called
it. And there was the license status issue: Was WHDH-TV present
as a "renewal applicant" or a "new applicant"? The others said the

station was clearly present as a new applicant, since it was operating on a four-month license only, which had expired. Bill Dempsey said, no. A four-month license was a *valid* license. Therefore its performance record must be taken into account. There was also an alleged violation of a complex rule called the "one percent ownership rule." And, like it or not, the Choate ex parte matter reared itself from poor Choate's grave. Sharfman asked somewhat plaintively how Choate could any longer be an issue in the case.

"That's easy," declared Gaguine, supported by the rest. Since Choate's views of the appropriateness of his conduct were shared by the Herald Traveler Board which had ratified his actions, and since George Akerson, the present chief executive officer, shared those views, the sins of Robert Choate must be visited on the successors in power.

In a brief filed later, probably the shortest brief ever filed at the FCC, Joe Maloney, on behalf of GBII, wrote, "I have been meditating for several months as to the best way to describe the effect of the death of Robert B. Choate on this case. I have come to the conclusion that I could not improve on the way it was said of another man and under different circumstances more than three hundred fifty years ago:

> "The evil that men do lives after them:
> The good is oft interred with their bones.
> So let it be with Beanie."

Meaning Choate.

Herbert Sharfman did not think it amusing.

"I fear," he said sadly, "that WHDH-TV will wear the Choate mantle like an albatross."

But possession is nine-tenths of the law. WHDH-TV was operating on Channel 5 in Boston. The others were on the outside looking in. All three opposing counsel knew the oft repeated axiom about the FCC: "The Commission giveth, but never taketh away."

So, the infighting grew more fierce as the months tolled by; summer, then fall, followed by winter, and into spring. Chief Hearing Examiner Cunningham urged Sharfman to "get on with it," wind it up. But how can you speed up a case with four parties? A case with more than one hundred witnesses and depositions? There were days upon days of intense cross-examination; then re-direct and recross. Fifteen days alone for Ted Jones, proposed general manager of Charles River. Outbursts were coming more frequently now. Bill Dempsey asked that Nathan David be ex-cluded from the hearing room for some obscure reason. Then, by osmosis, Dempsey became convinced that "David was listening through the grill." Sharfman didn't know what Dempsey was talk-ing about.

"The grill," Dempsey repeated. "There's a radiator grill in the hall that connects with the hearing room. Nathan David has his ear glued to it and is listening to everything I say."

Nathan David avowed that he had been listening to nothing more than the flush of the urinal in the men's room.

Charles River and BBI got into their own dogfight about whose programs were "farther out": Charles River, which had Robert Saudek, distinguished producer of *Omnibus* and winner of several Peabody awards? or the whole fantastic fabric of BBI's proposal?

"Outrageous," Charles River said.

"Completely unrealistic."

"How can BBI preempt so much prime time and still remain affiliated with a network?"

"How can so many of BBI's principals be integrated into its daily operation?"

Charles River said the BBI proposals verged on the "edge of fantasy." Its plan was branded as a series of "campaign maneu-vers."

"Its art is too precise in every part."

No matter what the degree of general skepticism shared by others, and to a degree by Sharfman, the hearing examiner was impressed. All that preparation by BBI, he thought with admira-tion, all those meetings; twenty-five stockholder meetings, some lasting eight hours; not to mention numerous "program advisory committee" meetings. All those surveys: monitoring and news-paper surveys; consultant reports; formal and informal interviews; program questionnaires; continuing surveys planned afterward with the aid of a computer; not to mention those "AB-X" surveys which Sharfman wasn't sure he understood. But they sounded impressive.

Not that Charles River was incapable of exaggeration. It was going to produce live plays produced from a list of: Strindberg, O'Neill, Buchner, Beckett, Osborne, Sheridan, Shaw and Albee. Its *College Focus* program might, among other things, feature an anatomy class (live nudes!) supplied by a medical school, which caused Sharfman to make an exclamation point in that portion of the record.

But, amid the snickers and smiles from competing applicants, Benny Gaguine, with Nathan David beaming approval, tirelessly charged forward with his case. "The stockholders of BBI are well aware of the income a Boston station can produce. They are nevertheless quite willing to accept a *reduction* of gross income, and to expand an uncommon proportion of that income in order to improve the quality and to extend the range and variety of locally-produced programs."

(What kind of heresy was this?)

"We do not regard the audience to be served simply an indiscriminate mass of viewers; nor do we believe that it is necessary to aim at a common denominator and especially the least common denominator. We think that rating services are of some help in ascertaining the services a station should render; but to know how many sets are turned to a particular channel is not the same as knowing what those people, and others who are not even tuned in, wish to watch."

Brave words, thought Sharfman. Did BBI have some magic rating formula of its own? A new kind of Ouija board, or magic wand?

"BBI is committed to avoiding the gross uniformity of television programing which implies an insensitivity to any facet of its audience except quality."

And—Excedrin number six or five for the networks: "To achieve its objectives, BBI proposes to follow flexible relations with its networks; specifically it proposes to keep free, extra prime time for programs of local origin and for exchange offerings from other stations."

Commendable, if possible.

"The television industry is in a state of flux," Gaguine continued. "Neither the course of its development nor its ultimate form and methods of operation can yet be divined. To improve its future programing and part of its program of maintaining close relation with the community, Boston Broadcasters intends to cooperate with nearby schools and other organizations engaged in research and in training personnel for work in television. Such groups as the Morse Communications Research Center at Brandeis University, Everson College, the Carpenter Center for Visual Arts at Harvard University, and Boston University's School in Public Relations and Communications will contribute considerable knowledge and criticism to the evolution of the medium. We intend to take advantage of their contributions."

Shades of "Boolah Boolah." BBI looked too good to be true!

One wit muttered caustically: "That's not a station I'd like to own stock in."

BBI's total commercial time would amount to only 76.8 percent of its schedule. Sustaining would fill the rest. Only 638 commercial announcements in a sample week of 160.5 hours, almost twenty-three hours per day. An average of only 3.9 commercial spots per hour! Only 53.3 percent of its schedule was listed as "entertainment." The balance, 46.7 percent was listed in areas of religion, agriculture, education, news, discussion, talk and miscellaneous.

Charles River harped repeatedly on the impracticality of these proposals. It was a factitious organization, they said; the brainchild of clever Nathan David, former Commission employee, who had put together a "paper-perfect proposal," and in doing so, had lost sight of the fact that it was so "artificial and excessive" that no reliance could be placed on it.

But there was no question that BBI's case was impressive. No angle was left uncovered. Eleven of its thirty members would be integrated to some degree into the operation of the station. And what a star-studded cast! A list of people with professional and academic pedigrees that filled the pages of half a dozen *Who's Who* volumes. Men like: Oscar Handlin, a Pulitzer prize-winning author and professor of American history at Harvard; Dr. John H. Knowles, a famous doctor and general director of Massachusetts General Hospital; Leo L. Beranek, famed acoustics expert; Charles Marran, president of Spencer Shoe Company; Alan Neuman, producer-director of Bing Crosby Productions; Louis P. Smith, industrialist and civic leader; Barry Wood, vice president of Metromedia Producers Corporation; Robert Gardner, anthropologist, filmmaker and professor at Harvard; Gerald J. Holton, professor of physics, Harvard; Henry Jaffe, president of his own company which produced the leading network show, *Producer's Showcase;* Jordan J. Baruch, president of Educom Company of Boston, and a lecturer at Harvard; and Nathan David, who, not unexpectedly, would be the expert in communications regulations.

Sharfman tried to remember a line he had written in reference to "civic participation and integration of ownership and management" in his article. He referred to it to refresh his memory. *"Civic participation and integration of ownership and management may have a basis in the admiration of sedentary bureaucrats for men of action. Shying away from grappling directly with program promises may represent an anti-intellectualism which rejects the appraisal of the merits of particular programs."*

But that didn't exactly fit in this instance. BBI's program proposals reached dizzying heights of alleged perfection. If the station could achieve only half of what it promised, it would be setting new standards for the industry. He read farther down the page of his brooding, introspective article to a passage that seemed relevant.

"To choose the best qualified applicant by the swatch-making method of the criteria is easier and superficially, at least, more satisfying than to gauge the wind of program promises. Preoccupation with the criteria is merely a manifestation of the same desire which bemuses all tribunals—judicial and quasi-judicial—and makes it easy for them to believe that they have solved their complex problems by handy formulas, if only to put an end to a squabble which may have become unendurable. Interest rei publicae ut sit finish litium has a personal as well as a social significance. Like court cases, comparative proceedings are played largely by the code duello, with the 'truth' desirable but incidental. Their purpose is to settle the dispute between the appli-

cants, and not to determine abstract rights and wrongs, or a disembodied 'truth.' Commission cases are in the great tradition.

"But whatever the explanation of the appeal of the criteria, it is clear that the FCC case suffers a double possibility of error: 1) The winner is chosen because he has scored well in 'criteria' other than direct assurance of good programing and its continuation; and 2) the criteria themselves bear only an untested relationship to the probability of operation in the public interest."

The final portion of the article bore the subhead: "Is There A Better Method." He felt too full of the Boston case to read it just now; especially the closing lines which said: *"It is perhaps hopeless, however, to suggest that broadcast applications be removed from this battleground and the public interest discovered in a calmer atmosphere. Among other immediate objections, it would be pointed out that there would have to be a revision of the Communications Act of 1934 and the Administrative Procedure Act. Short of so radical and impracticable a change—and presupposing that the coin toss and action are rejected as alternatives—it is hoped that there will be a serious study of the effectiveness of the present system."*

Herbert Sharfman put the article away forever, and wished he could put aside the disquieting thoughts that nagged at him increasingly as the hearing wore on. It must be the hearing, he decided. He again wished his colleague, Dave Kraushaar, had not seen fit to disqualify himself. After the Miami Channel 10 case, and the turbulent Edward H. Lamb case, dealing with the issue of Communism, he needed this case like he needed an ulcer. He only hoped he wouldn't lay claim to one before it was over. His gall bladder was acting up, a bad sign. Would there be a rest in a hospital after it was all over? He hoped not. At any rate, he would soon know. For now the long, seemingly never-ending hearing was drawing to a fractious close. All the issues had been put in. All the attempted character assassination had been tried. The name-calling and vituperation were losing their steam. The cast of his "clan" was getting tired. Soon all the worry-weary witnesses would be able to go home; the high-priced, high-powered counsel would be able to return to their other work. Some would begin praying in their favorite church or synagogue. Leaving Herbert Sharfman with the toughest job of all; that of reading over and over the ceiling-high record of testimony, sifting, analyzing, scrutinizing, adding up the merits and demerits of each side's case.

On July 16, 1965, almost thirteen months after it had begun, all participants ran out of things to say. It seemed hard to believe that the longest comparative hearing in the United States had finally ended.

4

Sharfman's Decision

Girl watching is great fun and so easy. You simply let your instincts do the job. Reading a profit and loss statement is somewhat more difficult because you must repress your instincts and let your above-the-shoulder "computer" do the work.

But reading a hearing examiner's statement is another kind of exercise. If one knows how to read one, it can be as much fun as the first and as informative as the second. Truly "reading" one is a challenge indeed. Few have mastered the art. Some call it a science. Others call it mumbo jumbo. But it really is an art in the sense that art is mysterious, unprovable; but like the deities themselves, immortal in their beckoning obfuscation. To really *read*, and *know*, an FCC hearing examiner's decision takes an education of an especial kind. Even "graduates" of the course in "reading FCC decisions" are wary about their ability to get passing grades from the twelve to fifteen apostles who are given the insuperable task of "understanding," and "trying to keep abreast" of the peregrinations of the Commission they serve.

If you are privileged to read a decision of Hearing Examiner Herbert Sharfman you have an even greater challenge. Can you, for instance, appreciate his piquant turn of phrase, his metaphors, his occasional flights of fancy? Can you appreciate his moods;

sometimes pensive, sometimes rapturous; other times brooding with irony, or etched in whimsy; or burdened with sorrow-laughter at this episode in the human comedy; sometimes acutely melancholic; never, however, downright bitter; and, as often as not, fey and gently smiling; as though he had all participants on his knee and was saying, not in a scolding mood, but softly reproving, with a glint in his eye, that could be Irish, or Jewish, in character: "Come now, all of you: why *must* we be here under *these* circumstances? Can't we do more important things with our lives?"

If you're a lawyer practitioner before the FCC, you read the decision from another point of view, a more pragmatic one. If you're Bill Dempsey, Benny Gaguine, Harry Plotkin or Joe Maloney, you get out a pad of paper and draw lines down the center. You make a tally sheet. You label the four columns; and under each, you put a mark, or note, for your side. Because *certainly*, if you lose, you will appeal. And if you end up with more good marks than the other side, you know *they* will appeal. So, why not begin with the very first reading, you tell yourself. Why wait, although you will reread the document dozens of times until you have it almost memorized. Yes. Since this is a long decision—226 pages, the length of a novel! —you say to yourself: get on with the tally sheet with the very first reading. A highlighter marking pen is also useful. And, while it's easy to flip to the very last page and get the *decision*, that is like cheating. Since you have confidence in your case and believe you are going to win, you take the other route; you follow the decision painstakingly through page after page of fine print, soaking up, not only the *intelligence* of Herbert Sharfman, but his *mood*. You are one year and thirteen days older than you were when you said good-bye to Sharfman on the final day of the hearing. And much older than that, really, in terms of wear and tear on the system. You have spent scads of your client's money. And now, with the document spread out before you, you know you have reached the point of almost no return.

So, you strike off the four columns, put the names of the four applicants at the top—and begin reading; and hold your breath, not to mention your crotch, your heart and your guts.

Herbert Sharfman began with the modesty that is traditional in all FCC Decisions: self-effacing almost; gentle; scholarly; no flair, style or flamboyance—not yet. Exchange the rhetoric of the first seventy-five pages with those of a decision written by any other hearing examiner and you could not tell the difference. Sharfman recited the charge placed upon him; laid in the issues; sedately covered all the points that must be covered before he could dare begin to be *himself*—that unfortunate person who was invested with the awesome responsibility of presiding as judge and jury over an economic and social entity worth more millions than he, or his ancestors, had ever made, or would make.

Then, rolling up his sleeves, but with seeming reluctance, he went to work. Looking at the mountain of record piled before him, he observed somewhat ruefully at the beginning of his "conclusions," "In this case, transcript and exhibit volumes, if piled up, would reach a mark higher than the Inca Atahualpa's when he indicated to Pizarro the amount of gold to be delivered for his ransom. Unfortunately, not all the contents of these volumes are of metaphorical gold. But this less noble admixture is inevitable in a long hearing in which an incumbent licensee, like the priests of Diana of the Woods at Aricia was shielding itself from lethal attack by aspirants to its place. ('In this sacred grove there grew a certain tree round which at any time of the day, and probably far into the night, a grim figure might be seen to prowl. In his hand he carried a drawn sword, and he kept peering warily about him as if at every instant he expected to be set upon by an enemy. . .')"

Vintage Sharfman, that. Proof that, despite his doubts about the system, he still had the zest, the yen, to get on with his task one more time.

First, however, there were some minor matters to dispense with. He did this quickly and crisply. The issue of legal qualifications of stockholders, officers and directors of the Herald Traveler Corporation, which involved the fact that WHDH had filed information on form 303 (for renewal applicants), instead of form 301 (for new applicants): Forget it, said Sharfman.

The obtuse "one percent ownership rule" charged against WHDH: No, said Sharfman. WHDH was not disqualified.

The citizenship issue regarding WHDH (U.S. television stations cannot be owned wholly, or in part, by aliens or representatives of foreign governments): No problem, said Sharfman. *Herald Traveler* stock was owned 92.6 percent by U.S. citizens. That was the best figure the auditing company could come up with because some people simply would not fill out questionnaires.

The transfer of control issue: Had the Herald Traveler Corporation changed hands? Certainly, said Sharfman, several times. But how can you prevent that in a publicly-held corporation? However, most of these stockholders were more concerned with their investment rather than attaining corporate control. So what difference did it make?

Transfer of management control: When the icon of power had been handed from Robert Choate to George Akerson, the Commission had not been properly notified; nor had approval been requested. Too bad, said Sharfman. Even regrettable; but *not* inexcusable.

In sum, he concluded in this warm-up portion, that in the area of "character qualifications," WHDH was not "adversely affected so that it should be disqualified from comparative considerations."

With these mundane matters out of the way—matters that had taken weeks, even months, of his time at the hearing, the examiner moved into the important, all pervasive issue of, "comparative issues."

This was the main arena. Here is where the game would be won or lost; where Dempsey-Gaguine-Plotkin-Maloney would begin aging with each succeeding paragraph; with each point; each nuance. Up to this time they were like four evenly-matched golfers. But now the handicapping would begin. Sharfman would begin playing God.

"In approaching a comparison," Sharfman began, as if with a sigh, "one is tempted to long, if only whimsically, for a relatively easy method of choice in which, to adapt Evelyn Waugh's phrase (from *The Loved One*): lamas would scan the snows for the Dalai licensee. Classically, comparisons are odious. In Commission proceedings they are also onerous, but of course they cannot be shirked."

He pointed out that this was no run-of-the-mill comparative

proceeding; that it was the longest such hearing before the Commission.

"A distinction which the hearing examiner would have gladly averted, had it been possible."

It was also the first litigated case to raise the question of transfer of control because of the trading of publicly-held stock. It involved a television operation without a regular license for a longer period than any case in the Commission's history. There was at stake the only VHF frequency in the top ten markets in the country which is not occupied under a regular license.

More importantly, he pointed out, it also tested the implications of the Commission's reservation in its policy statement on comparative broadcast hearings: "This statement of policy does *not* attempt to deal with the somewhat *different* problems raised where an applicant is contesting with a licensee seeking renewal of license."

But into the nitty gritty. "First, one must decide the status of WHDH. Here the ex parte contacts enter into the calculations. It has already been held that the Commission *never* held that Mr. Choate's heavy-handed attempts to impress his personality and ingratiate himself with Mr. McConnaughey were in the slightest degree effective; for all that resulted he might as well have sent letters to Santa Claus."

Bill Dempsey, put a mark on your tally sheet.

But, a moment later, Sharfman gives comfort to the others. "In this inevitable contest it could not have been the Commission's expectation that WHDH would be entitled to assert competitive advantages merely because it is a renewing licensee. . ."

On the other hand, Sharfman was quick to add: this "does not mean that WHDH loses the benefits, if any, of its television record, compiled since its original grant." Quoting from a past precedential FCC case, he said: "Under the circumstances (of an existing station with a good operating record, and of assurance of its continuance, competing against a newcomer for the occupied channel) it would demand a presentation by the newcomer extraordinary to a degree certainly not attained by Livesay (the newcomer) to justify ousting the incumbent."

What did that mean? Sharfman carefully explained, "This

means that a proven past record of good performance which may confidently be expected to continue is a safer index of future operation in the public interest than the mere promises of performance of the competitor, as the validity of the latter can only be assayed through the criteria. . ." A few lines later: "Like public officials charged with a public trust, a renewal applicant . . . must literally run on his record."

The all-important problem of Choate is still on his mind. Greater Boston II, Charles River and BBI would have WHDH forever damned by the Choate ex parte contacts, contending, in essence, that they generated a kind of equitable servitude to which WHDH must remain subject, or, to use a triter figure for the argument, that WHDH "wears them like an albatross."

Charles River and BBI had tried to prove too much, Sharfman complained. "The Commission did not make Mr. Choate an outlaw, or even send him to Conventry. Nothing that the Commission did made it improper for Mr. Choate's associates to recognize his competence as an executive and to avail themselves of his long experience. They did not, simply be reelecting him, approve his ex parte contacts any more than they necessarily approved anything else they might have known in Mr. Choate's past."

How long must the Choate matter go on, he lamented. "Does this mean that WHDH continues to bear responsibility until the Charles River ceases to flow? Or did the Commission exhaust the consequence of Mr. Choate's conduct by limiting WHDH's license to four months and thrusting it into a competitive hearing . . . ? WHDH as a corporation gained nothing from his efforts. It would have been immeasurably better off had Mr. Choate's idea died at birth. WHDH has suffered rather than benefited from his ex parte activity.

"In remanding the first proceeding in April 1964, the court of appeals envisaged an inquiry into the changes in 'the affairs and prospects of WHDH by the death of Mr. Choate.' If the hearing examiner correctly interprets this, the court did not exclude the possibility that Mr. Choate's death put an end to the baleful aftermath of his officious intermeddling. . .

". . . in the circumstances it would be almost sadistic to perpetuate a curse against a corporation for something which had not helped but had hurt it merely—for it comes down to this—to demonstrate the inviolability of the Commission's procedures. Such Biblical fury is not properly a part of the administrative process. There is no need to deter the present principals of WHDH and the *Herald Traveler* from doing what they cannot be charged with having done in the past; extending the disability would serve no prophylactic, but only an emptily minatory, purpose."

With that, Sharfman wound up the Choate matter firmly and with finality, *"It is therefore held that because of Mr. Choate's death his ex parte contacts are no longer a factor in the comparative consideration . . ."*

Bill Dempsey, put a *big* mark on your tally sheet! And consider your opponents as having been penalized at least two strokes.

Throughout the hearing Sharfman noted that both Charles River and BBI had tried to nail WHDH for "character deficiencies." He made short shrift of these efforts by saying, "Some of these proposals (by the two opponents) the hearing examiner passed over almost completely. Others he mentioned at greater length, but not always in the detail suggested. Thus, almost ignored have been findings on WHDH's alleged improper logging practices."

To make his point, he quotes from WHDH's own proposed findings, ". . . the game of needling the witness (to elicit testimony of mislogging) is held in somewhat the same regard among radio lawyers as pigsticking was held by the Bengal lancers . . ."

In full tilt now, one could see that the hearing examiner was enjoying himself. There might have been some "borderline errors" he conceded; but if so, he reminded everyone that these were of a nature and extent that ". . . the Commission has, in many, many cases, recognized as entirely reasonable. . ."

He scolded Charles River for having ". . . followed tradition in trying to make something out of the WHDH program logs and the composite week breakdown in the renewal application."

All of this he dismissed as legal rhetoric bordering on nonsense by quoting again from WHDH's proposed findings. "We submit

... that the examiner should also follow tradition and ignore this abortive effort as having no decisional significance.

"The hearing examiner agrees. There are probably few operating applicants who are not vulnerable to niggling complaints of the kind here rejected."

No comfort for Charles River or BBI here. Mark your tally sheets, gentlemen.

George Akerson's alleged "lack of candor" next came to his attention. Both Charles River and BBI had charged that there were major differences between Choate and Akerson on the "profitability of retaining the newspapers." Both opponents had attempted to prove that by introducing into the record a memorandum which Akerson had given certain union officials. This, they said, indicated a rift between the two men. And the fact that Choate's stock had ended up in the hands of a Midwest group indicated that there was a "residual hostility" on the part of Choate's widow. There was a third matter concerning a dispute between George Frazier, a former *Herald Traveler* writer.

Sharfman found nothing to concern him. He disposed of the "lack of candor" matter quickly. ". . . the atmosphere in which transfer of office (Choate kicked upstairs and Akerson made chief executive officer) . . . are not a part of the WHDH case, but are incidental to the affairs of the *Herald Traveler*, which, as such, has no case before the examiner."

These matters were, therefore, worth "only relatively brief disposition . . .

"Mr. Akerson's testimonial reliability has *not* been successfully attacked."

Programing was certainly one of the major issues to be weighed in the four-contestant fight. Everyone had picked on everyone else, with WHDH getting the brunt of a combined attack from the other three. Sharfman took cognizance of some of the allegations in this vital area.

In the six years WHDH-TV had been on the air, the station had a paucity of discussion programs—or so the others contended. An average of only one every 4 1/2 weeks, said BBI. Also, the station refused to carry a controversial program which defended the practice of abortion. Also, the station did not editorialize. And in the area of baseball, it carried an "overabundance" of programs—fifty-five games per year of the Boston Red Sox.

What applicant is there so well-balanced in programing that it cannot be subjected to criticism, Sharfman asked.

Indeed, what *was* "balance"? Who could define it? He quoted from another Commission decision, "There is no denying that the licensee may find it hard to judge the extent to which he can indulge his own predilections, condition programing by his individual tastes, or satisfy a mass interest only." Continuing, he wrote, "In (another case) the court of appeals recognized the strains upon a licensee's judgment: 'It may be that a licensee must have freedom to broadcast light opera even if the community likes rock and roll music, although that question is not uncomplicated. Even more complicated is the question whether he may feed a diet of rock and roll music to a community which hungers for opera.' "

On balance, Sharfman said, he had to give WHDH passing grades in programing. Bill Dempsey could tally another plus mark.

". . . it is fair to say that on balance WHDH's conception of its programing responsibilities is in reasonable, if not perfect, accord with the ideals positively and negatively suggested in paragraph 744 above."

But then, before Dempsey could put the pencil to his tally sheet, Sharfman, as he delighted in doing so often, if for no other reason than to inject suspense into his hard-wrought prose, took the edge off the gain by adding. "In only one general area—local discussion and failure to editorialize—was a reservation regarding its performance indicated."

Gaguine, Plotkin and Maloney could take a dollop of comfort from that.

Next, the hearing examiner turned his attention to "misrepresentations and concealments by WHDH to the Commission"—a pattern which the others had tried vigorously to develop in the hearing.

Sharfman seemed to frown as he began. "That recital was not one of unalloyed approval."

One visualizes Benny Gaguine grinding his teeth in delight.

"There is no doubt," Sharfman wrote, "that, as shown in the findings of fact, WHDH has been remiss in at least some of its reporting obligations, and that it has on occasion chosen to interpret Commission requirements by the standard of its own convenience rather than by that of strict compliance."

But then, with the whistle to his lips, he pulled back. "Nevertheless, and without depreciating the importance of candor and complete informativeness in reports to the commission, it must be concluded that the heinousness of WHDH's conduct lies more in the eyes of its opponents than in those of a more impartial observer."

Sharfman was revealing the pixie in himself.

"Viewed singly or in combination, it would be an unwarranted concession to advocacy to regard the resulting violations as a significant demerit."

Sharfman must know the counsellors are marking their tally sheets. Like jolly King Cole, he seems to be saying, with bemused finger to his nose, "All right, boys, how are you going to score *that* one?"

Repeatedly throughout the hearing, Sharfman had expressed amazement, to himself, and sometimes openly, at the quality of the individuals who were representing all parties, but in particular, Charles River and BBI. He felt the time had come now to pay them honor, and he did so with warm praise. "Probably no more distinguished persons than those numbered among the present applicants have ever submitted their qualifications for this agency's inspection. While wealthy businessmen are common in TV applicants, they seldom have as stockholders noted historians, and academicians, physicists, biologists, inventors, economists, anthropologists, physicians, captains of industry and services, financiers, judges, public officials and producers."

Benny Gaguine's heart had to swell with pride as he read the next line, "Most of BBI's stockholders are area residents and civic doers, and about two-thirds of its stockholders would be integrated, or would at least actively participate in station operation for a portion of their time varying from 100 percent down to a couple of hours a week. BBI has virtually no associations with any other communications media. Charles River has some association with other communications media, through Mr. Jones (their proposed general manager), and more remotely, geographically and personally, perhaps through Mrs. Lombard (wife of a co-trustee and director of Dow Jones Company)."

Then Sharfman put his pen in cheek to confound and dismay those who were too quick to put down marks for themselves. "Both BBI and Charles River had the wit to ally themselves with persons having broadcast or TV operating and production experience, BBI with Mr. Burdick and Mr. Jaffe's organization, and Charles River with Mr. Jones (as to whom it is probably more accurate to say that he had the wit to ally himself with a goodly group) and Mr. Saudek."

But enough of that, Sharfman seemed to say. He switched subjects, but kept the same tone of bemused irony as he commented on the internecine hostility between Charles River and BBI. "The incumbent," he began, "is bound by the past; its competitors are free of the future. They can organize corporations for which the (FCC) statement of policy could almost serve as character or by-laws, and they can make promises unfettered by a realization of bygone failures. They can canter briskly through preparatory campaigns and try to catch the eye of the Commission by means inappropriate to an existing station, which made its preparations long ago and now must rely on its operating record."

One can see Benito Gaguine crying out in pain; and Harry Plotkin reaching for the Excedrin bottle: *What did we do to deserve this?*

Both sides were guilty of exaggeration, Sharfman stated flatly. Then cautioned himself, "In a decision, facile suspicion must be avoided as much as gullible acceptance."

Then he began to muse and wonder how so many distinguished participating stockholders could find the time to contribute to the operation of the station. How could a man like Dr. Handlin (of BBI) find time to "wrench fifteen hours for the station from his already overcrowded work week . . ." and mindful of the famous Dr. Knowles (also of BBI) remark that he barely had been able to find time to appear one day as a witness at the hearing, he asked how Dr. Knowles could "find the two hours a week which he had evidently found it inadvisable to take from his hospital and writing work in the preparatory period." How could Dr. Beranek contribute ten hours a week; and Mr. Gardner, who would still travel extensively, contribute fifteen hours a week? Was BBI proposing "an actual working arrangement, or a superficially impressive plan of stockholder participation for comparative advantage"?

Despite his "skepticism," however, Sharfman insisted that he would not completely discard BBI's integration proposal as Charles River would have him do.

Now about that twenty-four-hour operation of BBI's? Sharfman plainly had his doubts. "BBI can only invoke brave generalities in its proposed conclusions in support of its claimed ability to carry out its local live proposals."

Still . . . maybe they could. "The hearing examiner does not share Charles River's scoffing at the proposed BBI twenty-four-hour operation for five days a week."

But he agreed with Charles River; "The proposal was calculated to impress the Commission."

He noted BBI's complaint that, "It is a transvaluation of values to criticize (BBI) for being 'too good to be true.' "

He replied, "If this had been the simplistic approach taken to (BBI's) case, one would be taken aback by the complaint. But the essence of the present conclusion is not merely that BBI is so nearly perfect in so many areas, but that its claims are consistently on the edge of credibility, when it is realized that it is as yet only an untried applicant. Its disparagement of its rivals' claims is correspondingly solipsistic."

This sent four lawyers running for the dictionary.

When it came to the subject of "surveys," Sharfman gave the impression that he had been surveyed to death by at least two of the applicants. "They indulged in an apparent ecstasy of self-abasement to the Commission's mandate that they 'consider the tastes, needs and desires of the public.' "

Even WHDH came in for a backhanded compliment, "Program

survey evidence is a constituent of a comparative case as oxygen (or perhaps xenon, an inert gas) is of the atmosphere. Even WHDH, an operating station, paid deference to the importance of a formalized ascertainment of public tastes by offering evidence about its program committee, a group which emerges biennially like a foxglove or the Internazionale d'Arte at Venice."

If he had to make a preference in this area, Sharfman gave the nod to BBI for its "elaborate, scientific and mechanized methods of ascertaining mass wants and approbation. It is an impressive display, but . . . the findings of fact indicated the difficulty of determining whether the platitudes gleaned from the survey substantially influenced (their) program proposals."

A plague on all your houses in this matter, Sharfman seemed to say: "For all the record shows, the surveys of both BBI and Charles River were as productive of the result as a Hopi rain dance providentially followed by a shower."

No question about it—Herbert Sharfman was *not* a survey freak! Still, unable to drop the matter, he concluded by quoting a former FCC decision: "Multiple surveys and banks of computers will not produce a poignant drama, a subtle comedy, a bold discussion of a troublesome problem or a clever pictorial essay."

Finally, as it must come to all hearing examiners, even the erudite Herbert Sharfman, the time came for "summation". That point where decisions are made, and explained; or not explained, as befits the muse of the author.

In a brooding, low key, Sharfman asked himself the question: How do I judge a case like this, involving three new applicants, and one with a station already on the air eight years? He isn't sure it can be done in a clear-cut, judicial, step-by-step checkoff of criteria: The "traditional mode of comparing mutually-exclusive applicants, in the mechanical or point-by-point manner especially advocated by BBI, would have been a sterile exercise. The cardinal probative attribute—for good or bad—of the incumbent was its operating record.

"The absurdity of judging an applicant for renewal by its conformity with the classical criteria pertinent in an all-newcomer contest is patent if one posits a case of two existing stations in the same city competing for a third channel there on condition the winner abandon his present channel. Applicant A is 100 percent locally owned by civic live wires with vast broadcast experience, and completely management-ownership integrated." (Media diversification being disregarded in this example.) Applicant A also has an operating record of "unexampled meretriciousness which it promises to continue. Applicant B is 100 percent absentee-owned, run by a hired staff without ownership interests, but with an excellent operating record it proposes to maintain. Clearly, as this paper conflict is posed, there is no contest. B should win hands down unless one overemphasizes the significance of the classical indices.

"In the present case WHDH should have cashed in its chips and gone home before the game started if it were forced to depend on its conformity to the traditional standards for preference. Its integration is small. Only if its long identification with the community through newspaper and station operation were regarded as a near-substitute for local ownership because it has enabled the applicant to acquire a knowledge of the community, could it claw a foothold. Facing the cleverly designed organizations and preparatory campaigns of locally-owned, civically-active opponents, each integrated to a different degree but more than it is, and proposing managerial direction by fairly experienced persons, WHDH's prognosis would be poor unless it could rely for a clincher on its operating record unabated by any substantial character or other defects."

My methods of comparison were, Sharfman claimed, those by which all applicants "were given the fullest opportunity to display their advantages.

"WHDH's operating record on the channel in issue, and the possibility of its continuance, were evaluated together with the proposals of the other applicants. Theirs are as yet only a hope and a promise, and estimates of the probability of their effectuation depend on characteristics which bear only a circumstantial relationship to them. It has already been explained that in the process adopted it was not intended that WHDH start off with a built-in lead, but that it was impossible to deny it the benefit of whatever superior persuasiveness its status as an existing station lends it."

And that record? Sharfman explains: "It is hoped that the chief defect of WHDH's operating record has not been scanted in this initial decision. But if there is inadequacy—an unwillingness to grasp the nettle of some local problems—as a whole its record is favorable."

Benny Gaguine, Harry Plotkin, Joe Maloney, fasten your seat belts.

"The hearing examiner has not allowed himself to be unduly influenced by the ferocity of the attack on the character of WHDH. The Choate ex parte contacts episode has, it is hoped, been entombed with fitting funerary remarks. WHDH's reporting lapses have been considered and found not to be a significant comparative factor; and in the circumstances variations between program promise and performance were held not significant. Mr. Akerson's alleged testimonial discrepancies, and his and the directors' failure to express repugnance toward Mr. Choate's conduct, have been weighed and it was concluded that WHDH's standing was *not* affected. Mr. Garfinkle, pictured by Charles River and BBI as a malign figure whose *Herald Traveler* stock ownership portends no good to the community, has been scaled down to a practical ineffectiveness."

How about the elaborate presentations by Charles River and BBI?

They are "flawed" says Sharfman by their very elaborateness. "Admirable, even star-studded as BBI's locally owned and civically-active group is, its promises are permeated by an exuberance which makes one doubtful of their fullfillment. BBI's program schedule, interestingly described and on its face adapted to the community's needs, contains so large a proportion of local live programs that, as BBI made its case, it cannot be confidently predicted that the applicant will produce them. Its integration and principal participation plan has not been criticized on the ground that it is impossible, but because it is proclaimed at the same high pitch as other parts of BBI's case."

The twenty-four-hour operation five days a week?

"Nor is there anything impracticable about the twenty-four-hour operation. Praiseworthy in itself, it is here mentioned together with the other matters because it is of a piece with them in its extremism, and helps to brand BBI's presentation."

Then he turns his scalpel in the direction of Charles River. "The luminosity of (its) group is of about the same order of magnitude as BBI's. Its principals . . . are locally resident and prominent. It proposes an excellent program schedule, though its charitable foundation stock ownership may have some impact on its service. A measure of its access to local program sources is its ability, because of the friendly relations of Mr. Jones and others of its principals with the Boston Symphony Orchestra, to propose to carry BSO concerts regularly." But Charles River is then faulted on the issue of integration, or "participation in station management by owners." He forgives, or ignores, other alleged weaknesses in its proposal, but concludes that its case, "is infected—though not to the same degree as BBI's—with the endemic taint of comparative applicants, exaggerated advancement of its claims."

The race to the barn has now begun in earnest. Messrs. Gaguine, Plotkin, Maloney have to be sweating. All of this *before* Sharfman gets into the all-important issue of diversification.

"It is . . . believed that this summation is sufficient to demonstrate, *before consideration of media diversification*, of the superiority of WHDH's claims to renewal against those of its competitors for initial license. WHDH's rest on a basis of achievement, theirs on promises, often glittering, but of relatively uncertain and unestablished validity."

Before moving on to the vital issue of diversification, however, Sharfman must dispense with GBII. He has implied what his position has been throughout the long decision (the longest written at that point in time) by giving short shrift to its position. Now he does it with irony and sarcasm—not his own, but that of BBI, for he quotes from BBI's proposed findings: "The descriptive word for Greater Boston II is 'tired.' It too has ardent desires for a television license which its principals have sought for years. But somewhere along the trail any zest they may have had for service to the community waned. Now, like old soldiers, they are preoccupied with old skirmishes won or lost more than with the current fray. They long for the good old days when the planning of a television operation and a television schedule seemed to them relatively simple and uncomplicated.

"Its application is a shadowy document, thinly supported at the hearing by vague descriptions of ghostly figures, with one or two partially-developed program ideas barely discernible in the mists. The only rational explanation of Greater Boston's application and its approach to the proceeding is that it has hoped to win, not on its own strength, but because of the *Herald Traveler*'s weaknesses."

A sad, final requiem to the group that, originally, had been selected over the Herald Traveler by Examiner Cunningham!

With that painful duty done, Sharfman tackles the ticklish issue of diversification.

Yes, he begins, diversification of media *is* a factor of "primary significance." It constitutes "a primary objective of the licensing scheme.

"In the 1957 first decision, WHDH was being compared with other applicants who, 'have connections in various degrees with other media of mass communication.' " At that time the Commission distinctly said that diversification "remains . . . a *comparative*, not a *disqualifying* factor." *Key words* in Sharfman's lexicon of hairline distinctions. Yes, he admits, BBI *is* virtually free of any media alliance. GBII is *entirely* free. And Charles River's alliance with other media is trivial. Nevertheless, he emphasized, ". . . in all initial license cases the Commission has *not* given lack of diversification disqualifying significance."

And: "In cases of a renewing applicant opposed by newcomers, absence of diversification has been even less of a comparative factor in Commission precedents."

In a final, dispositive paragraph, Sharfman says, in effect: No matter how you slice it, no matter what you inject to make it taste better, the diversification issue, in his judgment, is still baloney. Therefore: His "preference for WHDH is not materially affected."

That is the ball game. The taffy pull. Whatever you choose to call it.

Losers can head for the nearest bar. Winners can pop champagne. The longest hearing decision in history, 226 pages, needs only a scant few lines under the heading of "order." There are parts (a), (b) and (c). The only one worth reading is part (c) which *grants* the license to WHDH-TV for "the regular period," three years. Three safe, unencumbered years, provided a majority of the seven commissioners vote approval of Sharfman's decision.

The decision was unequivocal—final. For WHDH-TV and the *Herald Traveler*, eight agonizing years of harassment were over. Choate was resting in his grave, and along with him, finally, the ex parte issue.

August 10th, 1966—for WHDH-TV, the best day of the century.

For others a day that was black and bleak; worse than that— an apocalypse.

5

Oral
Argument

"Benny? This is Nate David up in Boston. Did you read it?"

"Don't bother me. I can't talk."

"Why?"

"I just slit my throat."

"I haven't read the decision yet. Somebody called me and read the bottom line. It's pretty bad."

"Worst goddam decision I ever read in my life." Benny Gaguine had a "thing" about losing. Nate reminded him that he said this about every decision he lost. Benny said, no, this one was different. Sharfman, he said, had put blinders on and kept them on throughout the yearlong hearing. The decision was full of errors. He couldn't understand what had gotten into Herb Sharfman.

Nate David got to the "bottom line" of his conversation: "What are we gonna do now?"

"Don't even want to talk about it," said Benny. "Leave me alone. Get the decision. Read it. We'll talk in a few days."

That wasn't good enough for David. "What am I going to tell the group?"

Gaguine searched his mind for something appropriate to suggest. He couldn't think of a thing—except the truth. "Tell them they just blew $300,000. And I'm sorry about it."

For the next few days the stunned losers licked their wounds and tried to recover from the shock. WHDH quietly exulted. The stock of the Herald Traveler Corporation began a steady rise to a new high of seventy-five. The *Herald Traveler* called the Sharfman decision a preliminary, but major, victory, necessary to final resolution of the protracted case and predicted that final Commission approval would be forthcoming in the near future. The *Boston Globe* gave the matter scant attention. The broadcast industry reacted with a yawn. Cynical veterans said: Of course! What did you expect? To a man, leaders of the major broadcasting stations and groups were pleased. *Broadcasting Magazine*, the industry's friendly "voice," gave the story thorough treatment. Its veteran Commission expert, Len Zeidenberg, gleaned from Sharfman's decision that WHDH's operating record had been the basis for the favorable decision.

Zeidenberg wrote: ". . . a 325-page document stressed what he (Sharfman) considered WHDH's creditable record on Channel 5 was a key factor in his decision."

And: "He indicated that WHDH's chances would be poor if it were an applicant for an initial license. It represents a concentration of control of mass media in Boston, and is not, he said, strong in such areas of Commission concern as local ownership and integration of ownership and management.

"But," he said, "the classical criteria pertinent in an all-newcomer contest should not be allowed to obscure that record achieved by an 'incumbent' in a comparative case involving a renewal application. He said the station's operating record was the 'cardinal probative attribute—for good or bad.' "

As for flaws of the losers, Zeidenberg wrote: "The examiner held that BBI's proposals 'are permeated by an exuberance which makes one doubtful of their fulfillment.' "

"BBI," he noted, "proposed to devote 45.3 percent of its time to local live programming, and to operate twenty-four hours a day."

Charles River was "critically weak in the area of participation in station management by owners." Greater Boston had failed to "ascertain community needs" and had not shown that it had an antenna site.

Back in Boston the principals of Charles River and BBI went into a funk that lasted for days. They were too depressed to talk about their defeat. Some of BBI's principals were resigned to taking their tax losses and fold the corporation.

Nathan David, however, did not see it that way. He and Benny Gaguine held further discussions and were in agreement that their group should proceed with a request for oral agrument; the only recourse remaining.

"We've gone this far. Let's go to oral argument. What have we got to lose?"

"More money!" one of his colleagues remarked, acidly.

"But nothing like the amount we've already spent," said Benny. "Oral argument is relatively simple and inexpensive."

"How much will it cost?"

"Only a few more thousand. Ten to twenty grand tops."

Several distinguished academicians winced.

Leo Beranek, the noted acoustical engineer, was willing to go either way—whichever way the consensus went. But there was no consensus. The group seemed evenly divided; looking for guidance, reassurance and leadership.

Nathan David provided that. "I recommend we hang in at least through the oral argument. Benny agrees with me."

"What does Benny say our chances are?"

Nate David paused. He knew the question was inevitable. But he disliked having to give the answer: "One chance out of ten!"

A pall descended on the BBI group. No one had the urge to break the deadlock. Finally Leo Beranek spoke. "Well, it's still better odds than the Irish sweepstakes. And the prize is much larger."

Judge Mathew Brown and Oscar Handlin laughed. You couldn't fault that logic. A vote was called. The group unanimously voted to authorize Gaguine to file a petition for oral argument.

As soon as that news leaked out, the other challengers voted to do the same thing. WHDH-TV reluctantly joined with its petition.

The FCC, not unlike other government regulatory agencies,

has one implacable rule: *Take your time. Haste makes waste.*

That rule certainly applied after all parties filed their briefs. The Boston case now disappeared into a maw of time.

After six months had elapsed, counsel for the challengers began calling each other.

"What the hell goes on? Have you heard anything?"

"Not a thing."

"I haven't even got any good rumors."

"I haven't either. Not even from WHDH."

Joe Maloney laughed. Rumors were continually emanating from the station or the newspaper. By now, however, the lawyers had learned to discount them.

"Maybe the Commission is waiting for Benny to cool down; or have a heart attack."

"Maybe they're waiting for the reincarnation of Beanie."

Such grim humor helped mask their frustration; but it did little to make the weeks pass faster. For WHDH, however, the situation was ideal. Time was decidedly on their side. If possession is nine-tenths of the law, that law was made more immutable by the passage of time. Not to mention the advantage of daily accumulation of profits. The various counsel debated whether they should, individually, or collectively, scream to the Commission for expedition of the case. They could do that properly through carefully worded petitions. But this could have a negative effect. Certain staff members could be alienated—if, indeed, they had any staff support. In any event, it was a last resort which no one wanted to pursue—as yet.

Benny Gaguine did his best to look for the bright side. Maybe the delay meant that the Commission was disturbed by Sharfman's decision, and were reading it over and over. But this, he knew, was unlikely. He and Harry Plotkin, with their long Commission experience, could not really find any good omen in the fact of delay. The reverse could just as easily be true. The staff, and notably, the office of opinions and review, might be quite *pleased* with Sharfman's "masterpiece." Maybe they were waiting to make things look good, so that, after the oral argument, when the Commission would quickly rule in favor of WHDH, no one could criticize.

Finally, in May, eight months later, the date was announced. Oral argument was scheduled to be heard on September 5, 1967; the day after Labor Day—leaving all parties four months to prepare.

Benny at once began drafting his remarks; page by page, handwritten in pencil. How do you boil down several filing cabinets of record into a thirty-minute presentation? What a mockery, he thought. Yet it was the last recourse they had. He liked trial work, knew he was good at it; but this business of trying to put your case before five cynical commissioners in a mere thirty mintues was almost a travesty.

Deep into the night, in his office, he worked on his presentation, analyzed his tactics, rehearsed before a mirror, assessed his chances. Position-wise he had a slight advantage. BBI would go third, after Greater Boston and Charles River. WHDH had the best advantage. Its position was last, since it was favored in Sharfman's decision. Date-wise there was some faint consolation: the day after Labor Day meant that all the commissioners would be back fresh from a long holiday weekend.

Adding to his distress was the fact that Kenneth Cox continued to disqualify himself from the case. As former chief of the broadcast bureau, the Commission's clearing house for its broadcast matters, Ken Cox had participated in numerous actions involving WHDH in years past. Therefore, there was no question that he must disqualify himself. If he did not, WHDH could, quite properly, insist that he do so. Benny knew this, yet had been hoping that perhaps his old friend would decide to take a chance and vote in the case; or, at least, sit in on the oral argument. As one of the most respected and brilliant of all FCC Commissioners, his opinions were listened to by everyone. Cox was a Democratic appointee and a liberal. A tough regulator. Cox would be inclined, Benny thought, to sympathize with the challengers; and hopefully he might find much in Sharfman's decision to disagree with.

This left only five commissioners remaining; for another, Lee

Loevinger, had also disqualified himself because of a minor inter-
locutory matter that predated the Sharfman hearing. Loevinger,
a Democrat appointed to fill Newton Minow's term, had come
from the Justice Department where he had served as assistant attorney general in charge of the antitrust division. A long time ago,
while at the Justice Department, he had signed a paper dealing
with a complaint against WHDH. Bill Dempsey, remembering
this, had suggested in writing that Loevinger not participate in any
Commission adjudication of the case. Although this was never
formalized, Loevinger had not involved himself in any discussion
of the controversial case.

This had been enough of a blow to Benny. Although Loevinger
was difficult to predict, and had not established any clear-cut voting pattern, Benny had high hopes that Loevinger, with his great
legal mind, would be persuaded to see the merits of his side. But
then Bill Dempsey felt the same way.

Now there were only five bodies left! An untenable situation. If
any other commissioner withdrew, it would make the vote con-
ducive to a two-to-two tie.

Benny hadn't indulged much in flights of fancy about how each
commissioner might vote in a case as important as this. He knew
how most of them stood on certain issues; but he also knew that
there was no commissioner who was "totally predictable." For that
he was grateful. It helped maintain the high degree of belief he
held in the Commission system.

Take Chairman Rosel Hyde, for instance. Hyde was a veteran
of thirty-three years with the Commission. He had been chairman
twice: from 1953 to 1954; and now again as a result of President
Johnson's appointment after the not unexpected resignation of
Kennedy supporter, William Henry. Hyde was a Republican; conservative; a Mormon who neither drank nor smoked. Mild man-
nered, he was inclined to let matters resolve themselves. He dis-
avowed strong advocacy as chairman, and preferred to let his
colleagues reach their own decisions in their own due time.

Robert E. Lee was more predictable, with fourteen years on the
Commission, he had a pattern on certain issues. He was a Republican, generally conservative, and a former FBI agent. He was an

outgoing Irishman from Chicago with a great sense of humor, a raconteur of considerable skill; immensely popular in the industry. Even those broadcasters who disagreed with him were able to say with bemused affection, "At least, with Bob Lee, you know *where* you stand!"

Where would Bob Lee stand on this case? Benny had a notion about that. Frankly, he had little expectation of getting Lee's vote. Bob Lee saw nothing wrong with newspapers owning radio or television stations. There was no ogre in "concentration of mass media"; he had said so numerous times in his career—to the delight of major newspaper-broadcast groups. Yet, Bob Lee could be reversed, thought Benny. Not likely; but at least there was a possibility. Bob Lee was tough on matters of hanky-panky. The Choate ex parte matter might swing Lee over.

James J. Wadsworth was a kettle of another metal. Wadsworth was *totally* unpredictable. And, some said, rather bored with his duties as a commissioner. After Henry Cabot Lodge left the United Nations, where Jerry Wadsworth had worked as Lodge's deputy, President Johnson, needing a replacement for Frederick Ford, had taken Lodge's suggestion and made Wadsworth a commissioner.

In no time at all, the hulking, six-foot-four, ex-Ivy league football star, made it clear that he was less than enchanted with reading the mountains of paperwork, and listening to boring recitals about how much a licensee should be fined because he failed to paint his tower. The carafe of water on his desk was really a carafe of his favorite gin, some said. Whether true or not, Wadsworth had a talent for quaffing martinis at lunch without visible effect. Except that, later, if he had to sit in at a reconvened Commission meeting, he sometimes fell asleep. Chairman Hyde would tolerantly abide Wadsworth's fatigue until Jerry began to snore; whereupon he would gently nudge Wadsworth with his foot.

My only hope, thought Benny, is to get Wadsworth's attention —and keep it!

Robert Bartley was another veteran like Hyde and Lee. He had fifteen years tenure as a commissioner. A Democratic appointee, he was neither liberal nor conservative in his voting pattern; yet he was predictable on certain issues. Unlike Lee, he was firmly opposed to newspapers owning other media in the same city. Otherwise, Bartley made few waves. He was in for the full twenty years and kept a low profile.

I should get Bartley, thought Benny. If I don't, I am *absolutely* dead. The trouble with getting Bartley was that, yes, he might vote *against* the *Herald Traveler* on the concentration of media issue; but, being a Texan, and suspicious of proposals that sounded too good, he might simply choose the challenger that had the briefest filing. He might be attracted to Greater Boston's proposal, or Charles River.

The last of the five men who would decide the fate of all parties was newcomer Nicholas Johnson. Truly the virgin of the Commission, and incredibly young, only thirty-two years old. He had been on the Commission (or would be the day of the oral argument) exactly fourteen months and four days. A firebrand who had made waves at the maritime commission, Nick Johnson, in his first year, was proving to be the toughest maverick in FCC history. Beneath the grinning, beguiling exterior of this gangling, raw-boned Swede, there was a burning spirit of regulatory zeal that had sent the broadcasting establishment into a state of shock. How could a "wild character" like this come from a solid state like Iowa, broadcasters wanted to know.

Such was the cast that Benny Gaguine, and the others, faced on the day of the fateful oral argument; the day after Labor Day, September 5, 1967.

Except that, when Benny entered the Commission's large meeting room, he found only *four* commissioners present!

Ken Cox was missing; but he expected that, and so was Lee Loevinger.

Chairman Hyde was there; so was Bob Lee, Bob Bartley, and Nick Johnson.

But where the hell was Jerry Wadsworth?

The news gave Gaguine a kick in the stomach, and the others as well. They sure needed all the *bodies* they could get!

The explanation was typical of Wadsworth. Jerry hadn't yet returned from his Labor Day holiday. He wouldn't be back until tomorrow.

My god, thought Benny, I need that big guy, even if he falls asleep during my remarks.

Benny asked permission to go "off the record" so that all attorneys could hold a brief conference to discuss the matter of Wadsworth's absence. The chairman agreed that this would be appropriate, and that it would also give the commissioners a chance to "give the matter of schedule some further thought."

A consensus was quickly reached among the four lawyers. A one day's delay would be ideal, but Hyde had not mentioned that as a possibility. He had suggested that it might not be possible to reschedule the argument until sometime in November. Nevertheless, all counsel agreed that, whatever the date, it would be preferable to proceeding today without Wadsworth.

Benny stepped forward and asked permission to go back on the record. "I think I can speak for all counsel with the exception of Mr. Reilly, who didn't participate: we are all in agreement that, if at all possible, we would prefer to have a rescheduling so that all members of the Commission could be present."

Chairman Hyde surprised them with good news: "I am authorized to change the time of the proceeding to nine o'clock tomorrow morning." If there was any change in that scheduling, each of them would be notified by phone, he added.

"The argument is recessed until nine o'clock tomorrow morning in this room."

The next morning Commissioner Wadsworth showed up looking bright and fresh. He knew this was an important case and apologized to Chairman Hyde for his delay. Frankly, he didn't know much about the case. He had merely scanned Sharfman's decision, knowing that, at the oral argument, he could get the nitty gritty of it all. He looked at the clock on the wall,, which read 9:15 A.M. Quick calculation told him that, with luck, if there weren't too many long-winded questions from his colleagues, some of whom took themselves too damned seriously, they could adjourn and have the matter over with, by lunchtime. Each party was to get thirty minutes to argue their case. The broadcast bureau would get the same. Afterwards, there would be a short rebuttal period;

then the commissioners asked questions. With any luck at all, they could be out by 12:30.

Jerry Wadsworth gave a yawn and placidly scanned the room. Gaguine tried to catch his gaze, but failed. At least he's *there*, thought Benny, quite unaware that this move, this maneuver, of requesting a day's recess, would turn out to be the most important, most fortuitous single action he would ever make in the fateful Boston case.

At 9:20 A.M., the chairman rapped for order. "We will resume the proceedings in the Boston Channel 5 television matter."

The battle of the blue light—or rather, *against* the blue light, had begun.

6

Fighting the Blue Light

Each counsel stood at a respectful distance before the five commissioners who sat clad, not in robes, but in business suits, behind a raised dais in high-backed, leather chairs, carafes of water before them, along with pads of paper for note taking. Directly below, the inevitable court reporter sat before his silent stenotype machine. Behind the counsel's lectern, rows of cushioned, theater-type seats with a capacity of about two hundred fifty, were all occupied by principals of all parties along with trade and general press reporters, plus interested spectators. As counsel looked ahead he could see a panel of colored lights—blue indicated that you had used your allotted time, unless you wished to reserve a few minutes for rebuttal. Speak fast and convincingly, that was the name of the game, for this indeed was prime time. With current estimates ranging between fifty and seventy-five million dollars as the value of the Channel 5 license, this was more expensive than an evening of prime time on networks! When the red light came on, you concluded your remarks abruptly. If you did not, the chairman did it for you.

J. Joseph Maloney Jr., counsel for Greater Boston TV Company, Inc., stepped to the lectern. "May it please the Commission: I think the chairman indicated yesterday that I should devote the first ten minutes of my time to what we call the old case . . ." Maloney was referring to the original Greater Boston group which differed in organization from the present group called Greater Boston II. Before he did this, however, he sketched expertly in a few minutes the general background of the complex case.

Then he turned without delay to the matter of Robert Choate. Noting that the Commission had adopted Judge Stern's findings of fact, but reversed Stern on his conclusion, Maloney quoted from that decision. "However, we do conclude that Choate demonstrated an attempted pattern of influence. He attempted, in effect, to influence the outcome of the case by presenting argument on a portion thereof to a member of the Commission ex parte. The very attempt to establish such a pattern of influence does violence to the integrity of the Commission's processes."

Again quoting: "There is no question that the attempted pattern of influence disclosed on this record reflects adversely on WHDH."

Maloney struck hard at Herbert Sharfman. "Examiner Sharfman, if I may use the expression, has wept crocodile tears at the thought of this corporation carrying an albatross around its neck in perpetuity; there must be an end to the punishment. I agree with that. Nothing should go on forever. I think the stigma or demerit should attach to the corporation only for this case, for the length of this case.

"I think that stigma should attach throughout the Channel 5 Boston case. If they wanted to apply for Channel 2 in St. Louis, I don't think the stigma would apply now to WHDH, Inc. They no longer have Mr. Choate and they are entitled to a fresh start someplace else. But in this case I say the stigma *persists* until the end of the case."

The diversification issue being WHDH's vulnerable spot, Maloney patted his ample girth and stressed that issue: ". . . the record in this case shows that in the five or six years from 1959 through 1964, WHDH, Inc. paid cash dividends of some seven million dollars, which was not distributed then to the stockholders of the Herald Traveler Corporation, but was used, in effect, to build a new plant and to further the corporate business of the newspaper.

"To me it is repugnant under the First Amendment. It is a subsidy to the press, and a subsidized press is not a free press. The reason I say it is a subsidy is this money flowed from the grant of Channel 5 in Boston.

"This may perhaps be a novel argument before the Commission, but to me, it is the most fundamental thing in the case.

". . . there are many things I could talk about, but to boil down some forty thousand pages into twenty minutes not being the easiest thing in the world, I will say, just in broad stroke, many of the witnesses who testified for WHDH were, in my opinion, somewhat evasive, not convincingly credible, in quite a few areas."

Again he went after Sharfman. "I have to say that Examiner Sharfman did not make this observation. I got the impression, frankly, that he is such a nice, gentle man that he doesn't want to see any evil, or hear any evil, or speak any evil about anybody. That theme runs through his whole initial decision. There were a lot of strong things brought out at that hearing which he manages to overlook, sweep under the rug or attach no significance to them."

Maloney then defended the major weakness of his own case: the fact that, if awarded the license, his group would take over WHDH's plant, personnel and continue the same programs. "What Greater Boston II did, was say that:

> 'Here we are, forty people who have lived in Boston all our lives. We watch television a normal amount and we know that WHDH is doing a good job, program-wise.
>
> 'If it had been determined that WHDH's programs were not good and did not meet the needs of the community, then, of course, we should go down the drain as not having made a proper survey.
>
> 'Examiner Shrafman says they have done an outstanding job of meeting the needs of the community. We took the course that we did at our own risk. We should have been punished for it if we were wrong.
>
> 'But . . . we live there. We know their programs are sound. We propose to continue them if we are the favored applicant.' "

From here he segued into an attack on the other losers. "The other applicants had the usual form of comparative hearing proposal. They were going to hire staffs and train them. They were going to change a lot of programs around. To my mind, they were the same old tired comparative TV proposals that certainly you gentlemen have seen a lot of in the last fifteen years," he said, singling out the three veteran Commissioners, Hyde, Lee and Bartley. "They are kind of put together by—with all due respect —legal carpenters. I mean no offense to Mr. Gaguine or Mr. Plotkin." (Both of whom made notes at this slur) "They are manufactured things. I think ours was a practical approach to an unusual problem. They didn't show any interest in this Channel 5 until the decision of September 1962 when . . . the Commission invited new applicants. A lot of people began to see the dollar signs before their eyes, and they put together these cases.

"Frankly, I don't think they are very good cases even of that kind, but I think that they are not at all realistic. It is a self-serving process, where they write memos to each other and themselves, and build a case. Frankly, I can't buy it.

"Unless there are any questions, I will reserve the rest of my time for rebuttal."

Chairman Hyde announced: "You have sixteen minutes remaining. Next is Charles River Civic Television, Inc."

Harry A. Plotkin arose and immediately requested that he "get the blue light at plus twenty," meaning that he wished to reserve the balance of his time for rebuttal.

Brushing almost disdainfully over the case of Greater Boston, he concentrated on WHDH, attacking on a number of points, and as inevitably as Maloney, soon got into the Choate matter.

"The conduct (Choate's) as described by the Commission was unpardonable, unforgiveable. I would not want to use stronger words myself. The examiner, however, would overlook the conduct of Mr. Choate at this time because Mr. Choate is now dead, and he said it would be Biblical fury to pursue Mr. Choate and WHDH for conduct that was done while Mr. Choate was alive.

"I have three answers to that. In the first place, Mr. Choate was an integral part of the applicant. He was really its personification, so far as the Commission was concerned. He was the individual to whom you looked. He was the individual to whom the corporation looked.

"Not only did the directors of WHDH (not) undertake to take any measures reprimanding Mr. Choate, or removing him, but, on the contrary, after they were fully conversant with all the facts, they proceed to reelect him unanimously; in effect, to condone his conduct."

Then Harry Plotkin struck at the present chief executive officer of WHDH, Inc., George Akerson, who, "on the stand in this very proceeding, has indicated that, so far as he is concerned, unless he was specifically deterred by counsel, he today sees nothing wrong with his coming in and trying to talk to a member of the Federal Communications Commission while the case is in adjudication. . .

"Mr. Choate never learned, the directors never learned, and Mr. Akerson never learned. It seems to me, in the face of that, to say that this corporation is qualified, in light of this history, would be a travesty on justice."

Plotkin reminded the Commission that WHDH was no longer a New England or a Massachusetts based corporation. "Only 27 percent of the stock is owned by New Englanders." Henry Garfinkle, the controversial magazine distributor, now owned about 18 percent. John Blair and Company, the station's sales representative, owned "just short" of 10 percent. The estate of a New Yorker, Herman Muller (now dead) owned 5 percent. A Midwest group owned 10–15 percent. The Commission knew very little about the background of these people, Plotkin stated. As for Garfinkle: "He showed himself to be a witness who was not always careful about the accuracy of his remarks".

Plotkin then launched into a diatribe on the "very elaborate promises" that WHDH had originally made to the Commission.

William Dempsey, WHDH counsel, interrupted him, "I wonder if we are going to hear an argument entirely outside the record in this case, or whether we will confine ourselves to the record."

Plotkin retorted, "Mr. Dempsey will have the opportunity to rebut, Mr. Chairman, if he thinks I have gone outside the record. I don't think he should interrupt counsel."

The chairman didn't think so either. He instructed Plotkin to proceed.

"On promise and performance . . . what happened? Mr. McGrath, who has been the general manager throughout the whole period, was called as a witness, and I must say made a very frank witness. We went through every single program that they had described in their 1954 application upon which the Commission made the grant, and on virtually every single one of their types of programmings Mr. McGrath said, 'We are not broadcasting it'; and on almost every single one said, 'We never broadcast that type of programming from the beginning.'

"The examiner gives this very light treatment. First he says on promise and performance we know that people can't really live up to their promises; things change.

"Then he said, 'However, they have had a very, very good operation and, therefore, since they have a record of good operation and you people only make a promise, you are not entitled to comparative consideration at all because they have shown they can do it and you haven't shown you can do it.' " Plotkin's exasperation brought color to his face. *Of course we haven't shown we can do it. We can't do that until we are in a position to do it!*"

"Then he (Sharfman) says it is a good record of operation without comparing it with their promises, and, secondly, without in any way undertaking to compare it with what is the standard, what *is* a good record of operation. The Commission in the comparative criteria statement has said that, "We will not record something as unusually good unless there is unusually good emphasis on local live programming.

"In this case, the programming looks at the best mediocre. It is the type of program that the Commission in its comparative statement has said we expect applicants to carry out."

Then, after a strong thrust at the diversification factor, Plotkin began extolling his own group. *Quality* was his theme. Thomas D. Cabot, their chief principal, had made the Cabot Corporation "into a major factor in world production of carbon black, both here and overseas." He served on the governing bodies of such schools as Harvard, MIT, Radcliffe, the Fletcher School of Law and Diplomacy, the Hampton Institute and others. Ted Jones, their proposed general manager, was the principal owner of a good music station, WCRB, in nearby Waltham; a station that broadcasts concerts of the Boston Symphony Orchestra. Robert Saudek, creator of *Omnibus,* was "a truly creative genius on the American television scene."

He defended the fact that Charles River uniquely was to be owned by a charitable foundation with its profits going to a charitable trust for the purpose of supporting education in the Boston area.

"This is not just a mere gimmick. These people, knowing that the channel was available, did not want to come in and get something for their own private use. They said, 'Here is an important resource that we want to use. We are not asking for a credit, saying that the Commission ought to give us a credit because it is going to be for charity.' This explains the kind of people they are, their motivation.

"They said, 'We are not going to come in like vultures and try to seize an important asset and use it for our own personal good. We will run it as a commercial enterprise, but the benefits thereof will not inure to our own benefit but for charity.' "

Then Harry Plotkin came up with a point that caused several commissioners to make notes. "We have made an offer to WHDH which they do not have to address themselves to until after a final decision so they are not under the gun, to pay up to five million for the assets and good will of the station.

"So we are *not* trying to steal anything from them . . ."

Plotkin was running out of time. The blue light had switched on and he knew he must reserve a few minutes for rebuttal. He concentrated, in his final moments, on BBI. They were not so great, he said. Some of their principals did not have very strong Boston roots. Their integration of principals within their daily operating schedule was "meaningless." A make-work sort of thing. "For example, sixteen of their principals will be active on one particular program. They will fall all over themselves! I don't know what sixteen people who have no experience in producing programs are going to be doing. This is a paper presentation. It is window dressing."

The Chairman said: "You have two minutes remaining."

Harry Plotkin said he would reserve the balance of his time for rebuttal.

Benito Gaguine, representing Boston Broadcasters, Inc., now stepped to the lectern. Short, portly, volatile Benny was staring hard at James Wadsworth. The diffident member of the Commission, so far, had shown considerable interest; but in the last few minutes, his interest seemed to have waned. He had to "grab" Wadsworth, and therefore aimed much of his argument directly at the huge ex-football player.

"I would like to reserve five minutes of my time," he snapped.

Feeling that Harry Plotkin had gotten across some telling points, he concentrated on Charles River. "Charles River is comprised primarily of wealthy and of elderly persons. During prime time, it proposes to do little more than perform switching services for the CBS network. Its overriding objective, as described by its stockholders, is the charity angle." Profit distribution to its parent foundation would "assist them in carrying out what they consider to be their charitable obligations with the least strain on current income and on their estates." Certainly Charles River did not merit any preference over the great BBI group. As for Greater Boston II, he gave it scarcely a paragraph. "This is a retread of Greater Boston I without the famous Mr. Henry. The examiner properly found it to be disqualified."

Then, rising to the tip of his five feet four inches, Benny put on his best expression of righteous indignation. "This is the longest comparative case in the history of the Commission, but it can be one of the easiest for you to decide. The initial decision granting WHDH just cannot stand. Let me stress that your decision to grant an applicant other than WHDH will *not* open what some of you may fear to be an administrative Pandora's box. It will *not* have any significant effect on future renewal cases." That point, Benny knew, was an important one to make, vital, in fact. The Commission had *never* taken away the license of a major market television station. The first time it did would bring forth a roar of panic, shock and fear from the broadcast industry. The Commission had to be sold the idea that this case was *sui generis*—one of a kind.

Then, turning to his own group, he reminded the Commission

what Sharfman had said about the distinction and quality of the principals in both Charles River and BBI. Sharfman had said: "While wealthy businessmen are common in TV applicants, they seldom have as stockholders, noted historians, academicians, physicists, biologists, inventors, economists, anthropologists, physicians, captains of industry and services, financiers, judges, public officials and producers."

Never one inclined to excessive modesty, Benny added: "The examiner undoubtedly had BBI in mind for it is the *only* applicant with at least *one* representative in *each* of these categories. The people constituting BBI are truly outstanding representatives of the community."

Yet, BBI, he insisted, was not merely a "star-studded cast," as Sharfman had said. Its proposals were feasible, doable and practical. The examiner was wrong to characterize BBI's efforts as having been done "in an ecstasy of self-abasement." The principals were not "window dressers." They were "doers and not drones." Sharfman was doing grave injury to "insinuate that outstanding people of the stature and of the character described by his own findings would join together to put a counterfeit proposal before you." Yes, this was a group that would *not* maximize profits. It would reduce commerical clutter in Boston, operate well below the outer limits of the NAB broadcasting code. Not only would commercial messages be reduced "sharply," but BBI would editorialize, whereas WHDH had a policy "against editorializing"; and Charles River couldn't editorialize on political subjects "without losing its tax-exempt status."

BBI alone, he reminded them, proposed that all political broadcasts would be free. BBI alone proposed a twenty-four-hour operation. BBI alone proposed procedures by which it would get "assistance of community leaders and of viewers in determining future program changes." He expressed dismay that Sharfman had conceded that BBI's proposed integration of principals was feasible; and then, at the same time, "faults its motives." Although terming the BBI proposal as "excessive," the examiner had been unable to find that "it cannot or will not be effectuated." "Instead," said Gaguine, "he seems to view it as so nearly perfect as to indicate some kind of lack of sincerity. If all of you want to reward mediocrity, you can adopt this logic; but if you want to improve telelvision programming, you have to reject it."

Boston, explained Benny, was a market that generated in excess of thirty-five million dollars per year in advertising revenues. In 1966 it provided TV stations with "a profit in excess of nineteen million dollars.

"Surely part of this can, and certainly should, be plowed back into local programming . . . Can it be doubted that a need exists for at least *one* Boston station with the guts to switch off some network program during prime time and give the public a choice?"

Now, in a staccato, rapid-fire tone that accelerated in tempo and ardor—was Wadsworth paying attention?—yes, he was!— Gaguine listed eight reasons why WHDH was not deserving of consideration.

WHDH had *not* made a survey of community needs in the past ten years. WHDH had *never* followed through on its use of its program advisory committee. WHDH's integration was minimal. WHDH was now dominantly owned by interests in New York and the Midwest. WHDH, from "the minute it went on the air in 1957, scrapped its program proposal." WHDH had two newspapers, a 50-kilowatt AM station, an FM station and CATV interests, but despite this, Sharfman had given no comparative consideration to the factor of diversification of media. WHDH was guilty of "testimonial excesses." And last, WHDH had violated the communications act and the Commission's rules in connection with "transfer of control, multiple ownership and many other matters.

"And WHDH's witness and principal," said Benny reaching a crescendo, "and here I am going to use a strong word—committed *perjury* in this proceeding—" Bill Dempsey turned pale at this charge. Gasps of astonishment came from the dais. Now color flooded Dempsey's face, especially in the region of his neck. Dempsey was livid.

". . . committed perjury in this proceeding, so these derelictions are explained away or forgiven. The initial decision, in short, cannot stand! Its conclusions must be completely replaced."

Benny was not through yet. "I have only mentioned some highlights of WHDH's sordid record. Now I would like to expand on a couple of items." There was undeniably a transfer of control, he charged. In addition, both Akerson and Garfinkle had perjured themselves when questioned about a certain article in the *Wall Street Journal*. The two men were *not* in accord, as Akerson had testified in the hearing. There were "fundamental differences of opinion" between them.

"I have suggested that a decision granting one of the other applicants will *not* open a Pandora's box. The case before you today is *sui generis* both in law and in fact . . . your decision today will be a ticket for *this* train, *this* trip, and *this* day only. It will *not* affect subsequent renewal cases. It will *not* prove a hindrance to orderly Commission processes . . . this case is so unique that the Commission need have *no* concern that a denial of WHDH will serve as a precedent for wholesale attack on renewing licenses." Now, in a new fervor of zeal, Gaguine rattled off a litany of some of the charges he had made before: Attempts by Choate to subvert the hearing process . . . *perjury* . . . unreported violations of the Commission's multiple ownership rule and of other reporting requirements . . . arrogant and callous disregard of its responsibilities . . . a mediocre past broadcast record . . .

"The record compels the conclusion that the application of WHDH cannot be granted!"

Benny Gaguine had made his case with all the considerate passion he was able to muster. He knew it was time to get off stage. Besides, he was tired. He would like, he said, to reserve the rest of his time for rebuttal.

The chairman acknowledged that Benny had five minutes of time remaining. He glanced at his colleagues. After these impassioned remarks, it looked like a good time to take a rest.

"We will recess for a five-minute break," said Chairman Hyde.

Following the recess, the FCC's Broadcast Bureau, through its counsel, John F. Reilly, put in his case. It was brief and low-key, which came as a relief after Benito Gaguine's high-pitched argument. Reilly had little to say, because the role of the Broadcast Bureau, by custom of the Commission, had been a limited one.

There *was* a transfer of control in WHDH-TV, said Reilly. Greater Boston II did *not* perform a program survey in accordance with the Commission's policy. It also had not met the burden of proving that it had an antenna site in the event it was to be awarded the license. In general, said Reilly, the bureau supported the conclusions reached by the hearing examiner in his initial decision. "As a matter of fact, it is somewhat the other way around. We support (the decision) because he (Sharfman) adopted the positions of the Broadcast Bureau with respect to these issues, except with respect to transfer of control."

Chairman Hyde had one question regarding WHDH's transfer of control issue: "Does the bureau have a suggestion or an opinion as to when an application for a consent to transfer of control should have been filed?"

"Certainly, sir," replied Reilly. "One should have been filed under section 1.541 of our rules when Mr. Akerson succeeded Mr. Choate upon Mr. Choate's death."

Commissioner Bartley had a question: "I got the impression that there had been, in fact, a transfer in influence and power, at least, from Choate to Akerson prior to Choate's death."

Reilly hedged: "Choate was not active from some point in October 1963 because he was then ill; he was going into his final illness. Akerson was taking over more and more power with Choate still alive. There is a debatable area."

"Thank you," said Rosel Hyde. "WHDH, Inc. is next. Mr. Dempsey?"

The final act of the expensive drama was to begin. William J. Dempsey stepped to the lectern. He set his papers down carefully and scanned the faces on the dais. Handsome, gray haired, and urbane, Dempsey made a striking impression. Like Gaguine and Plotkin, and so many of the other top lawyers who practiced before the FCC, Bill Dempsey had served the Commission. As general counsel, Dempsey at one time had been senior to Rosel Hyde. The FCC was a place to earn your reputation; a natural stepping stone to lucrative law practice. This case had helped support Bill Dempsey and his partner, William Koplovitz, for twenty years. It had helped Bill put his son through law school.

As a youngster, Dempsey's son had watched his father present arguments in the first comparative hearing in 1954. Now young John Dempsey was sitting in one of the seats toward the rear, still learning, still learning from the Boston case.

In terms of histrionics and shrill advocacy, Dempsey knew he was no match for the others, particularly his old friend, Benny Gaguine. Nor had he any desire to try. His role today would be simply to defend Sharfman's decision. There it was, all on the record. Sharfman had recognized the truth and wrote it in his decision. That was the only tack he need take.

Point by point, in measured, quiet tones that were in striking contrast to Gaguine, he defended the WHDH record.

On Choate: "The Commission found that, in neither of the Choate-McConnaughey meetings, was there *any* discussion of the merits of the pending case. It found that under the circumstances, and I read from the decision, 'It would be unrealistic to conclude that he'—meaning the chairman—'was influenced by Choate's contacts, or that the grant was actually secured as a result of improper activities.'

"And they found the ultimate conclusion: 'Mr. Choate is *not* guilty of offering any material inducements to influence the outcome of the proceeding, or of actually arguing the merits of the case ex parte; but, rather, of attempting to establish a personal relationship with a member of the Commission with the hope of creating a favorable bias in that gentleman's mind which might be calculated to operate in favor of WHDH in the event of a close decision.' "

Dempsey said he was not inclined to argue the Commission's decision of July 1960, nor the Commission's decision of September 1962 when it concluded that Mr. Choate had a pattern of influence in mind when he held his meetings with Mr. McConnaughey. But certainly Chairman McConnaughey had found nothing improper in what Mr. Choate did; nor had Judge Horace Stern. He reminded them that Commissioner Frederick Ford, in 1962, concluded "on reflection, that he had been *wrong* in attributing an improper motive to Mr. Choate."

Then he voiced the old lament; how long must this issue go on?

"The question is," said Dempsey, "does that motive live longer than Mr. Choate? Does it, like the grin on the Cheshire cat, remain *after* Mr. Choate has departed the scene, to haunt WHDH?"

Turning to his rivals, particularly Ben Gaguine, his voice took on bitter, scathing sarcasm. "With respect to BBI promises, Mr. Gaguine has made my argument for me. The *excess* beyond the bounds of *any decency* or *advocacy* that Mr. Gaguine has indulged in has been *typical* of the BBI proposal and representations throughout this case. He would have this Commission assume its examiner sat there smiling complacently and even paternally at witness after witness from WHDH who got on the stand and perjured themselves, that Commission counsel, who was there to protect the public and the Commission, nodded pleasantly and did nothing whatsoever about it, because neither the examiner nor the Commission's counsel, found anything like the things Mr. Gaguine has *shouted* at you this morning."

Now Dempsey swung his hardest punch: "It is my considered conviction that, when this Commission has a chance to consider the record, its *final* decision will contain a severe *censure* and *rebuke* to Mr. Gaguine for his statements today." Benny Gaguine glared back defiantly. Dempsey returned to his theme: the *record* . . . judge this case, we beg of you, on the *record*. "It is the *record* that will determine that, and not my writing strong language to answer his strong language. I leave it at that."

In a sense, Dempsey had both an easier and a more difficult problem than his zealous challengers. It was always easier to be dramatic and go on the attack. Standing on one's record did not make for a Pyrrhic victory in terms of an oral argument; but on reflection, when, in more sober moments, the commissioners read the official report of these proceedings, they would certainly have to take note of the record—the record of the station's performance; and Sharfman's favorable decision.

He harped over and over again on this theme: "The *record* is going to determine this case . . . We believed then, and believe now, that the Commission will determine whether WHDH should be renewed based on the *record* it made, not on a predetermination made in December 1962 before the Commission had examined its application. Thank you."

"Thank you," said the chairman. "Mr. Maloney, you have time available for rebuttal."

Joe Maloney returned to the lectern and defended his group from charges made that Greater Boston II's case was minimal.

"I would like to remind the Commission once more just what it is. We propose the programs of WHDH which the examiner has found to be of exceptional quality. We propose to use their staff and facilities. We see nothing wrong with their operation as such."

He took issue with Benny Gaguine's statement that BBI was the only applicant which intended to editorialize. His group *also* was going to editorialize. As for their failure to take surveys of their community's needs, in light of WHDH's excellent schedule, which already was fulfilling the community's needs, why go out and make new "blue sky" surveys? And, inevitably, he ended with the matter of Choate.

"Mr. Dempsey makes much of the fact that the commissioners found that, while Mr. Choate tried to influence Mr. McConnaughey, he didn't. Since seven years ago I have wondered, myself —and this is the first time I have said it out loud—when it was known that he tried to influence him, and when Mr. McConnaughey voted for him, how can anyone *know* whether he had any success or not in his efforts to influence him?" Maloney paused. "I just don't *know* how *anyone* knows."

He paused again.

"If you adopt the view that Mr. Choate's death ends that aspect of the case, from a very practical point of view, what you are doing is putting a *premium* on finding people with short life expectancies to make ex parte contacts!"

Harry Plotkin stepped up next to deliver his rebuttal. He had scarcely begun when Commissioner Robert Bartley interrupted him: How about editorializing?

The attorney was quick to reply. "The station *will* editorialize." It might have to go easy on supporting, or opposing, candidates, but otherwise, there would be no restriction.

Commissioner Wadsworth surprised everyone with a sudden question. "How about legislation?"

Plotkin replied, yes . . . "so long as it doesn't constitute a substantial part."

To Wadsworth, and perhaps the others, the answer seemed vague. Wadsworth asked, "If the station should actually support legislation either before the Massachusetts legislature, or before the Congress, it would be rather injurious, wouldn't it, to your standing as a nonprofit organization?"

Harry Plotkin shook his head in disagreement. "Mr. Cabot indicated that he, for one, and he is the one who originated the idea, would be prepared to see them lose their tax exemption. In other words, pay another set of taxes."

Commissioner Nicholas Johnson then put some questions that revealed the trend of his mind. He wanted to know more about Charles River's programming proposals. How much live? How much network and news?

Plotkin told him. Twenty-six percent local live; about 50 percent network. The balance would be news and film.

Johnson wanted examples. Plotkin referred him to the record. "We are going to carry the Boston Symphony Orchestra, for example. We are going to carry some broadcasts from a museum in Boston. There are specific proposals, programs in conjunction with universities, and so forth."

Young Nick Johnson was not satisfied. "The kind of local live that you were talking about sounds to me somewhat similar to the kind of local live that the Boston educational station does."

No, said Plotkin. There *was* a difference. "We will have excellent operating revenues to undertake some of the ventures that WGBH (the educational station in Boston) cannot undertake."

Johnson probed further. Were they going to take their profits and put them in programming? Or turn them over to the foundation for charitable expenditure? Plotkin assured him that Charles River was committed to many specific programs whether sponsored or not. "The Boston Symphony, for example, will be on an unsponsored basis."

Concluding, Plotkin warned about "glib promises." Charles

River would hope that "profits would be at a level so that the educational institutions would get some of it; but they also committed themselves in a very, very specific matter to prestige types of programming. . . . The Commission's experience has shown all along that promises easily made are not so easily kept."

"Thank you," said Johnson.

Benny Gaguine was already at the lectern eager to begin. He couldn't resist a barb at Johnson's interruption of another counsel's rebuttal time. "Mr. Johnson," he said, "I hope you will ask me those questions on your *own* time."

The commissioner smiled, but was not pleased. Almost before Gaguine could get started on his rebuttal, Johnson interrupted caustically. "Mr. Gaguine, if I may, *on your time*, ask a question relating to what you have just spoken to, Mr. Plotkin did raise the question of your principals, and you chose not to direct yourself to that, presumably for good reason. . . . If you wish to remain in that position, that is very well, and we will refer to the record."

Benny Gaguine lost his cool. His anger flared. "Sir, can I answer that on *your* time? We have Professor Handlin, who is a Pulitzer Prize winner."

Johnson seemed to relish giving Benny the needle. How about the three gentlemen Plotkin had referred to, men who had little contact with Boston, Messrs. David, Burdick and Pickard?

Benny gave quick, scant answers. Nathan David was educated in Boston and still lived there, although he had been away for a while. Mr. Burdick had been partially educated in Boston. Mr. Pickard had spent a number of years in Boston as head of a news department for the Westinghouse TV station. All the rest came from Boston. Keerist! Why do I have to spend *my* valuable time on these piddling matters, Benny thought. "Sir, I asked for an hour and I got thirty minutes. I tightened up what I could to twenty-five, and I was trying to save five for rebuttal."

Commissioner Johnson grinned, immensely pleased with Benny's frustration. "Your answer is quite adequate."

"Thank you, *sir*," Benny said, his voice tinged with sarcasm. Now he launched into his (hopefully uninterrupted) rebuttal.

"An applicant is people," he began. Compare our people "to

Choate, to Akerson, and to the largest beneficial stockholder of WHDH, Garfinkle.

"I have made strong charges against these two gentlemen. Apparently I have offended Mr. Dempsey; but I meant every word of it. I suggest that you *accept* his challenge, to which I add mine, that you review the record with utmost care and see whether my charges are warranted.

"I am convinced that they are. On Mr. Dempsey's argument that somebody can go out and buy both a license and a record, I would like to point out, and this is just theoretical . . . and perhaps Mr. Dempsey will quote me of excesses again, that the Cosa Nostra, which is now being highly publicized, could probably buy control of an applicant and under his theory acquire the status of an existing license!"

Benny had done it again. Eyebrows went up. Notes were taken. Perhaps he was going too far, but this was the last desperate shot he had. At least there was *no* question about having their attention. Even Jerry Wadsworth was leaning forward.

"About Choate's activities, Mr. Dempsey seems to ask for a preference for Choate's acts. Nowhere has this activity ever been anything less than improper. Nowhere was it condoned, either by the Commission or the court. And even in this proceeding it was termed by the examiner as inexcusable.

"One last thing. Mr. Maloney suggests that you read Chairman Minow's dissent. I agree. Let me refer to just one sentence. 'However, the majority, by granting only a four-month license to WHDH, does provide the opportunity for the filing of competing applications at an early date. So far as I am concerned, the existing temporary licensee will *not* enjoy a preferred position in any such proceeding.' "

Benny's pace quickened as he tried to get in every last ounce of advocacy: more local live programming than any of the others . . . preempt certain CBS programs for "good, solid, locally-produced programs . . . a promise not to extract every last nickel of profit, "either to support a newspaper and to build wings and equipment for newspapers, or to turn it over to charity . . .

"We think it is a novel, good, fresh and desirable idea to take some of that money and put it back to the people who pay for it. We *have* the people; we *have* the staff; and we *have* everything that is required to put that programming on the air. If you don't think we will do it, we challenge the Commission: give us a four-month license, or give us a one-year license, and call it up for renewal, and see if we back up our programs."

Commissioner Bartley wryly interjected: "I can't help but remark, I don't think it is a *novel* proposal. I think it is just an *old-fashioned* one."

Thanks, thought Benny. I needed that! "It is old-fashioned enough, I think, to have been the original proposal of WHDH back in 1954. I agree with Mr. Plotkin that WHDH sure didn't follow through on it."

"Why," asked Nick Johnson, "do you think there will be *less* pressure on you in terms of the amount of money you have available to put into programming than there would be on the Charles River proposal?"

"It is very simple, sir," replied Gaguine. "Let me just go back to people. We have, as a member of our group, Professor Handlin. He is a professor at Harvard, one of the brightest ranking professors. He has received a Pulitzer Prize for his work. He is a noted historian.

"We invited him to join our group. He was friendly with one of our stockholders. He was intrigued with the idea and he told us that, before he joined the group, he wanted to see the policies. In effect, he said he wanted to go farther than that. Before he joined the group he wanted to write out the policies that he wanted to live by and then to see whether we would accept them.

"He *wrote* those policies. They were debated. They were written, rewritten. He joined us. He is going to participate and he is going to see to it that we follow those policies. The same thing can be said for Dr. Knowles, the head of the Massachusetts General Hospital."

Johnson interrupted, "Professors have been known to make investments, Mr. Gaguine."

Gaguine nodded. "This is a group that is willing to make a good investment. Again, when it comes to character, this is a group composed of individuals, some of whom don't really need a lot of money . . . they don't need every nickel they can get. Dr. Knowles, the head of the Massachusetts General Hospital, told this Commission on this record that he wanted to join this group because he wanted to get a message concerning health across to the people, that he didn't think television was doing the job it should.

"This is the kind of group it is. You can only rely on them if you look at them and see that they are the *kind* of people you can rely on. We think that is what we have."

"Thank you," said Johnson.

Suddenly it was all over! After one short, final point in rebuttal by John F. Reilly of the Broadcast Bureau, Chairman Rosel Hyde said, "This, I believe, concludes the proceeding. The matter will be taken under advisement."

Commissioner Jerry Wadsworth looked at his watch, only 12:20, excellent! No worry about reconvening after lunch. He could look forward to a leisurely, relaxing meal at the International Club which he had founded.

The stenotype operator packed up his machine.

The tense counsel mixed with their respective groups and made small talk. No one ever felt satisfied after an oral hearing. The ignominy of it, thought Benny Gaguine, was that, after all this time, all this expense, all this mountain of record—and then to be thrust before a ridiculous panel of lights and told to talk furiously until the blue light went on! Benny's gut churned. He felt as though he had been kicked in the stomach; and he was certain the others felt the same way.

He sat there brooding as he watched *Herald Traveler* reporters, along with Akerson, Harold Clancy and other executives from WHDH-TV, cluster around Bill Dempsey, congratulating him on the excellent job he had done. Suddenly he realized how tough, really tough, it was fighting a station owned by a powerful newspaper. I've blown it, but good, he thought. What he had intended to be the best oral argument ever presented at the FCC had turned out to be something less—much less—maybe a debacle. He probably had alienated *all* the commissioners with his perjury charge. But damn it, as far as he was concerned, it was true. Why Sharfman had glossed over certain discrepancies in the testimony of George Akerson and Garfinkle, he never would be able to understand. And, he brooded, if he hadn't hurt himself with the perjury charge, he had certainly blown his chances of getting Nick Johnson's vote. What an insolent sonofabitch! He's as tough as I am. Also, that Cosa Nostra remark hadn't gone over too well either.

Keerist, he thought with deep melancholy, my wife and two sons were out there watching me!

7

How a Decision is Reached

After an oral argument, discussion of the case usually is held immediately afterward, or sometime during the same day. If a consensus is reached it is not unusual for a vote to be called by the chairman on the same day.

In the Boston case, however, Rosel Hyde made no attempt to speed the discussion process. This case was far too important. Also, it was a case that, personally, gave him much trouble. In some ways it was the most vexing, most difficult licensing case he had ever had, for several reasons:

The ex parte issue, for one, deeply troubled him. He remembered the odorous conduct of some of his colleagues in the free-wheeling era when the Commission was a pressure tank of ex parte attempts. Rosel Hyde deplored Richard Mack's drinking habit, his slurred speech at Commission meetings. He recalled the great pressures to have television licenses granted after the 1953 freeze on licensing when the Commission faced a backlog of hundreds of important VHF applications. Attempts at ex parte were made to him directly, usually by members of Congress, just as attempts were made to the other commissioners. Strong, powerful applicants were chafing to get licenses granted in their markets. Public opinion was with them. Network programming was beginning to flourish. Networks needed major market affiliates. People demanded to see these programs. Rosel Hyde had acted in an ingenious way to break this backlog at that time. Although criticized by some members of his staff, it had turned out to be a correct solution. He had suggested that, in markets where there were multiple contenders, competing applicants should pool their resources; and if they did, the Commission would act quickly to authorize grants. This became known as the "Hyde Plan" and he was proud of the fact that it helped to speed up the establishment of a truly national television service.

But he was not proud of the ex parte taint on WHDH's record. However, he agreed with Herb Sharfman and the contention of WHDH: how long must the station continue to wear this albatross? In the past, he had voted originally against the station on the issue of diversification: later he had voted to grant the station a four-month license on the basis of its operating record.

On the issue of diversification he knew that WHDH was unquestionably weak. But when a station had done as good a job as WHDH . . . when it had demonstrated by its performance that it was conscientiously broadcasting in the "public interest, convenience and necessity" . . . do you then, in the name of diversification, ex parte, or any other combination of issues, take away . . . actually *take away* its license? Would that not undermine the whole Commission licensing scheme? Would that not discourage venture capital from investing in television stations? Would it not create such a furor politically that Congress, spurred by broadcasters, would demand an investigation?

The applications of the three challengers were impressive, Hyde thought. No question about their quality. Particularly those of Charles River and BBI. Of the two, he guessed BBI had a slight edge; but if he voted for BBI, he had a special kind of problem: Benny Gaguine had once served as his legal assistant during Benny's long and distinguished career at the Commission. This could cause eyebrows to lift even though it would be ridiculous to assume that friendship ever could influence his vote. It never had in the past. Benny knew this. Everyone at the Commission knew this. Nevertheless it could become a point of controversy. And if he voted for Charles River, what then would Benny think? That he had over-reacted because of his sensitivity on this point?

These were only a few of the problems that tormented Rosel Hyde as, without enthusiasm, he called for discussion of the Boston case following oral argument. He wondered how soon a consensus would become apparent. There was much to discuss. It might take weeks. In the past, certain chairmen, particularly Newton Minow and Wayne Coy, sought to get a consensus quickly after oral argument while issues were fresh on everyone's mind. He saw nothing wrong with that, although it did have its faults. In the past, under Chairmen McConnaughey and Doerfer there were some bad leaks on important decisions. *Broadcasting Magazine* and *Television Digest,* both enterprising trade magazines, sometimes had the correct prediction of a vote before the vote was actually taken. So, seeking an early vote was not Hyde's style, nor was advocacy. Some chairmen saw nothing wrong in urging their own points of view. Hyde liked to let matters take their own course. He seldom urged his views on his colleagues. And during the initial discussions of this case he sat silently, listening to the conflicting views of the various, complex issues.

Robert E. Lee, however, was not reticent about stating his views. He believed that WHDH-TV had an outstanding broadcast record. The best indication of that fact was its high percentage of local live programming—22 percent!

"How many stations can show that kind of record?" he asked. "That's a higher percentage than most of your so-called good operators. And extremely high for a network-affiliated station."

On diversification, Lee said: "I've said it before, and I'll say it again: being owned by a newspaper is not, of itself, wrong. The question is: Is the station well operated? Is it doing a good job? I say that WHDH-TV has done an excellent job!" On this controversial issue of diversification, Bob Lee stood with his colleague, Lee Loevinger, who was fond of saying that criteria only constituted general guidelines, and that each case must be examined and judged on its merits. To Bob Lee, the critical question was: do you take away the license of an excellent station like WHDH-TV in the face of the favorable decision written by Sharfman? Or do you support Sharfman?

When it was time to vote there was little doubt where Lee would stand.

"How about the Choate matter?" someone asked.

Bob Lee grimaced as though he had bitten into an unripe key lime. Sooner or later, he knew, that question was bound to come up.

"Choate?" he replied. "That poor guy is dead. Can't we let him rest in his grave?" Then, as an afterthought, he chuckled, and his Gaelic sense of humor came to the fore: "It's like that old joke: Schultz is dead!"

Everyone laughed.

"No, I can't get worked up over the Choate matter any longer," Lee continued. "And I don't have any serious problems with the other issues." Lee's implication was clear. He was ready to vote anytime the chairman called for one. But Rosel Hyde scrupulously avoided any such call. He urged more discussion of all issues. He secretly hoped that discussion would go on for a long time and that it would be cautious and filled with soul-searching deliberation, for he was convinced that if this decision went the wrong way— against WHDH-TV—it would rock the industry. Perhaps, he told himself, I am hoping there will be no consensus! Perhaps if one of us withdrew . . .

Withdraw? The idea came with the force of a blow. Yes! That was it! Why not withdraw himself? He had lain awake nights thinking about this tortuous case. No matter which way he voted he knew he would have misgivings afterwards. He simply could not vote with any conviction for either side. But this was a coward's way out. Or was it? No, not really. One owed it to his own conscience to vote with *conviction;* with *decisiveness;* one should *not* vote for the lesser of two evils; one should not vote, in a case of this importance, with anything like a sense of compromise. No, he thought, if I withdraw and not vote at all I will be doing the *judicious* thing!

Having reached this decision he asked himself what reason, what explanation, could he give his colleagues? How he envied Ken Cox and Lee Loevinger for being disqualified. But, the devil with explaining myself, he reasoned. Why should I? I can do that later if I choose.

"Gentlemen," he spoke in his quiet, well-modulated voice, "I have something I must say at this time. This case has given me considerable problems. For reasons I don't care to explain at this time, I must follow what I consider to be the most judicious course I can take, which is that I no longer participate in the discussions of this case. And . . . I hope I never have to vote on it. Therefore, I am going to leave the room. As the next senior in tenure, and because I think it his turn to handle the processing of a major Commission matter, I designate Commissioner Bartley to chair the discussion from this point on."

With that, Rosel Hyde left his astonished colleagues.

Three down! Only four Commissioners left!

A bare quorum remaining—if one more left, or refused to vote, or died, or became ill, the case could not be resolved!

Robert Bartley, who had no particular qualms about the case, accepted his responsibility with his usual equanimity. A taciturn Texan, he was easily the most unflappable member of the Commission.

"Okay, let's get on with it. Who was saying what when Rosel walked out . . . ?"

Bartley was a Democrat, appointed by President Truman in 1953. He believed, with the President, that "If you can't stand the heat, get out of the kitchen." A product of the early days of radio, Bob Bartley had seen nothing to dissuade him from the view that diversification of ownership, and integration of management, were the two major caissons upon which a sound broadcasting service should be built. Sometimes he was an enigma to his colleagues and members of staff. Sometimes he agreed with what they said, yet voted against them. When he lost his temper his voice grew softer; his smile almost malevolent. When a staff lawyer once returned with a decision, saying, "Commissioner, I can't agree with this, I simply cannot write this decision the way you want it." Bob Bartley nodded gently and fixed the young lawyer with a steely glint: "That's fine, son. Go find someone who can."

He prided himself on his "feel" for things. Such as the time he called Sol Taishoff, publisher of *Broadcasting*, and asked, "Is there a rating survey going on this week for radio stations in Washington?"

Taishoff did not know, but promised to find out. The next day he called back and said, yes there was.

"I thought so," said Bartley.

"Why do you think so?" Taishoff questioned.

"Because half the stations in town are running wild-ass giveaway contests to hypo their ratings."

Yes, Bob Bartley had a distinct "feel" for many things. He also had scathing contempt for pomposity and verbosity; and for those who took themselves too seriously. Harry Truman was his idol, along with FDR, and Sam Rayburn who was his uncle.

He remembered Harry Truman's advice when the President appointed him. "Bob, I don't think it will ever happen, but if I should ever call you about a case, don't pay any attention to it. And if anyone from the White House calls you about a case, don't pay any attention to that either."

Bartley adjourned the session shortly after Rosel Hyde left, and a few days later called another meeting. Bob Lee still supported Sharfman's decision. Jerry Wadsworth remained noncommittal. But Bartley and Nick Johnson found that they had something in common as further discussion went on: they had no clear idea as to whom they were *for,* but they were in strong agreement as to whom they were *against.*

They were against WHDH-TV. And for the same reasons: diversification and integration of management.

"I can 'buy' much of Examiner Sharfman's findings," said Nick Johnson. "But I can't 'buy' his result. I come out with an entirely different result."

"I agree," said Bartley.

"Sharfman admits the diversification weakness of WHDH, then proceeds to ignore it. I find that issue alone disqualifying."

"There are some other issues that Sharfman is soft on," added Bartley."

"And there is that Choate matter . . ."

"Choate?" Bob Lee exclaimed. "Haven't you heard? Choate's dead. So is Schultz."

"He's not dead in my book," said Johnson.

"Which one? Choate or Schultz?"

After the laughter died down, Bob Lee pleaded that the case be decided on some other issues rather than the Choate matter.

"Yes. Let the poor devil rest." The speaker was Jerry Wadsworth who, until now, had spoken little.

Nick Johnson was surprised, but agreed.

We're making progress, thought Bartley. At least there is a consensus on *that* point.

But not for long, because Wadsworth interrupted, "That isn't what I said. What I said, and your interpretation of what I said, are two different things."

"Sorry," Nick Johnson jibed. "What is your interpretation of what you said, Commissioner?" at the same time flashing one of his sudden, disarming grins.

"Choate is dead," explained Wadsworth. "I said, let the poor devil rest. But *not* the issue."

The others glanced at Wadsworth quizzically, trying to divine his meaning. Maybe, thought Bartley, a consensus is closer than I thought. Maybe there would not have to be a two-to-two tie. When Hyde had walked out, Bartley would have given odds, and bet heavily on the fact that, with only four men remaining, the final vote would be deadlocked.

Discussion continued at further sessions after that and progress seemed to be made, but slowly. Bartley, however, did not care. Debate could go on till Christmas; he was not going to be accused of rushing matters.

One of the most heated arguments centered around the complicated method of comparative evaluation of the parties. How do you compare a station that is not on the air, and seeking renewal, with three new applicants? The Commission had wrestled with this problem in the past and had yet to come up with a satisfactory formula.

"WHDH wants to have its cake and eat it too," declared Nick Johnson. "They have been living on borrowed time. Now they say, 'we should retain the license just because we're already operating the station'. WHDH should be entitled to no more status than a new applicant."

Bob Bartley agreed.

Jerry Wadsworth said nothing. He hardly seemed to be listening.

Bob Lee vehemently disagreed. "How can you disregard, or discard, a good operating record like theirs?"

"Their record is not beyond the bounds of average performance."

Oh hell, thought Lee. Are we going around that tiresome track again? The Commission, a few years earlier, had tried to set down a policy statement that would deal with situations like this one. He had gone along with that decision, but reluctantly, believing that it was impossible to set down policy that would cover every kind of renewal situation. Here was a classic example: a *renewal* applicant pitted against three *new* applicants. The policy statement did not fit at all. He recalled Rosel Hyde's intelligent dissent in that murky decision.

"The filing of a new applicant—organized according to formula—to challenge a renewal applicant could lead to a facile, but in many instances, unfair and arbitrary decisional process. Is the Commission now ready to read out established broadcasters, not locally owned, but otherwise without blemish in favor of the locally-owned applicants? Is the Commission now ready to read out established broadcasters who do not have an ownership interest, in favor of applicants who propose to operate the facilities themselves? Is the Commission ready to accept a new applicant formed to meet this preconceived mold in preference to an existing broadcaster who does not fit into such mold regardless of other circumstances?"

That had been a good dissent, thought Bob Lee. He also remembered stating then that a preferred applicant could very well be one with newspaper and CATV interests. As Commissioner Loevinger reiterated, every case had to be judged on its own merits. How could one wash out the excellent record of WHDH with blue sky proposals tailored to meet the Commission's hypothetical dream formula? What kind of equity was that?

"You fellows are talking nonsense," Lee said. "Remember: 22 percent local live! Compare that with other applicants. WHDH is *above* average in my book."

"Sharfman didn't say so."

"I get the impression from reading Sharfman," retorted Lee, "that he thinks their record was damned good." Their obstinacy on this point rankled him. He was now beginning to discern at least one of the reasons why Rosel Hyde had bowed out. His WBAL case had set what, up to now, had been precedent for deciding how renewal applicants should be judged. If WHDH lost this battle it would set an entirely new precedent. What a furor it would create! The value of TV licenses would depreciate overnight!

It still irked Lee that Hyde had pulled out. And, when the going got rough, when it became clear that he was perhaps a minority of one, he began toying with the idea of pulling out himself. If he did, there no longer would be a quorum. But he postponed coming to grips with this alternative, at least until Jerry Wadsworth revealed his intention.

But, as the discussions wore on, Jerry Wadsworth revealed little. He sat there silently, sometimes bored, sometimes daydreaming.

When it came to a discussion of the merits of the new applicants there was common agreement at least on one point:

"Sharfman is right on Greater Boston TV. It is disqualified."

Everyone agreed; even Wadsworth.

"How about the other two new applicants, Charles River and BBI?"

"Both have over promised," said Bartley.

"I prefer Charles River," said Johnson.

"Why?"

"I like its integration factor. That fellow Jones seems to run a good radio station in Waltham. And I think their foundation idea is a good one."

Bob Bartley said he preferred BBI. For several reasons: he liked BBI's twenty-four-hour proposal; he liked its extensive amount of local live—36 percent; he liked the quality of its principals. And, remembering his early days as a vice-president of the Yankee Network, he admired BBI for promising to share 25 percent of its equity with key executives. He had never heard of anything like that in his life.

Bob Lee said that if he had to make a choice between the two new applicants he would give a slight edge to BBI; but that was academic because everyone knew he was going to vote for WHDH-TV.

"Jerry, what are your thoughts?" someone asked.

"I say, let's bring this case to a vote and get it over with. We've talked about it long enough."

"Really?" Bob Bartley couldn't have been more surprised. "You mean you think we've discussed the issues enough?"

"Certainly. Let's vote."

Hell's bells, thought Bartley. I must be hearing things. But that was good enough for him. "Let's do it then," he said tersely. "Let's see if we have a consensus. As chairman of the group. I'll forego my privileges of voting last. I am for BBI." Then he turned to Nick Johnson, who said:

"I am for Charles River."

"Commissioner Lee?"

"WHDH-TV."

"How about you, Jerry?"

Without hesitation, Wadsworth answered, "I will vote for BBI."

The others sat there, stunned, as though only now realizing what they had done, stunned at how Wadsworth had voted. Jerry Wadsworth had shed his conservative Republican stance and had voted in a manner that no one expected. Why? How? What were the reasons behind it? These burning questions ran through Bartley's mind as he quickly adjourned the meeting for lunch, suggesting that they consider this only a tentative expression of a consensus; and that, after lunch, they convene again for more discussion and another vote.

Bob Lee ate lunch alone at his usual table at Traymores. Today, however, he was so deeply immersed in thought he scarcely knew what he was eating. A corned beef sandwich, he thinks it was, but isn't sure. He was grappling with the fateful decision of whether to bolt from the room when it came time to vote, thus destroying the quorum. It was the only action left that could stop this unbelievable course of events.

That afternoon they would be taking away the license of a VHF station that was worth between fifty and seventy-five million dollars!

That afternoon they would be dooming the jobs and careers of hundreds of men and women!

In the name of what, diversification and integration of management? What if the Boston *Herald Traveler* did not survive? What then? What kind of diversification would that be? What in hell had gotten into the guts and soul of Jerry Wadsworth? And where was Rosel Hyde when he was needed? The three Republicans who should be coming to the defense of the *only* Republican paper in Boston! Over and over again he weighed the pros and cons of Loevinger's advice: if you think the case stinks, walk out of the room when a vote is taken. Destroy the quorum.

"Coffee sir?" a waiter asked.

"Yes, the coffee is very good," Bob Lee said absently.

The waiter stared. He hadn't even served coffee yet.

Bob Bartley and Nick Johnson, at lunch, quickly resolved their differences over whether Charles River, or BBI, should get the golden apple.

"I'm not hung up on either applicant, insofar as the comparative merits go," said Nick Johnson. "As long as it is *not* WHDH."

"BBI has the better program proposal," insisted Bartley. "The foundation angle of Charles River is an intriguing one; but it's not one of substance if you think about it."

Nick Johnson smiled. "I'll go along with BBI." He paused and turned grimly serious. "The key to me is that, for the first time, in our ten or eleven largest cities, there will be *one* VHF, network-affiliated station that is truly *independently owned!* To me, this is a significant step toward the goal the Commission has been preaching for years . . . media diversity and local ownership."

Bartley agreed. "The question is," he added laconically, "how will Jerry vote when we get back?"

Nick nodded. Yes. It all depended on Jerry's mood. Was he euphoric from martinis? Would he have a change of heart? Had Bob Lee gotten to him?

The fact of the matter was that Jerry Wadsworth also dined alone. He returned fresh, alert and more businesslike than he had been.

"Gentlemen," Bob Bartley began, "is there a need for further discussion of any issues of this case?"

No one spoke.

"Okay. Let's get on with it. I suggest that we put the Channel 5 case to a second vote. This, of course, is only a tentative expression of a consensus. Any questions?"

Bob Lee half arose from his chair. If he was going to make his move, now was the time to do it. Simply excuse himself from the vote, thereby eliminating the quorum. Yet something held him back. Something old-fashioned involving ethics and training and character. To leave the room, to inflict an artificial block, would be of itself a form of copping out; adding only one *more* absurdity and obfuscation to a case that was already overburdened with obfuscation, inconsistencies and ironies. As much as this whole sad affair pained him, he could not bring himself to play "one more game" to thwart, or abort, the decision so that it might never be resolved. Right or wrong . . . good, bad or indifferent, this case *had* to be settled! He prepared himself for the worst, Jerry Wadsworth now being his last hope. Perhaps Wadsworth would come to his senses . . .

"I am still for BBI," said Bartley.

"WHDH-TV," said Bob Lee.

"BBI," spoke Johnson.

"I am still for BBI," said Wadsworth, adding: "It may be of interest to you why I vote as I do. Anyone who tampers with the Commission's processes, or attempts to do so, as Robert Choate did, with the obvious condonation of his colleagues, who said that they saw nothing wrong with it, and who also said as I believe the record shows, that they would do the same thing again . . . well, that, gentlemen, is wrong! Not only stupid, but just plain, damn, simple downright wrong! In fact it's reprehensible! I don't go for that kind of hanky-panky. I never have. I never will! As long as I am in public office, or in a position of public trust, I will have nothing to do with people who try such things. This is why I vote as I do. For no other reason. I vote, not so much for BBI, as I vote *against* those people who tried to tamper with the Commission process. I thought you'd like to know this. And I hope I'm not called upon to explain my position ever again."

"Thank you, Commissioner," said Bob Bartley. "You've explained your position quite clearly. Now we'll proceed to have drafted a decision that tries to express the consensus of the majority."

"I'll have a dissenting statement," interjected Bob Lee.

"Fine, Bob. Go to work on it. Gentlemen, let's get back to our offices and catch up on our other work. And remember: this is *not* going to be an easy, or quick, decision to write. It'll take some doing. Let's try to keep this news to ourselves. If it leaks out there'll be hell to pay!"

Later that day Jerry Wadsworth continued to turn the difficult decision over in his mind. Troubled thoughts that he could not bring himself to tell the others. Such as the high regard he had for the name Choate. It was a name that, as a youngster, he had venerated. Hadn't he gone to Choate School? He remembered with great fondness his many conversations with Joseph B. Choate, Jr., the father of Robert Choate. This is what had disappointed him most of all, the fact that, somewhere in the testimony, he had read that Robert Choate had said that he was convinced that he had committed no wrong, and that under the same circumstances he would do the same thing again. His extraordinary sensitivity about human behavior that could be questioned in terms of ethics was, for better or worse, a quirk of his. During his long career in public service he guessed that he had made half a dozen similar decisions —decisions that more practical, more pragmatic public servants might find difficult to understand. But that's the way he was, he reflected. It was too late to change now. Every man had hang-ups that were peculiarly his own.

8

The
Decision

The decision indeed was a difficult one to write. No better testimony to that fact exists than the time span alone.

Fifteen months and sixteen days!

All of the year 1968 passed, plus twenty-two days of January, 1969, before the working majority could approve a document that they were willing to sign. Draft upon draft circulated secretly between Bartley, Johnson, Wadsworth and staff lawyers who did the writing.

To this day none of them have any other explanation for the delay except that: "It was a tough job."

The decision, they agreed, had to be written "correctly" so that it would stand up under the inevitable appeals. Bob Bartley wanted it brief. He got his way. The decision filled less than thirty pages. No time was wasted getting to the point:

"We have reviewed the examiner's findings of fact in light of the exceptions, and we are of the view that they are substantially accurate and complete. Accordingly, they are adopted with the modifications noted herein and in the appendix."

Herb Sharfman would like that. But he wouldn't remain happy for long.

"However, we view those findings as warranting substantially

different conclusions and a different ultimate result. For the reasons set forth below, our judgment is that grant of the application of Boston Broadcasters, Inc., would best serve the public interest, convenience and necessity."

The Choate matter? Skip it, they said. Sharfman had stated that, with Choate dead, the ex parte issue was no longer a factor.

"In view of our denial of the WHDH application on *other* grounds, it is unnecessary to determine whether the examiner reached a proper result on this question."

The past program record of WHDH would not enter into the "comparative evaluation" since it was merely "within the bounds of average performance."

The issue of diversification took only five succinct paragraphs to shut the door on WHDH. The *Herald Traveler* owned AM-FM radio stations, along with a company that manufactured CATV cable components. Also, the station failed to editorialize; and on one occasion the station withheld the announcement of a major news story about the Massachusetts Crime Commission until after the newspaper had printed it.

As for a comparison between Charles River and BBI, the latter was given a "slight preference."

Integration of management? Equally brief. Both challengers were given the edge over WHDH; and BBI was given a "significant preference" over Charles River.

As for the "proposed program service," all those surveys and elaborate preparations of the challengers were no better than "acceptable."

And for BBI, with its 36.3 percent local live promise in a schedule of almost twenty-three hours per day, seven days per week, the decision was dismayingly harsh. How can we believe such extravagant proposals, the decision asked. Where is your substantiation? Anyone so brash runs the risk of "having a demerit attached to its showing." Whereupon a "slight demerit" was assessed with the blunt charge: "Insufficiently supported"!

Charles River's charity foundation angle? A nice gimmick, the decision commented. So good, in fact, that it also merited a "slight demerit"!

The total score? Charles River and BBI's demerits were "offsetting in nature." Neither one deserved an edge. And since WHDH was "within the bounds of average performance," all three were rated even in the program service evaluation.

As to "other factors," Greater Boston was disqualified for not having found a transmitter site; and for not having ascertained the community's needs.

Both Charles River and BBI were favored over WHDH under "diversification and integration criteria," plus a demerit for WHDH for unauthorized transfer of control.

BBI was awarded a slight preference on the diversification factor; and a "signficant preference on the integration factor."

Therefore: "Because of its superiority under the diversification and integration criteria, we conclude that the public interest, convenience and necessity will be best served by a grant of the application of BBI and denial of applications of WHDH, Charles River Civic Television, Inc., and Greater Boston TV Co., Inc."

Chairman Rosel Hyde, still torn by doubts, filed a statement that was to become more perplexing to his colleagues, and to the industry, as time went on. "I have abstained from voting in this case. This case has roots extending far back and has always been a difficult one, at least for me.

"On the first round I voted against WHDH, Inc. On the second round, in light of certain changed circumstances, I cast my vote for WHDH, Inc. This is now the third round and it is no less difficult for me to choose among these competing applicants.

"In view of my previous participation and finally the fact that my vote is not essential to resolution of the matter, I have simply abstained."

Robert E. Lee, true to his word, filed a vigorous statement of dissent. "My major disagreement with the majority is the basis for comparing these four applications . . . WHDH, Inc. should be preferred.

"Vast expenditures for facilities and goodwill have been made which it would be inequitable to declare forfeited unless the licensee has operated *against* the public record."

On the diversification issue, asked Lee, how come the *Boston*

Globe, after this record closed, had obtained a 50 percent interest in Channel 38 in Boston?

WHDH-TV, he stated, had operated all these years under a four-month license; yet it had been found to be "qualified under all applicable sections of our act and rules."

As to the integration of management factor, "this must be weighed in the light of the record which shows that WHDH, Inc. has done an above-average job in the past."

And how about all the matters that were *not* resolved? Or ignored? The ex parte matter, for instance, "This . . . leaves a disparaging connotation as WHDH, Inc. is now in the position of being charged with a serious offense but its guilt or innocence is forever left in limbo." Judge Stern, he reminded, had absolved the station of this charge. Hearing Examiner Sharfman had said the issue was no longer a comparative factor. As to failure to editorialize, "We have no rule which *requires* a station to editorialize. Rather this responsibility ultimately devolves upon the individual licensee."

In his judgment, said Lee, he found the programing of WHDH-TV to be "above average." Remember, 22 percent local live! And even if, as the majority contended, WHDH was only "average," the other proposals were "not found to be above average.

"In such a case, preference should be given to the *known* past rather than speculative future promises."

He agreed with the majority that there was a de facto change of control, but: "There was no attempt to mislead or deceive the Commission, and this violation is not the type which should be considered either as absolute or comparative disqualification."

As far as he was concerned, all the facts in the case "which both the majority and this dissent accept, dictate a grant of the renewal to WHDH, Inc."

Lee concluded his dissent with a prediction of the horrors to come if WHDH-TV lost its license; and it did, indeed, send shudders up and down the spine of the establishment; especially the 155 publishers who owned a total of 260 television stations in the United States:

"I am very much afraid that this decision will be widely interpreted as an *absolute* disqualification for license renewal of a newspaper-owned facility in the same market. Competing applications can be expected against most of these owners at renewal time."

Nick Johnson was not content to let the decision speak for itself. In the flush of victory, he wrote a "concurring statement" which he showed to Bob Bartley.

Bartley had misgivings about the statement; thought that it did nothing to enhance the decision itself. Why gild the lily, he thought. With no particular enthusiasm, he told Nick, after reading it, that he saw nothing wrong with it. Later, however, he regretted not having tried to change Nick's mind.

"I don't know if I could have talked Nick out of it, but I wish I had tried," he later said.

Johnson began by stating that he really felt "no passion about the selection of the ultimate winner." A weighing of the merits of both Charles River and BBI was "not overwhelming." But the case had roots in time far predating his tenure at the Commission, therefore he was voting because his vote was "necessary to constitute a working majority for decision."

However, he added: "In America's eleven largest cities there is not a single network-affiliated VHF television station that is independently and locally owned. They are all owned by the networks, multiple station owners, or major local newspapers. The decision to not award Channel 5 to the *Herald Traveler* is supported by good and sufficient reasons beyond the desire to promote diversity of media ownership in Boston."

Johnson avowed that he took no strong position on the merits of continued newspaper ownership of broadcasting properties in markets where there is competing media, but he did think it "healthy" to have "at least one station among these politically powerful thirty-three network-affiliated properties in the major markets that is truly locally owned, and managed independently of the other local mass media."

Then with carefully couched sarcasm aimed at the Commission itself, he dropped the first of several depth charges that were to have the effect of creating a tidal wave of fear amongst station owners. "It is a step, however small, back toward the Commission's often professed but seldom evidenced belief in the benefits of local ownership and media diversity. It is, at the very least, an interesting experiment which will be watched carefully by many."

The next was even more threatening: *Renewal applicants should have the same standards of comparison as new applicants!*

To be forewarned is to be forearmed, Johnson reminded the industry. More of this kind of thing was coming. It was open sesame now . . . open season from this date on. Cases in the past had been overruled by the court of appeals, he reminded; cases where licensees "with substantial media concentrations were able to retain their license under a renewal comparative challenge.

"The door is thus opened for local citizens to challenge media giants in their local community at renewal time with some hope for success before the licensing agency, where previously the only response had been a blind reaffirmation of the present license holder."

So, the stage was set.

In terms of precedent, and stability in the billion dollar broadcast industry, the bomb, when dropped, would have an effect as far-reaching as the big blast at Hiroshima.

And the bomb was dropped on January 22, 1969.

9

Meet
Harold Clancy

Broadcasting Magazine set the tone of what was to come. "MUL-TIPLE OWNERSHIPS NOW UP FOR GRABS" screamed the headline in the January 27th issue. "FCC Yanks Channel 5 Boston. Spells Out How Rival Applications Can Attack Renewals And Win."

"Multiple owners throughout the country were put on notice last week that they are vulnerable to challenge by local groups with the funds and determination to oppose the renewals of their broadcast licenses."

A box on the same page called it the "50-Million Giveaway," citing that figure as the value of a VHF station in Boston, the nation's fifth largest market. Nineteen-sixty-seven had been a "poor year" noted *Broadcasting*. Boston revenues had been only 37.1 million dollars.

Variety ran a banner headline across its main television page.

FCC BOMBSHELL IN BOSTON
WHDH Decision Rocks Industry

In colorful *Variety* prose, Larry Michie wrote: "Sounding more like the Tower of Babel than a Federal regulatory agency, the

FCC in a landmark case last week voted 3–1—not even a majority of the 7 man commission—to take away Channel 5 in Boston . . . The ruling left the broadcast industry with knees as wobbly as Joe Namath's, but with far less assurance."

On the same page *Variety* tossed in one of its infrequent editorials: "CLASSIC FCC PERFORMANCE."

"When clarity and forcefulness are needed, the FCC all too often responds with a decision like last week's on Channel 5 in Boston.

"It is almost as though the FCC decided to ensure that the court, not the supposedly expert Commission, will make the final decision."

The lack of a true majority of the entire Commission bothered *Variety.* "Perhaps that is unsurprising in light of the leadership it got from its chairman, who declared himself so confused he declined to vote at all. Rosel Hyde has been with the FCC since the days when it was the Federal Radio Commission and if he hasn't made up his mind by now, he must directly be implying that his colleagues are presumptuous to vote at all."

It concluded dolefully: ". . . last week's FCC decision seems to have proven nothing."

TV Digest called the case "The Strange Boston Decision," which "sent shivers throughout the industry last week . . ."

The Commission had given clear warning, said the *Digest*, that a "station's broadcasting record doesn't mean anything, as against a newcomer who has glowing promises, unless that record is extraordinarily good or bad.

"Maybe this case is unique," it continued, "but a lot of hungry applicants may think FCC has set up some sitting ducks for them to shoot at when renewals come up.

"It was a weird 3–1 vote . . . Chairman Hyde abstained, issuing a strange statement . . . District of Columbia Court of Appeals retains jurisdiction in the case, and decision is back in its lap." Then a disturbing prophecy to the industry: " Based on past performance, it's assumed court will *endorse* FCC decision."

The national press was somewhat more decorous, yet obviously perturbed. The *Christian Science Monitor, Time, Newsweek, Wall*

Street Journal, New York Times, the wire services, and major newspapers from coast to coast gave the story prominent attention.

Time laconically called it an "unprecedented ruling" under the heading: "Media Barons," and said: while the present philosophy of trying to achieve widest possible dissemination of information was "admirable," it was also "complicated in practice." Papers were ailing in many U.S. cities, *Time* pointed out. Some were able to keep going only because of profits from their owned TV stations. The *Herald Traveler* was a case in point. It had given up its "losing afternoon competition" with the *Boston Globe* in 1967 and now published one combined daily paper which was lagging behind the morning *Globe* by 217,000 to 237,000.

Newsweek, under a headline: "FCC BARES ITS FANGS" also termed the action "unprecedented"; one which "set the operators of every TV station in the country reaching for the Excedrin bottle."

And: "Widely regarded as a benign watchdog when it came to renewing licenses, the FCC has suddenly bared its fangs."

Newsweek was the first to come out with the blunt question that was already on many minds: could the *Herald Traveler* continue to survive? The paper "is reportedly in delicate financial condition."

Barrons business weekly took the occasion to cast a pox on *all* of television. Its banner proclaimed: "A REALLY POOR SHOW: THAT'S WHAT BOTH TV AND THE FCC LATELY HAVE STAGED."

Barrons was angry at many things: the FCC for announcing its intention of banning cigarette advertising; the networks for their "painfully biased" coverage of the preceding year's political conventions; the recent shift in licensing policy of the FCC; the WHDH decision, and several other matters. The salvation, *Barrons* said, lay in subscription or pay television.

By now *Broadcasting Magazine* began warming to its task. Its next issue carried a blazing editorial: "BOSTON STAKE: $3 BILLION"; that being the estimate of the value of stations that were being put in jeopardy.

Sound the alarm, the editorial cried; especially to those naive broadcasters who refused to believe that the Commission was serious in March of 1968 when it "proposed to prohibit the acquisition of more than one full-time broadcast station in any community."

Now, every broadcaster "in his right mind is aware" of what is going on. The FCC intent was nothing less than to break up the entire industry!

"The alarm has sounded from coast to coast," trumpeted Sol Taishoff, the publisher. "The headquarters of the National Association of Broadcasters has been stirred to action."

Only the *New York Times* took a different view. In a long editorial on February 9th, it came out with outright approval of the decision:

"The most crucial function performed by the FCC is the awarding of broadcasting licenses to radio and TV stations. Yet, franchises are usually rubber-stamped with no regard for station performance in the public interest despite a legal requirement for consideration of that yardstick.

"The FCC decision not to renew the license of Boston television station WHDH shows a welcome awareness of the need to examine management promise and performance in passing on licenses."

Among the dramatis personnae, reactions varied greatly. Chairman Rosel Hyde was stung by the snide remarks in the press over his failure to vote. It was hardly fitting, or fair, he thought, to reward a man thusly after more than three decades of public service. But that was the way the game was played. One was only as good as his latest decision. In addition to criticism on this case, Hyde was also catching hell from the Hill, particularly the Congress, over a variety of irksome issues. He decided quietly that the time had come to hang it up. After thirty-five years of government service it was time to get out. And if his failure to vote on the Boston case was to remain a stigma on his escutcheon, so be it; at least he could face himself in the mirror and say that it was not a burden on his conscience. Rosel Hyde continued to smile to his friends and associates; but it was a mechanical smile. And he closed his ears, and eyes, to the persistent questions that were, not very discreetly, being flung at him about his failure to vote.

Nine more months, he decided, after counseling with his wife. Then he'd retire.

Nicholas Johnson had another kind of reaction. His was one of unalloyed glee. He was positively giddy with euphoria over the waves he had helped make in the industry.

"How are the reviews today?" he would ask his staff each morning. "Any good new ones? Any with cuss words in them?"

Indeed, there were some with, if not outright obscenity, at least vituperative language that one seldom found in stories about public officials. Nearly every story gave prominent display to Johnson's "concurring statement." Publications could scarcely avoid this, for if Nick's "open door" policy was to apply, it certainly would change the pattern of broadcast ownership.

When *Broadcasting Magazine* singled him out for most of the blame he chuckled with sheer delight. He loved to tilt with rock-conservative Sol Taishoff who fought most of the industry's battles in his highly regarded weekly trade book. Sol wrote: ". . . this brash thirty-four-year-old, self-annointed savior, who was removed from his last job as maritime administrator, jams the FCC processing lines with his dissents, editors and pundit-columnists . . . maintains a private mailing list at government expense, and stands accused of brow-beating FCC personnel."

"Couldn't have written that better myself!" declared Nick.

"It is shameful," continued one of Taishoff's editorials, "that at the root of most of the troublemaking is Nick Johnson who . . . has made a fetish of throwing sand in the FCC machinery while accusing his colleagues of flaunting the law, or worse."

"Beautiful!" exclaimed Nick. For two years now he had been espousing a hard regulatory line within the Commission. Ken Cox agreed with him on most issues, but Commissioner Cox believed in working "*within* the system," not taking his case to the public with flamboyant statements and speeches that were sometimes devastatingly critical of the Commission itself.

"Won't work," Nick would reply to Ken's line of thinking. "That's been tried and it doesn't work. To effect any changes in the system one has to take his story to a larger forum—the people."

With the Boston decision there was no doubt that Nick had succeeded in taking his story to the people. His "concurring statement," and other embellishments obtained via personal interviews, received almost as much attention as the decision itself.

Ken Cox warned him about the whiplash effect. To which Nick replied, "Let it come. Let's see how strong it can be." He was hopeful for the first time since he had become a commissioner that there could be some changes in the system; that monopolies could be broken up, or at least splintered; that independent voices could make themselves heard; that alternative choices could be offered in programing. Only last summer the Justice Department had rocked the industry by going even further than the Commission, which had suggested that the time had come for media monopolies to be held in check. The Commission had merely said that, from here on, no owner should be permitted to acquire more than one full-time broadcast station in any community. The Justice Department had gone further and said, why not broaden the rule? Why not make it retroactive? Why not *dissolve* media concentrators in major markets? And only last week the Commission had announced a general inquiry into the ownership of broadcast companies by conglomerates. Yes, from Nick's point of view, 1969 looked like it was going to be a "good year." As for the Boston decision, he considered it a great accomplishment. He had finally succeeded in sending the establishment fleeing for the bomb shelter.

Robert Bartley, on the other hand, remained indifferent to all the sound and fury. It was only another decision, he thought; maybe more important than some others, but let's get on with the backlog of cases that are waiting to be decided. As for this furor, he couldn't help wondering if Harry Truman's hands-off policy, which, as far as he knew, President Johnson had also maintained, was going to prevail now under the new Nixon Administration. He was certain there would be an immediate appeal for reconsideration. And he was equally certain he was not going to change his vote. But how about the others? Would they waver? Poor Rosel, he thought; Rosel must be getting incredible pressures. But to hell with it, Bartley told himself. Let the chips fall where they may; let's get on with other business . . .

Among the most disappointed principals was Hearing Examiner Herbert Sharfman. Gentle, scholarly, Herb Sharfman who had to go about his business as though the decision did not really affect him; when, in fact, it affected him greatly. He was bitterly disappointed.

Not that he found any novelty, or surprise, in being overruled; that happened about a third of the time. But to be overruled in *this* decision which he had worked so hard on. It was particularly galling to note that the majority (even Bob Lee) had *accepted* his findings—then had blithely gone ahead and come up with entirely *different* results! What kind of logic was that? And all that nonsense about WHDH being only within the "bounds of average performance"? If he had known they were going to take *that* tack he would have used much stronger language: "WHDH *far exceeds* the bounds of average performance." But then the majority would have come up with some other absurd rationalization. In retrospect, it seemed to Sharfman, that WHDH was doomed from the beginning; that there was some weird, but real, expiation theory at work there. The odious days of the "Whorehouse Era" at the Commission were long since gone. Oh, one could still find plenty to complain about in terms of red tape and delays; but the conduct of the Commission and staff was impeccable, in Sharfman's view. Yet, because of that long-ago sordid past, there seemed to be a determination to expunge . . . expiate past sins, even though Judge Horace Stern had ruled that Choate's contacts with McConnaughey were not culpable. Yes, mused Sharfman, there could be, psycologically at least, *a law of expiation* at work here. How sad! And to think it all stemmed from those two lunches. What expensive eating! Well, I am not the one who is going to be hurt, Sharfman thought proudly; *they* are going to have to choke on their decision; *they* are the ones who are making the Commission a laughing stock. It makes the entire Commission process, murky and convoluted as it already is, nothing more than an exercise in futility.

Robert E. Lee, on the other hand, found some scant comfort in the numerous press references to his vigorous dissent. The broadcast trades, and many of the nation's major papers, applauded his views. *Variety* called it ". . . a lonely argument that deserves to

be disproved rather than capriciously ignored." The press emphasized his prophecy that, as a result of the decision, "competing applicants can be anticipated against most of these (multiple) owners at renewal time." Nevertheless, Bob Lee remained troubled.
He still had lingering doubts about the question he knew his colleagues were privately asking: why hadn't Bob Lee destroyed the
quorum?

Of the four Commissioners who voted, James J. Wadsworth,
however, remained the chief enigma. Why had this conservative
Republican voted as he did? What had gotten into him?

Jerry Wadsworth found the turmoil easy to ignore. There were
rumors that the White House was perturbed. The devil with all of
them, he told himself. He had voted in good conscience; had no
second thoughts; and knew that he would vote the same way again
when the case came up for reconsideration. What his colleagues
didn't know, and what he had no intention of telling anyone—at
least at this time—was that, a short time before the vote was
taken, he had been confronted with, and *affronted* by, an ex parte
attempt. In another proceeding a respectable broadcasting executive had brazenly tried to influence him. This had turned his
stomach; convinced him more than ever that he was voting the
right way.

And now Wadsworth had come to an important, personal decision. This Commission post was not for him. It hadn't turned
out to be as interesting, or challenging, as he had been led to believe. Endless days of quibbling over piddling matters, trying to
wade through lawyers' rhetoric that was a language all its own; it
certainly was not English. What kind of job was this for a man
who had served with distinction in state and national government
for twenty-four years? A man who had been Permanent U.S.
Representative to the United Nations; who had written two books
on international affairs; who had headed numerous important
diplomatic delegations. No, Jerry Wadsworth quietly made plans
to resign from the Commission later in the year. Fall would be a
good time, he decided; when the rolling hills of his large estate in
upstate New York would be a riot of color; when he could do
some hunting; and get to see more football games than in the past.

Up in Boston, the principals of BBI were understandably ecstatic, also somewhat incredulous. After waiting so long . . . after reaching the point where they no longer dared talk about, or predict, the outcome . . . then to have victory drop out of the blue!

After Benny Gaguine got through with them, however, they were not so sanguine.

"The only good thing about the decision is the bottom line. The rest of it stinks!" Benny told them.

"My god! How can you say such a thing? We won, didn't we?"

"We won, but in the wrong way. For the wrong reasons. It's not a *sui generis* decision, but one that applies to the entire industry. We don't need *that* kind of victory."

The only member of the BBI group who agreed with Benny was his old cohort, Nate David. He agreed that the decision, as written, would have the industry up in arms; and justifiably so. And Nick Johnson's "concurring statement" was something akin to disaster.

"We've got to get this thing in the proper perspective," Benny told them, and then, to their utter astonishment, he told them that he was filing an objection. Something called a petition to supplement and clarify the Commission's decision.

Their reaction was something like horror: my god! leave well enough alone. We've won! Don't tamper with the results . . .

"Nate," one of them said, "tell Benny to cool it."

"No," said Nate David. "The Frenchman is right. The decision can't be allowed to stand as it is. Don't worry, you'll get a chance to read it before it's filed."

"Please, Nate, tell Benny to lay off . . ."

"Forget it. Benny always knows what he's doing."

"This time he could be wrong. There can always be a first time."

"Forget it."

After getting over this shock, the BBI principals asked how long further litigation would take. Nate's answer was vague.

"There'll be an appeal to the Commission for reconsideration. That shouldn't take more than six months; probably less."

"Will we be upheld?"

"Benny sees no problems. Then it goes to the district court of appeals. That's where the real ball game will be played."

"Will we win there?"

"Who knows."

"What does Benny think the chances are?"

"Sixty-forty. Either way."

Benny Gaguine was never generous about giving himself odds. It made you look better if you won; if you lost, it lessened the blow.

"How long will *all* litigation take?"

"Well, after the battle at appeals, the case undoubtedly will go to the Supreme Court. The whole thing should not take more than a year."

"That's still a long time."

"Are you kidding? Compared to the time we've already spent in this donnybrook, that's like an hour!"

Then Benny gave them a piece of good news. And it showed the kind of mow-em-down spirit that made Gaguine such a gutsy lawyer. "I'm asking the Commission to specify August 1 as the date they should get off the air. I'm sure we won't get that date, but we might as well start pushing for a termination date. Get your bank credit lined up. You'll be buying equipment soon!"

Harold Clancy prided himself in being a highly controlled individual. He worked best under pressure, when he was in a state of suppressed rage. After the decision he found his self-discipline tested as never before. Apoplectic rage was a better term to describe how he felt.

And that was approximately his state of mind as he sat at his desk reading an offer by BBI to buy WHDH-TV's plant and equipment. The offer was quite specific and detailed: BBI would purchase the station's physical facilities at replacement cost; assume its studio leases and contracts; engage all but its executive personnel. A reply, said the letter, was requested by March 3. If no response was forthcoming, BBI would proceed with alternative plans to acquire its own facilities and equipment.

"The nerve of those bastards," Clancy muttered to himself. The phone rang. It was George Akerson calling from his office next door in the newspaper plant. George wanted to drop by for his daily chat about "the situation." George was now chairman of the board, but Clancy was actually his boss. The two had exchanged positions nine months ago as a result of several circumstances, chief of which was the fact that the *Herald Traveler* had had a bad year in 1967. A deficit, in fact, of $104,795, as against a profit of $1,978,453, or $3.60 per share, in 1966.

"Come on over," said Clancy. He knew what the routine would be like: What's new? Had he heard anything today? Any new rumors? Had Bill Dempsey finished his petition for reconsideration? Then George would assure him once again that morale was high on the newspaper side.

Indeed, morale was high throughout the organization, Clancy reflected. Partly because the decision itself was so incredible! Not everyone could believe it. And his own firm, decisive statements had helped. "I cannot imagine any ground for overturning Mr. Sharfman's findings and rejecting his conclusion that can survive the appelate procedures within the Commission itself or within the courts."

A firm hand was needed now more than ever, and he was damned well going to give it that. He resigned himself to Akerson's visit. He wasn't really in the mood to talk today, but it was a necessary part of the stiff-upper-lip routine. Relations had continued reasonably well between the two men despite their switch in positions, although at times Clancy suspected that he detected a touch of hidden resentment in George. Why not, he thought sympathetically. I'd feel the same way. Yet they still made a good team; had weathered many a crisis since the days when Robert Choate had been kicked upstairs and George had taken over. Maybe, he thought, all of the turbulent past was a prerequisite to winning this life-or-death struggle. Both had matriculated through the newspaper ranks, although Harold had quit the paper after reaching the level of managing editor; after Robert Choate had told him: "You have gone about as far as anyone named Clancy is likely to go in the *Herald*." Taking his cue from that remark, Clancy had begun the study of law at night, while still supporting his family. After obtaining a law degree, and practicing for several years in Boston, he had returned to the *Herald Traveler* as vice president and assistant to the publisher.

The phone rang again; Bill Dempsey this time, calling from Washington. While listening, Clancy glanced idly at some of today's fan mail. A special kind of fan mail, this. Letters and telegrams from the broadcast industry; from major executives of networks and station groups. A spontaneous outpouring of vows of support that, by their number and their vehemence, quite surprised him.

"I've got the petition ready," he heard Dempsey say. "Can I read a couple of new paragraphs?"

"Go ahead."

As Clancy listened, phrases from some of the letters and telegrams leaped out at him.

"An absolute outrage in government's long history of bungling . . ." From the president of a major broadcast group.

"What can we do to help? We stand ready to testify . . . to send money . . . anything!" From another large group.

"We hope you are prepared to go all the way to the Supreme Court . . ." From one of the networks.

"A tragic decision that cannot stand if we are to maintain a free broadcast system. Count on our unqualified support . . ."

One from a newspaper-TV group: "Running front page editorial. Doing spots on our stations editorially in support of WHDH-TV."

It was hardly a coincidence that the strongest letters came from newspaper ownership groups, thought Clancy with a tinge of amusement. They'd better be with us! *They're in the same boat!* What was surprising, however, was the mail they were getting from non-newspaper groups. That was a good sign. But his reporter's sense of cynicism came to the fore: I wonder where they'll be in December? When the chips are *really* down! That time wasn't far off.

When Dempsey had finished, Clancy said: "I think the petition sounds fine, Bill. Go ahead with it."

"We'll have it on file tomorrow."

"What do you think the chances are?"

"At the Commission? Not good. Not with the likes of Henry Geller leading Rosel Hyde around by the nose. The real battle is going to be at the court of appeals."

"And?"

"Tough. It's going to be tough, Hal. But with all the heat this case is generating, I'd say we stand at least a fifty-fifty chance."

George Akerson came in as Clancy was on the phone. Hal waved him into a chair and shoved a sheaf of the "fan mail" at him. A minute later he finished with Dempsey, hung up, and told George what Dempsey had said.

Akerson, a tall, distinguished-looking man with premature gray hair, smiled and said he was glad to hear that the petition was ready for filing. Morale amongst the troops was good, he said. "You know something that surprises me? Makes me feel good? Our guys *believe*—actually *believe* we're going to come out on top!"

Hal Clancy's stern, poker face, almost always inscrutable, turned dark, giving himself away. He was certain that George had not intended his words to convey *that* kind of meaning; but the manner in which he spoke irritated him.

"Of course they're right!" he retorted sharply. "There is *no way* we're going to lose this station. Remember that, George. No eternal stinking way!"

George laughed. At times like this Clancy reminded him of no less than old gutbucket General Patton. And he admired him for his iron determination. "I'm not disagreeing with you, Hal. Yet we must be practical. You and I, at least, must consider that the worst can happen. If it does, how long do you think it will take?"

Hal Clancy did not particularly like this question either. He answered it grimly, in a clipped tone. "A minimum of three years. We'll spend those guys broke. That may not be good English but it conveys what I mean. The longer we can stretch it, the deeper they will have to dig. But the point is: it's *not* going to happen!"

"I'm with you on that."

"You and I, George, will never see the day that WHDH-TV signs off the air. It just can't be! This case is too unjust, too much of an abomination, an outrage! Justice shall prevail. Don't ever forget that."

Akerson shrugged. There wasn't too much more one could add to that. He tossed the letters back on the desk. "One thing for sure: our fan mail gets better each day."

Clancy smiled skeptically. "We shall see."

George spent a few more minutes, had one drink of scotch, and left. After he had gone, Hal wondered if he had been too sharp with his old friend and comrade. He was really a hell of a guy; one that you could count on when the chips were down. But did he have the deep-down conviction that was necessary to win this battle? Was he, Harold Clancy, the *only one* who believed with heart and soul in the justice of their cause? Maybe I'm the one who's crazy, he thought somewhat ruefully as his mind drifted back to that important day last summer when he had been made president of the company and publisher of the radio and television properties. A heavy burden had been placed on him. He sometimes wondered if he was up to it. Earnings had been down when he had taken over. There were disquieting rumors drifting up from Washington about the status of the case. Nevertheless, despite the problems, he had gathered his family around him in February of 1969 and asked for their counsel. He wasn't a believer in Democracy when it came to raising a family. With eight kids, how could there be anything but a benevolent dictatorship? But in this situation, because of what he intended to do, he felt he must counsel with his family. Especially with the youngest. For the money he and Ernestine had saved would ultimately be for their education.

He had said to his family that night, "The company has entrusted to me a heavy responsibility. I feel I must show, and prove, my faith by doing something that affects each and every one of you. I want to put every dollar we can get our hands on into *Herald Traveler* stock. Now this is a risk. I want you to know that. Yet I believe so much in the righteousness of our cause that I want to take that risk. On the other hand, our money is your money. It's for your education; to help each of you get started in life. So, in a sense, I am gambling with what is yours. So you must tell me if you want me to do this."

"Ernie" Clancy waited expectantly. No need for her to answer. Hal knew how she felt. Besides, the question was put to the children. Tears came to her eyes as each of them—from little Peter who was only nine, to Mike who was twenty-one—solemnly said, yes, they wanted their father to do exactly as he suggested: invest every penny in company stock.

Which is what he had done, every penny, at over-the-counter prices, not at special option prices or on favored terms. Until finally they had purchased all of the stock they could find the money to buy. Sixteen thousand shares at prices ranging in the fifties.

Since then, since the decision of January 22, the stock had dropped 55 percent!

Did that faze him? Not in the least. Because Hal Clancy *believed!* As only an Irishman descended from County Kilkenny can believe. Kilkenny was fabled for its fighting cats. Well, he swore to himself, BBI had a fighting cat to contend with from now on.

The phone jangled again. It was another major broadcaster calling from the Bahamas where he was escaping the frigid climate of his native Midwest.

"Hal?" came his unctuous, molasses-sweet voice. "I've had a devil of a time getting through to you. The phones are so bad down here."

"Glad to hear from you, Jack."

"Hal, I just wanted to tell you how upset I am by this unbelievable decision. I've already talked to my congressman, my senator, the NAB, and of course to Sol Taishoff. I told the NAB to get off their ass and DO something about this. Maybe Dick Nixon will have to do something about it. If that's where we have to go to get this thing straightened out, then I say, let's do it! What else can I do, Hal? Tell me. Anything!"

"Thanks, Jack," said Clancy. "You've done enough."

"No I haven't. There must be something else I can do. I want to do more!"

"If I think of anything I'll let you know."

"Please do, Hal. This is a catastrophe!"

"Enjoy the sun, Jack. I wish I were there with you."

"Will you come down as my guest? I'd love to have you. Won't cost a dime. We have a trade deal you know . . ."

Hal Clancy laughed. Was there a broadcaster in the country who did *not* have a trade deal? "Thanks, but no, Jack. Enjoy yourself. Remember: we're going to win!"

After hanging up, Clancy resumed what he had started earlier in the day. That lousy *New York Times* editorial. Those damned lies had to be counteracted, but quick. Already he had listed twenty-five misstatements of facts. He was going to ask them for a face-to-face meeting, and wondered if they would have the guts to face him.

"Gentlemen: After reading your editorial, and throwing up, I take pen in hand . . ."

No, of course not, Clancy, calm down, he told himself. Take a deep breath and start the kind of letter that everyone will expect a top executive to write.

He took that deep breath, but for a long time the words would not come.

PART II

1969-1972

10

Preparation
for
Appeal

As far as the broadcast industry was concerned events had now clearly gotten out of hand. More than one "expert" noted the irony that the Boston decision had come only two days after the inauguration of Richard Nixon as president. But of course, they were quick to add, Nixon could in no way be blamed for the situation. Now that he was aboard, they predicted, the industry would stabilize. (Their definition of "stability" of course meaning a return to the laissez faire attitude of governmental commissions which had existed under Eisenhower.) There would be a period of tranquillity; business as usual, no interference, no inquisitions, no attempts at esoteric rule making. There were those leaders of networks and broadcast groups who asserted openly that the proper role of the FCC was that of defender of broadcasting against outsiders; against usurpers; against those liberal congressmen who were trying to make overnight reputations at the expense of the industry.

"The problem is," industry leaders bemoaned, "we are too visible. We live in the world's largest fishbowl." Which was true. But it was also true that the "fishbowl" would never become invisible again.

But, with Nixon as leader, there was much to hope for—or was there? The president had a curious sense of ambivalence toward broadcasting—as the industry would learn with increasing dismay as time passed. For Richard Nixon had mixed feelings about both broadcasting and the press. This stemmed from past events. He had revealed a certain brooding resentment at the treatment he had received from both media in his unsuccessful campaign against John F. Kennedy.

The key appointment to watch for was that of successor to Rosel Hyde as chairman. Hyde had announced his intention of retiring in the fall of 1969. There was speculation, not to mention some fervent hopes, that Hyde might retire sooner. Hyde, fine old gentleman that he was, clearly was not the right man to meet the "critical situation."

When rumors began circulating that Dean Burch was likely to become the next chairman, there was a collective sigh of relief. The "book" on Burch was that he was a no-nonsense fellow; decisive, middle of the road, a believer in minimum regulations and possessed of a brilliant, incisive legal mind. Burch would be the man to cut through, and stop, the trend of events, which if allowed to continue, would "destroy" free-enterprise broadcasting.

But, as the first quarter of 1969 passed, there was no sign that Hyde intended to retire early; or that Nixon would expedite the appointment of his own chairman.

And so the "nonsense" continued. A group called The Voice of Los Angeles had the temerity to challenge the license of the NBC owned-and-operated station in that city. The group admitted that it would not have gone forward if it had not been for the Boston decision, which represented to them, the first time in which an incumbent would be treated equally with newcomers.

In the last days of the Johnson administration, the Justice Department had informed the Gannett newspaper chain that it must divest itself of its television station in Rockford, Illinois where it had recently bought, not one, but two newspapers. About the same time the Justice Department ordered the Frontier Broadcasting Company in Cheyenne, Wyoming to break up its "mass-media communications monopoly."

If there was any letdown at the Commission itself, it certainly wasn't noticeable. In late March the FCC announced two decisions that gave the industry apoplexy. By a vote of four to two, it voted to withhold the renewal of KRON-TV, San Francisco; it further ordered a public hearing into various charges, among them a charge that the station "managed" the news to benefit its owner, the powerful *San Francisco Chronicle*.

The next day the Commission sat for hearing charges from a competitor against WCCO AM and TV in Minneapolis. These stations were owned by two powerful publishing companies— Cowles with morning and afternoon papers in Minneapolis; and Ridder with two papers in St. Paul. The Ridders held a substantial interest in the Minnesota Vikings and Minneapolis Twins, and the broadcast licensee held a small interest in the Twins. It was alleged by a competing station that WCCO controlled the broadcast rights to these teams and that the combination of four papers promoted heavily the coverage of the games by the stations.

Nick Johnson, meanwhile, was "riding the range" with his usual gusto. He lashed out at the industry continually; seldom a day went by when he did not make a slashing attack on, not only the industry, but the slothful ways of the Commission itself. His utterances made fascinating reading. Some station managers could hardly believe what they read. Could this really be happening in America? Had things gotten *this* far out of hand? Newton Minow had been bad enough, as far as they were concerned, but, when you analyzed Minow's career (brief—only 2½ years) one had to admit that he had not forced, or produced, any restrictive legislation. He had shaken a few trees, hoping the bad apples would fall; he had scared the hell out of everyone; but his regime was surprisingly devoid of new, or "restrictive," rule making. Minow himself liked to recall this, pointing out that, in terms of actual fact, his was a sound, stable and productive period. A period that saw the establishment of satellite TV; the first public television law; and the all-channel rule, in which all receivers, after a certain date, would have to be equipped to receive UHF as well as VHF signals.

While Nick Johnson was saying things like, "Television does to your mind what cotton candy does to your body . . . it attracts your attention, makes you want it, and then leaves you with nothing but an empty feeling and a toothache" . . . there was only one VIP, besides the editorials of Sol Taishoff, to come forth and speak out about the "mess" things were in. This was Lee Loevinger. *Ex*-Commissioner Loevinger, for he had resigned in mid 1968 and was now a partner in the large Washington law firm of Hogan and Hartson.

Loevinger, today, refuses to say how he would have voted in the Boston case; but, had he been eligible to cast a vote, and judging from the warm comfort he gave to broadcasters attending the NAB convention that year in March of 1969, one can come to a reasonable conclusion. It was time, said Loevinger, that Congress got into the act. The National Association of Broadcasters should "urge" Congress to set legal standards guaranteeing broadcasters "a reasonable expectancy of renewal."

Current FCC policy on renewals was something of a horror, he said. No rational man could afford any longer to make more than a minimal investment in a station. The setup was an open invitation to quick-buck artists. "You are engaging in a lottery, or roulette, when licenses expire every three years."

Paul Porter, another former FCC chairman, went a step farther at this same NAB meeting. Obviously encouraged by the warm and sympathetic audience, he said it was his conviction that things had gone so far that, yes, Congress definitely should get in the act. Congress should be asked to consider a law making licenses *perpetual!* His remark produced thunderous applause.

Nick Johnson did not show up at the NAB convention in Washington. Nor was he asked to appear. But he showed up every place else; luncheons, meetings, bar mitzvahs and Irish wakes. He was available to any reporter and his quotes were juicy. When he wasn't speaking somewhere, taking his case "to the public," he was writing articles or dissents to decisions.

When the Senate began hearings on a proposed bill which would have all but granted stations lifetime licenses (a license would have to be *revoked* before a challenger could file against it) Johnson remarked: "It's like saying you can't oppose an elected official unless he's impeached."

As for the Boston decision, Johnson insisted that the case truly was *sui generis;* that it had been in the courts almost forever, and that, despite all the talk, the Commission had yet to transfer a single license from a broadcaster to a protesting group because of poor program performance.

The bill before the Congress was sponsored by Senator John O. Pastore, a Democrat from Rhode Island and chairman of the Senate Commerce Subcommittee.

Of the Pastore Bill, Nick Johnson said, in July, that "even if the FCC were to take away two or three licenses a year—something it has yet to do during its forty-two-year history—we would still be providing rubber-stamp renewals to 99.9 percent of the stations." (At a time when there were 7500 stations, of which 2500 came up each year for renewal.)

The passage of the Pastore Bill, or anything like it, said Johnson, would "leave a frustrated people with no recourse, except to engage in more violent protests and other actions that serve the interests of no one."

In May 1969, the FCC turned down WHDH-TV's petition for reconsideration along with those of the other losers. The decision was not unexpected, but the speed with which it came was a shock to WHDH. It had taken sixteen months for the Commission to act after the oral argument, hence it was logical to reason, and hope, that in this instance, another year or more would elapse. Because now, more than ever, WHDH knew that it must play for time. Now that Nixon was in office and a new chairman was coming aboard in November, it was reasonable to expect that time would bring additional forces to bear in their favor.

However, the Commission acted quickly. May 19th—only three months after petitions had been filed—it denied the plea for reconsideration. The vote was the same. And it is clear now, with hindsight, that WHDH would have been better off had it bypassed the Commission and gone straight to the court of appeals. For, the petition to reconsider gave the Commission a chance to tidy up its own decision, to shore up certain weak spots, some of which were brought to light by Benny Gaguine's petition on behalf of BBI.

As Gaguine had suggested, the Commission, in its new turn-down, went out of its way to reassure the industry that the Boston case decidedly was "one of a kind." It definitely was not an ordinary renewal case. The Commission also buttressed its position that the FCC policy statement of 1965 *did* apply, and that WHDH-TV *had* been given fair consideration within the purview of that statement. It raised an admonishing finger once again at WHDH for not editorializing; and for not providing for the discussion of certain controversial problems of "local interest." (Referring to a program about abortion which the station had refused to air.) In a wonderfully obscure passage the decision stated, "In the difficult task of evaluating a past performance record, we believe that the terms 'within the bounds of average performance' and 'unusual attention to the public's needs and interests' are as 'concrete as possible.' "

In another effort to ease its conscience about the diversification issue, the decision stressed that the Commission "does not discriminate against newspaper interests, but rather gives appropriate comparative consideration to all diversification elements." Charles River's request that the channel be put under an "interim" operation until final action by the court of appeals was flatly denied. BBI's request for an August 1 termination date was also turned down. You have the construction permit, the decision in effect said, but no termination date can be given at this time. WHDH was reminded that, since September of 1962, the station had been operating under a license that was good for only four months because the Commission had been concerned with the ". . . inroad made by WHDH upon the rules governing fair and orderly adjudication . . ." And all of the "unique events and procedures" that had followed, placed WHDH in a "substantially different posture from the conventional applicant for renewal of broadcast license."

One could almost hear the Commission specialists in legal rhetoric saying to themselves: There, that ought to do it. That should shore up the few weak points, and also, calm the industry down.

Now, another twist of irony entered the case: The Commission itself—torn, divided, and bitter as it was over this case—now this every Commission must *defend* its decision before an obstreperous, cantankerous U.S. District Court of Appeals.

Hence the stage was set for the critical, final battle. Attorneys for all parties began preparing their appeals and their oppositions, which, when filed, would lead to another oral argument before a panel of three of that court's twelve judges. How long would that take? No one would hazard a guess. WHDH hoped it would take forever. BBI hoped for the quickest decision possible. But certainly it would take a year, and perhaps two, in a case of this magnitude.

At least now, and for the next many months, the Boston case would be off the front pages—or would it?

Nick Johnson, that summer of 1969, continued making his caustic statements. *Broadcasting Magazine* continued to rail and cry havoc. And in August of that year, Hearing Examiner Thomas H. Donahue, after a long renewal hearing, recommended that the license of another major VHF station be taken away. This was KHJ-TV, Los Angeles, owned and operated by RKO General, a subsidiary of General Tire and Rubber. Donahue's harsh litany read something like a catalogue of all the sins that Nick Johnson, and other staff liberals, had long been expressing: KHJ-TV specialized in old movies, and "miserably failed to serve the public interest"; like four other RKO stations, it did not editorialize. As an independent station, it made no effort to compete with network affiliates in news, documentaries and programs of special interest to the community.

KHJ-TV, said Donahue, dedicated most of its time to "the service of the young, the congenitally gullible and those not very bright." In a survey of one week, the station had depicted 181 murders, ninety-eight attempted murders, fifty-five "justifiable killings," eighteen shootings and eight kidnappings.

The parent company was also involved in dubious trade practices with General Tire's Los Angeles dealers.

After excoriating the license, Donahue turned to the competing applicant, Fidelity Television, Inc., a group comprising eighteen local businessmen and headed by former agent in charge of the FBI, William G. Simon. Here, Donahue found himself in a dilemma. Fidelity, he confessed, was not so great; his decision was more *against* KHJ-TV than *for* the challenger. He recommended Fidelity "without much enthusiasm" and concluded with the rueful observation that a hearing examiner's life would be a lot easier if he had better guidelines to follow. Likewise, he added, KHJ-TV would not be in this "pickle" if the FCC published minimum standards for use of air time.

11

Henry Geller Sells a Package

On October 31, 1969 Dean Burch was sworn in as the fifteenth chairman of the FCC. Rosel Hyde was drummed into retirement by the new administration and accorded full honors by a grateful industry. He was a good man who had served without blemish for 23½ years. On balance, his record was not without distinction. But clearly he was not the one for these turbulent times. What was needed now was new blood, a fresh viewpoint, an outsider, a man with a strong cutting edge, a sense of impatience and urgency.

Dean Burch clearly filled that bill. He had served as assistant to the attorney general of Arizona, had been administrative assistant to Senator Barry Goldwater; and later, was chairman of the Republican National Committee. From 1940 to 1948 he had lived on Alcatraz Island, because his father had been a guard with the Federal Bureau of Prisons. He was lean, lithe, small of frame, taut, cryptic and caustic—some said, too intense; humorless. Others who knew him disagreed. Everyone agreed that he had an intense focus on problems before him; no one questioned his brilliant mind.

Like all chairmen before him, particularly outsiders who came to the Commission from civilian life, like Newton Minow, Burch did not like what he saw at the Commission. Minow was affected by the odorous hangover of the scandal era; Burch was appalled by the "due process" slowup; by the logjam of cases and rule makings; and most of all by the renewal policy crisis caused by the Boston decision.

That matter, regrettably, he confided to friends, was out of his hands. The final battleground, and test, for that case was the U.S. District Circuit Court of Appeals, and there was nothing he could do about it except hope that the court would overrule the Commission, or remand it back to the Commission in whole or in part.

But one thing he could do—indeed, it was imperative that this be done—was to insist that the Commission hammer out its own renewal policy. Senator Pastore badly needed to be taken off the hook from which he was still dangling: his own two-hearing protective renewal bill which had backfired the previous summer. Pastore, called by some a wind-up doll for the broadcast lobby, had been sincerely disturbed by crime and violence on television. As a kind of quid pro quo he had offered to help the broadcasters out of their Boston-induced panic if the industry would make a genuine effort to reduce crime and violence in programs. Nobody seemed to know what happened to the latter part of that quid pro quo, but everyone knew about the uproar the Pastore Bill had caused, and was still causing, in the fall of 1969 when Burch succeeded Rosel Hyde as chairman.

Community interest groups, particularly black groups, criticized Pastore in harsh, ugly terms, characterizing him as a racist and stooge of the broadcast lobby; therefore, not the kind of man who should represent the Democratic voters of Rhode Island with its sizeable black constituency. Pastore growled whatever excuses he could think of, and vowed not to be so quick in the future to rally to the side of the broadcast industry. It was nice to have powerful friends, but there was a strange, self-defeating dichotomy of dynamism in broadcasting—it was so all-pervasive, so ubiquitous; every citizen had opinions about broadcasting—that Pastore learned a hard lesson that many others have yet to learn: It is all right to be friendly with broadcasters, but don't get *entirely* in bed with them. Perhaps that is the reason why broadcasters, with all of their considerable power, find it difficult to mount an effective lobby. As that group president had remarked: "We're too visible! We live in the world's largest fishbowl!"

Dean Burch rolled up his sleeves and gave an order to his staff and six colleagues. He wanted a renewal policy "as soon as possible." By ordinary Commission definition that meant at least six months. Not with Burch. He took over Hyde's desk on November 1 and said: "I want a renewal policy out by the first of the year."

He got his wish. Two and a half months later, on January 15, the Commission released its own renewal policy—to the immense relief of Senator Pastore who now could go about mending his fences with his constituency.

The author of that policy statement was Henry Geller, then general counsel. Indefatigable Henry, they called him. The brilliant architect of many of the Commission's past policies. He was a slender wiry, self-effacing man; the kind of man no one noticed. He had the manner of a middle-aged law clerk, a staffer who shuffled papers and saw to it that the pages were numbered correctly and that each copy was stapled in exactly the right place. Important broadcasters who came to the chairman with their lawyers to "pay their respects" and "clarify some matter" (deciphered, that means asking for something) would leave the chairman's office and ask each other in the halls, "Who was that little guy with glasses in the back of the room?"

The chairman knew who the guy in the back of the room was. Geller was something of a legend at the Commission. He was, it was said, their one-man think tank. "If something is impossible, give it to Henry." Geller was so smart he was held in something like awe by the staff.

Burch and Geller made strange bedfellows. The chairman, a staunch conservative, believed in less regulation rather than more. Geller, a liberal, had his own clearly-defined definition of that most ephemeral of all Commission doctrine, which is the foundation stone of FCC policy: ". . . the public interest, convenience and necessity."

Geller's renewal policy, modified somewhat, changed here and there in numerous meetings, had the desired effect of calming down the industry. It still had many features that were objectionable to broadcasters; but at least it was a step "in the right direction" and would go far in easing the nightmare of the Boston decision. In terms of a vote, it produced a rather remarkable consensus. The vote was six to one. Only Nick Johnson dissented, and his dissent was considered unusually mild. There followed the usual, inevitable appeal by a community interest group for reconsideration, and subsequently it went to the court of appeals.

Meanwhile, Geller had other work to do. Foremost on his agenda was the Commission's defense of its Boston decision before the court of appeals. The date for that oral argument was set for May 26. As general counsel, Geller had the choice of assigning the case to his assistant, John Conlin; but this was a tough one. And Henry Geller liked to handle the tough ones.

Unlike other lawyers, Geller thinks the oral argument is a useless process serving a doubtful purpose. "After all, everything is in the briefs," he says. "A judiciary body should not be *that* impressed with a thirty-minute recital of the high points of a case." Most judges and lawyers, however, disagree. Nevertheless, Geller knew the ordeal of the oral argument must be endured. The sometimes archaic way of "due process" must be followed. "The system seldom changes, and then only slightly, but one must work within the system." So he spent four days saturating himself with the record. And on the morning of a balmy spring day on May 26, he stood before Judges Tamm, Leventhal and MacKinnon, the three-man panel of the twelve-man court that was chosen by lot to hear counsel of all parties.

This, of course, was it. The last hoorah for WHDH if it lost. Oh, there would be a pass made at the Supreme Court; but there wasn't a great chance of the highest tribunal overturning the court of appeals; there was even doubt whether the Supreme Court would accept the case for review.

Geller talks without notes. But every point is numbered and filed in tight compartments of his mind. He looks at his black-robed judicial peers and extends his hands in an apologetic, almost supplicating manner as if to say: look at me! I don't know what a little guy from Michigan is doing here in these august surroundings. But, you see, we have this case, and I must admit, it has given us all kinds of problems. I thought it might be helpful if I point out some of these problems and tell you how the Commission views them.

On he goes, talking *to* the panel, not *at* them; but maintaining eye contact always through his large, tortoise-shell, framed glasses. Smiling, sometimes laughing self-deprecatingly at himself, and at the Commission, for having gotten the case so extraordinarily complicated; but always making his points with short, simple words; his ideas flowing so lucidly, so logically, that the panel begins to see how really simple it all is.

Geller has lost very few oral arguments, despite the fact that he thinks they are overrated and unneccessary. Yet he is a master of the art because he is so modest in manner, so beguiling and disarming that everyone wants to help him. There is, of course, another reason: his brilliant legal mind.

Geller began by admitting to the court that this case, taken *in toto,* was badly muddled up. (Certainly the court didn't need to be told *this,* but it was refreshing to hear such candor from the general counsel of a major government commission; especially the FCC, which, at times, seemed to have a genius at muddling things up.)

Geller's candor went farther. The original decision against WHDH-TV, he said, was badly written. No question about that. He didn't know who had written it and didn't care. The second one wasn't so hot either. Taken at their then face value the two decisions really couldn't be defended too well unless, and until, one went to a certain key paragraph in the second Commission decision (the one that attempted to tidy up, and shore up, the first decision). This was paragraph forty which *did* separate this case from all other renewal cases, and made it absolutely *sui generis.*

He then read paragraph forty:

> "In closing, we think it should be made clear that our decision herein differs in significant respects from the ordinary situation of new applicants contesting with an applicant for renewal of license, whose authority to

operate has run one or more regular license periods of
three years. Thus, although WHDH has operated station
WHDH-TV for nearly twelve years, that operation has
been conducted for the most part under various
temporary authorizations while its right to operate for
a regular three-year period has been under challenge.
Not until September 1962 did WHDH receive a license
to operate its television station, and even then its
license was issued for a period of four months only
because of the Commission's concern with the
". . . inroads made by WHDH upon the rules governing
fair and orderly adjudication . . . ." Again, unlike the
usual situation when an applicant files for renewal of
license, after WHDH filed its renewal application we
issued an order directing that new applications for
Channel 5 would be accepted within a specified two-
month period. Such applications were filed, accepted,
and entered into the proceeding herein. Those unique
events and procedures, we believe, place WHDH in a
substantially different posture from the conventional
applicant for renewal of broadcast license."

"Now that," he continued, "is the crux of the whole matter.
Without that paragraph I have serious doubts whether the original
decision was the correct one. I think the application of the 1965
policy was erroneous if you leave this paragraph out. If this case
were to be considered a regular renewal situation, then, obviously,
WHDH-TV should retain the license.

"Here is where we get into trouble," he argued. "The Commission, in its first decision, said it did not want to resolve the Choate
ex parte matter. I don't know why it said that, because it makes no
sense to say that. For, the ex parte matter goes to the very roots of
this case. It has been there from the beginning.

"In the second decision the Commission did come to grips with
the matter with paragraph forty. That is what I think you must
recognize. All through the years there has been this taint. A long
time ago, when the Commission gave the station a four-month
license, and at the same time invited new applicants in, I think
the Commission was saying to WHDH: Look, you can't have

your record to go on. The fact of the matter is, it was a good record. But, of course, the station was under the gun from the beginning, and a station in that situation, always does a good job. However, that wasn't the point. The Commission was really saying: You're in trouble because of this ex parte taint; therefore you can't have your cake and eat it too. You are going to be on *even keel* with the other applicants."

That, Geller knew, was the big hurdle he must get over first— admit the imperfections of the two decisions, focus on the key, *sui generis,* ex parte taint, and *then* go on from there. If the court accepted this argument, then the rest of the case flowed evenly and properly. In applying the other comparative aspects, there was no way WHDH-TV could win. In terms of diversification, WHDH, with its newspapers, its AM and FM media counterparts . . . Geller shrugged apologetically . . . it was too bad . . . there was no way WHDH could win on that comparison. I'm sorry, his smile seemed to say; but I didn't write the rules. It's not my fault.

As for integration of management? Same thing.

From here on, he was able to be more emphatic, because the case did flow properly. The danger in his approach, he knew, was that the court might reason: We've read paragraph forty, but the Commission has muddied up this decision so badly, Mr. Geller, that we want you to take it back and clarify it.

Which was all that Chairman Dean Burch wanted!

Geller recalls that he felt good making his argument that day. Leventhal interrupted frequently, but he was asking intelligent questions, so that didn't bother him. In fact, that was a good sign. Stony silence from an appeals court panel could mean indifference, boredom or a closed mind.

The courtroom was packed that day. Every wire service, network and trade magazine was represented. Industry lobbyists and lawyers filled every seat. Bill Dempsey did his usual excellent job. Benny Gaguine did not have one of his best days, but the burden was on Geller, not himself.

When Henry Geller finished, knowing smiles were exchanged around the courtroom. The modest, unassuming little guy from the back of the room had obviously done it again. His points had been made informally, in almost a chatty manner, but he had gotten them across precisely in the order he wanted; and it was apparent to the lawyers among the spectators that Judges Leventhal, Tamm and MacKinnon had "bought" Henry Geller's "package."

Geller wasn't that sure. He knew it was one of his *good* arguments, not his best one, nor his worst, just one of the good ones.

But, for him, that was good enough.

As he walked out of the courtroom he made a wry face to Gaguine. "You know something, Ben? Grown men shouldn't have to do things like this!"

Five months later, on November 13, the court of appeals panel handed down its decision.

It upheld the FCC, thus administering the *coup de grace* to WHDH, and ultimately the *Herald Traveler*.

The court agreed that WHDH-TV was *not* in the position of an ordinary renewal applicant. "Unique events and proceedings . . . place(d) WHDH in a substantially different posture from the conventional applicant for renewal of broadcast license."

The theory of *sui generis* was thoroughly subscribed to by the court.

Ironically, like an echo from the past, Herb Sharfman came in for unexpected praise. The court noted that the Commission had been diligent to take a hard look at the problem areas and that it was "aided in no small measure by the initial decision of the hearing examiner, and the examiner's careful and indeed, exhaustive review of the evidence and issues, and comparisons of the applicants in regard to each of the pertinent criteria." Which, in turn, attested to his care that his decision, "was useful, although the conclusion was reversed." This belated praise gave Sharfman scant comfort.

Finally, the decision expressed the main core of its reasoning. As Henry Geller had argued, also Benny Gaguine, it was paragraph forty from the second Commission decision which the court took pains to stress: "Not until late September 1962 did WHDH receive a license to operate its television station, and even then its license was issued for a period of four-months only because of the

Commission's concern with the '. . . inroad by WHDH upon the rules governing fair and orderly adjudication . . .' "

WHDH had argued that the Commission had erred in not applying its new, 1970 policy statement. Not at all, said the court. Footnote thirty-five in that statement indicated that the new statement did not apply to "those unusual cases, generally involving court remands, in which the renewal applicant, for *sui generis* reasons, is to be treated as a new applicant."

This case fitted that category, said the court, reminding that the Commission, in its decision of July 14, 1960, when it reviewed the record, had concluded that "Robert Choate, who was then principal officer of WHDH, had 'demonstrated an attempted pattern of influence.' "

It quoted a paragraph of that 1960 decision which had recited the strong remonstration: "The very attempt to establish such a pattern of influence does violence to the integrity of the Commission processes . . . The facts revealed on this record persuade us that the Commission processes can best be protected in this instance by exercising our discretion to void the grant of WHDH."

Why had the Commission erased the strong operating record and experience of WHDH and its principals? What the Commission had done, said the court, was to hold WHDH to a *higher* comparative standard than that required of renewal applicants generally in order to be able to invoke a past record as a reason for rejecting the promise of better public service by new applicants.

"The Commission . . . was more concerned with keeping the parties as close as possible to a new application situation, without undue advantage acquired from the physical fact of operation under a temporary authorization."

To be sure, this decision was fraught with certain "novelty," admitted the court. But, "in the evolution of the law of remedies some things are bound to happen for the 'first time.' "

What a first for the *Herald Traveler!*

Then, in a burst of ingenious rhetoric, the court closed the door forever on the incumbent: "Handcrafted orders and procedures are particularly appropriate for unique fact situations. On the unique facts presented, WHDH was neither a new applicant nor a renewal applicant as those terms are generally construed . . . that body soundly formulated an intermediate position for the instant case."

Finally the chilling words that tell a lawyer he has had it. *"There was no error."*

The industry reacted with its customary shock and dismay. Was it now *really* over? Yes, it now was really over. Only a last desperate appeal to the Supreme Court remained. Broadcasters and the trade press remained incredulous. Some miracle would happen yet. Something like this simply could not happen in America!

And where was the Commission's renewal policy? That was bogged down in the same U.S. Court of Appeals, a court that, in the past few years, seemed to take delight in overturning most of the Commission decisions and rule makings that came before it.

In fact, a year later, the same court, but a different panel of judges headed by Skelly Wright, threw out the Commission's renewal policy entirely, leaving the industry more frightened and bewildered than ever. Indeed, there is still no renewal policy that gives broadcasters guidelines on how they will be treated at renewal time. Some say there never will be clear-cut rules; that Congress will not act; and that, whatever the Commission comes up with, will be reversed at the court of appeals. Others say that there does not need to be a policy—that, because of the enormity of the disenfranchising of WHDH, the Commission will see to it that no major station is *ever* taken away again, except on the grounds of outright fraud, or total irresponsibility of operation.

Only time will answer this question. The KHJ-TV, Los Angeles, case has not yet been decided. The WNAC-TV, Boston, case has not been decided, nor WOR-TV, New York. The WPIX-TV, New York, case has not been decided. Some thirty other renewal challenges have either been decided in favor of the incumbents, or not decided at all.

What does Judge Leventhal say? Obviously, he will not talk for the record, but he is reported to have expressed misgivings about the Boston decision. He is reported to have said that, if he had it to do over again, he would not have voted against WHDH-TV. The later collapse of the *Herald Traveler* is said to have disturbed him greatly. All of which gives scant comfort to the former employees and stockholders of the Herald Traveler Corporation.

As for the vote he cast, Judge Leventhal gives the credit (or blame) to Henry Geller. Leventhal is reported to have confided to friends that, going into that oral argument, he was prepared to overrule the Commission; or remand the case for further study because he did not want to be a party to a deed of such magnitude as taking away a major TV license.

But Henry Geller talked me out of it, he said. When he finished his oral argument he turned me around 180 degrees.

As for Dean Burch, disgusted as he was with the outcome, and helpless to do anything about it, and as diametrically opposed as he was to Henry Geller's philosophies—Burch proceeded to do a strange thing. He took the unassuming little man from "the back of the room" and asked him to become his assistant in special projects. As someone said, they did indeed make strange bedfellows. But Dean Burch recognized talent when he saw it. He also knew that, with a Republican administration in power, the sensitive post of general counsel required a loyal, resolute Republican. Richard Wiley, of Chicago, fit that bill. Meanwhile, Dean Burch could keep an eye on Geller, and at the same time, use his outstanding abilities in vital areas of policy making. Geller was to perform capably in this job for the next three years, until disenchantment set in and he resigned the Commission and joined the Ford Foundation.

12

The
Crotch
Fight

There are several kinds of fights; fair, unfair, the surprise attack, a fight by rules and the no-holds-barred fight. But the worst kind of all is the crotch fight. In this kind, one aims to maim; to inflict the maximum damage in the most vicious manner possible.

What happened next between the two adversaries from this point until the last bitter day was a crotch fight. The fact that WHDH-TV extended its survival for seventeen more months is dramatic testimony to how effective its tactics were. Legally and in every other way the tactics used by both sides comprise a kind of classic handbook in corporate homicide.

(Clancy: *"They infiltrated us. They got to someone inside our organization. We found out about it quite by accident. The first reaction was to fire him. I said, no, we'll keep him in there. Feed him phony information. This will help confuse them. Which is what we did. It worked. He was a reporter. He's still a reporter. He works today for one of the two remaining papers in Boston."*)

(BBI—Nate David: *"We were convinced our phones were being bugged. Too many leaks were occurring. To prove it, we fed a couple of phony stories out on one phone that we knew was being tapped. Sure enough, they bit and took action on the incorrect information we put out. It confused hell out of them."*)

Harold Clancy, by now, was convinced that WHDH and the *Herald Traveler* were victims of a monstrous conspiracy; a sinister and evil conspiracy that, somehow, had to be exposed. He, like Herb Sharfman—although they never discussed it—subscribed to the expiation theory. This case had its umbilical cord, in point of time, back to the "Whorehouse Era" of the FCC. But *only* in point of time, in Clancy's view, because Judge Stern had *absolved* Robert Choate of any guilt as a result of those two expensive luncheons with Chairman McConnaughey. Hearing Examiner Sharfman had *eliminated* the issue. The first Commission decision of January 22, 1969 had *bypassed* the issue. The ex parte matter had only been restored four months later when the Commission came out with its drastic revision of its decision. To Clancy, this only proved that "they" were out to get his side.

Who were "they"? "They" were a motley group of liberal staffers: that renegade anarchist, Nick Johnson; Mr. Machiavelli himself, Henry Geller; and that grudge-holding obstructionist, Robert Bartley. Yes, he thought, there was no question about it; psychologically, at least, the expiation theory fit.

At any rate, the time had finally come, he decided, to let it all hang out. Until now he had been forced to remain under wraps; but with the case decided by the likes of Tamm-Leventhal-Mac-Kinnon, there remained only the spin out of time through legal procedures involving appeals, delays and finally, a shot at the U.S. Supreme Court. Yes, now the time had come to speak out. Everyone, he told George Akerson, must *know* about this monstrous conspiracy. The industry must know. The Commission must know, the courts, the Congress, yes, even the president—above all, the people! Everyone must know what he knew, or sensed, about the travesty of justice that was being perpetrated.

What were some of the matters that bothered Clancy? They were varied, and many. He intended to talk about them all.

Rosel Hyde's not voting, for instance. What did Benny Gaguine have on Hyde? Was it merely that Gaguine had once worked as Hyde's assistant? Or was it something else? He preferred to believe the latter, although he had no proof. But if he could find anything . . .

Commissioner Wadsworth. That to him was the most suspicious angle of all. Joe Kessler had been Wadsworth's legal assistant. Joe Kessler, prior to that, had worked for Gaguine's law firm; he had gone to work for Wadsworth directly from the firm of Fly, Shuebruk, Blume and Gaguine. Wadsworth wasn't known to have much enthusiasm for his job. Kessler, he explained to Akerson, led Wadsworth around by the nose. "When Wadsworth went to the bathroom, Kessler was there to show him where it was."

In Harold Clancy's mind there was no question about Kessler having influenced the commissioner's vote. "How could he *not* have had an influence? His other assistant was Dan Jacobsen, who was an engineering assistant. Was he going to get advice from an engineer? Hell no! Engineers don't get into political matters."

There were other matters that disturbed him. Henry Geller had hung his entire argument on the attempted "fix" imputed by paragraph forty. To Clancy there was a much more sinister "fix" lurking in the background of this incredible case.

How, for instance, had BBI been able to know, according to a tip he had received, the *exact day* the Tamm-Leventhal-MacKinnon decision was to be handed down?

And the *New York Times,* bleating its pride over BBI's victory —when Alan Neuman, a director of BBI, he knew to be closely *related* to one of the top executives of the *New York Times!* No wonder BBI got a good press from the *Times!*

And Bob Bartley, rolling his eyes over the Choate luncheons. He knew Bartley from Bartley's Boston days, when his uncle, Sam Rayburn, had helped put Bartley in as chief executive officer of WNAC, Boston, long enough to help that station straighten out its license renewal problems with the FCC. Shortly after that, Bartley had gone on the Commission himself, through Sam Rayburn's influence. Bob Bartley was a practical, pragmatic horse trader who no more cared about ex parte trivia than he did about ballet. To Clancy, "his hypocrisy was of the highest magnitude"!

These were just a few of the things Clancy decided to get off his chest. As far as he was concerned, BBI was not clean. They were nothing more than a group of opportunistic, buccaneering academicians motivated by only one thing—greed. He assigned several reporters to begin digging into the backgrounds of each of the BBI principals. He worked on this surveillance aspect with George Akerson, while at the same time, planned with Bill Dempsey a legal campaign that would stretch the case out as long as possible.

To get his story out, he chose a small, obscure, but respected, New England adverstising trade publication called *Ad East*. He would give an exclusive interview, he said, if certain simple ground rules were followed. The interview must be taped and the transcript of it must be printed unedited and unexpurgated.

John H. Griffin, publisher of *Ad East,* and the interviewer, was delighted to accept the conditions. Harold Clancy was hot copy. Any paper, magazine or wire service, would jump at the opportunity to have Clancy "speak out."

Clancy was interviewed shortly after the Tamm-Leventhal-MacKinnon decision. The story appeared in the December 1970 issue of *Ad East*. It was truly a remarkable interview; an extraordinary purging of one man's long pent-up emotions. The December issue of *Ad East* sold out quickly; Xerox machines in many areas of the country were kept busy grinding out extra copies. Today that issue of *Ad East* is a collector's item.

Clancy began by noting the impact the case had made so far. The company's stock had declined by more than thirty million dollars; the jobs of some two thousand employees were in jeopardy; approximately 1500 stockholders faced severe economic injury. Not to mention the whiplash effect the decision would have, and was already having, on the broadcasting industry.

Did he think their cause had been treated unfairly?

"I think we have been the victim of the most unconscionable injustice in the history of the Federal Communications Commission." The Commission, he said, had invoked a set of rules which "state within their own language that they are not to apply to renewal proceedings and, what is even more appalling, a set of rules that was not promulgated until *after* the record in our case had closed."

Griffin: "Is it being suggested that the FCC has discriminated against WHDH?"

Clancy: "I'm not suggesting. I'm stating that as a fact."

There was an especial uniqueness to this case, he said. "We stand as the single case in the history of the FCC of a renewal applicant whose operating record has been held to be irrelevant and who has been forced to compete on the basis of the artificial criteria that are usually used in connection with new applicants only."

Griffin asked, "Why was your past performance irrelevant? What was the basis for that?"

Clancy answered, "I can only say that it was excluded on the basis of comparison with a non-existent norm, a fictitious average, without any record basis for saying what was average or how we compared.

"Furthermore, the Commission did not, as a matter of indisputable fact, possess any reservoir of data for the period involved in our renewal application, by which it could determine, even from data outside the record in our case, what constituted average performance in the nation, or how we compared with other stations nationally.

"They would, for example, have found that we presented *more* educational programming than the combined total of the other two stations; *more* religious programming than the combined total of the other two stations; *more* agricultural programming than the combined total of the other two . . . Is that average?

"The Commission, by quoting the examiner out of context and giving a grossly misleading import to his words, blithely concluded that we have been deficient with respect to airing controversial issues. Had we been compared to the past performance of the other two VHF stations in Boston, the Commission would have discovered that we had presented *more* discussion programming than the total of the other two stations combined. Is that average?

"In the vitally important category of local live program origination our performance was *more than double* the total of the other two stations combined. Is that average?

"Comparison of those applications would also have revealed that WHDH-TV interrupted its programing with *fewer* commercial spot announcements than either of the other stations. Is that average? . . . It would be absolutely impossible to reach a rational conclusion that WHDH's performance, in comparison with other Boston stations, was merely average or anything other than superior."

Griffin: "Mr. Clancy, in your judgment, has WHDH operated above the FCC bounds of average?"

Clancy: "There are, in point of fact, few stations in the United States that can point to as many awards and citations for public service, for educational programming, for the excellence of its news coverage.

"Nowhere in the decision of January 22, 1969, does the Commission reveal any basis to support its holding that the past performance of WHDH was merely within the bounds of average. It does not because it cannot.

"The examiner did not find, and the Commission does not hold, that any station in the United States—much less those stations within the bounds of average—had a past performance which on the whole was equally favorable."

Griffin: "You weren't treated like others applying to renew their licenses?"

Clancy: "It is much worse than that. To deny us the regular status of a renewal applicant was, by itself, a gross injustice. But we were told categorically that we were a renewal applicant. We were misled. We were plainly misled."

Clancy then talked about the awards the station had won. Some sixty-seven of them in a category that could be called "prestigious." Hundreds of other lesser awards. Recently the Boston Press Photographers had given WHDH fifteen of their total annual twenty-three prizes for TV excellence, plus a first-time all-inclusive award as "New England News Film Station of the Year."

"The walls of my office are covered with awards," he said. "I didn't win them, the station won them; our talented and capable people won them for serving our community."

Then Clancy launched into a long defense of the Choate luncheons. Yes, Choate *did* have those luncheons. No question about it. But what did they talk about? They talked about the Harris-Beamer Bill which would "prevent discrimination against newspapers by the FCC." Senator John Kennedy's name came up again. Choate had sent his "amendment" to Kennedy at the latter's request. Then FCC Chairman McConnaughey had testified on the Hill regarding the bill. Choate, after studying McConnaughey's position, agreed with him; but there were technical defects, Choate thought; they could be corrected by a simple amendment. That was all Choate had in mind. And McConnaughey had refused to discuss even that. That was all there was to it. Judge Stern had later agreed with this interpretation. However, there had been some genuine scandals back in this era of the late fifties, Clancy admitted. Serious scandals, which involved "licensees and applicants and even certain commissioners." There were instances of unrepaid loans of money. Evidence of behind-the-scenes influence and overt attempts to exert secret influence. "It was a horrible mess and everybody was shocked and angry."

The expiation theory again.

"Let me put it this way—no question as to the propriety of Choate's conduct would ever have arisen, in my opinion, had it not been for the genuine scandals, the very real scandals, that were coming to light at the same time in connection with other cases. Because there was evil in them, many assumed that we were, somehow involved in the same or similar misconduct."

Griffin: "Was Mr. Choate's conduct investigated by any government agency other than the FCC?"

Clancy: "We were investigated by just about everybody who had the time and inclination to do so. We were investigated, I would say, to the point of harassment.

"Everyone with a motive for injuring us or opposing our license was encouraged to come forward, usually without our knowledge or ever finding out their identity. The most incredible allegations were made and they were investigated with the full resources of the United States Government. One columnist whose column had been discontinued by our newspaper evened the score by printing the most outrageous succession of falsehoods about us, and the anti-trust division of the Justice Department sent agents—teams of agents—to check out every one of them. A competing newspaper, the *Boston Globe,* had a field day savaging our reputation and many wildly false allegations from that source were diligently pursued by the government.

"The FBI checked out several phony leads. Agents from the Legislative Oversight Committee popped in and out of the city without warning. Sometimes they would want to interrogate one of us, mostly all we would know would come from an item in the *Globe* telling the public—the same public we were asking to buy our newspapers—that government agents were back in the city again, investigating us again in connection, once more, with scandalous involvement in television proceedings. After a while, of course, some people began to wonder if there was fire behind all the smoke. Our circulation began to suffer. Our reputation took a terrible beating, both locally and nationally, by the constant publication and republication of false or savagely distorted defamation and most of all, perhaps, by cruel and snide innuendo . . . In my case, for instance, one agent began by getting a copy of my birth certificate, and doggedly researched me year by year through school, military service and through my working career. He found it dull going. Our rival applicants, of course, conducted their own investigation.

"We found ourselves being followed on foot and by automobile. On one occasion someone broke into the files in the publisher's office. On two occasions we discovered and had removed unauthorized and illegal listening devices on home telephones. Altogether, it was an agonizing ordeal.

"The really amazing thing about it all is that no one—not the anti-trust agents, not the FBI, not the Congressional sleuths, not the rival applicants, not the sundry firms of private eyes, not any of the assorted types with real or fancied grievances against our business, or against us individually—not one of them came up with a single fact of adverse significance, not one single, solitary, isolated fact.

"I can only wonder how many of those involved could have survived a similar experience unscathed."

Griffin: "Returning to the Choate topic, if I may—why was the Commission harder on Choate than others? The same climate, as you called it, existed when some of the other things happened.

Why was he singled out?"

Clancy: "Like many of the other perplexing questions to this case, Mr. Griffin, if I had the answer to that, I might have the answer to the whole puzzle because there is a great deal of mystery that surrounds this case."

John Griffin now entered the raw-nerve area of individuals. Rosel Hyde, for instance. Why hadn't the chairman voted?

"There was some far-fetched speculation that he might have abstained because the counsel for the successful applicant, Mr. Gaguine, had once been Mr. Hyde's legal assistant in the Commission. I certainly hope that had nothing to do with this decision because abstaining must have helped BBI. It is unthinkable that he could ever have espoused the wild doctrine proclaimed by Commissioners Bartley, Johnson and Wadsworth in the WHDH decision of January 1969."

How about Bartley, Griffin asked.

"Bartley was employed in Boston with the Yankee Network from some time in 1943 and the network's Boston radio station was involved in a proceeding before the FCC. Choate was at odds with the network which he accused of pirating news from the *Herald Traveler.*

"At all events, Speaker Rayburn's nephew was made general manager of the radio station and the Commission renewed that station's license the following year. Choate believed Bartley disliked him because of the dispute over the news and because our papers editorially supported the Republican party and tended to be critical of many Democratic leaders including, on occasion, Speaker Rayburn."

Griffin asked about Commissioner Nick Johnson's vote. Clancy contemptuously replied that Johnson wanted the doors open to challengers of the wildest kind. Come one, come all. Open sesame. "All of this was consistent with his established philosophy . . . it is manifestly in the public interest that many take a close look at what he and two other commissioners have done."

Griffin: "Were you surprised by Commissioner Wadsworth's vote against you?"

Clancy: "I was astounded. The policies (the decision) espouses are opposite—180 degrees opposite—to Commissioner Wadsworth's position on the same matters in all previous cases. The decision represented on its face a complete abandonment of his established philosophy and his abrupt conversion to a totally new and diametrically opposite philosophy.

"It seemed to me the height of irony that his stunning turnabout should have coincided in point of time with the decision in our case—a case in which apparent coincidence had so often arisen to injure and frustrate us.

"It was also ironic because in ordinary circumstances Commissioner Wadsworth would not have been able to participate in the decision. He was not present on the day set for oral argument. Had he missed the oral argument he would not have voted in the decision.

"However, BBI—which had complained indignantly about delays in the past—asked for a delay in the holding of oral argument in order to make it possible for Wadsworth to participate . . . Had BBI failed to make that motion, Wadsworth could not have voted to deny our renewal of license and to give the license to BBI.

"But then, only a couple of weeks after the WHDH decision, the Commission released decisions in several other matters and there was Wadsworth—back at the old stand, as it were—reverting with undiminished vigor to the policies and positions and philosophy he had abandoned when he voted in our case. That made the mystery doubly enigmatic. That meant that he had completely reversed his position on identical issues, not once but twice, and all within the space of two weeks.

"If I had been astounded and chagrined by his reversal of philosophy in late January, and I certainly was, I was obviously delighted to see his second reversal in early February. It appeared to mean logically that he would want to reconsider the decision in our case and vote for a result consistent with his latest change in mind.

"However, as you know, Wadsworth voted against reconsideration of the WHDH decision, so that destroyed the impression that he had undergone two complete changes of philosophy in early 1969. At that point, frankly, I wondered if Wadsworth knew what he was doing when he voted for the January 1969 decision. He was not a lawyer and there was nothing in his background, so far as I knew, to suggest that he had any particular familiarity or experience with administrative law generally or the complicated and highly specialized law administered by the FCC in particular. I wondered about the quality of legal advice he was receiving in our case and I looked up the name of his legal assistant . . . I discovered that one, Joseph J. Kessler, was Wadsworth's legal assistant and, further, that the announcemennt of Mr. Kessler's appointment was approximately one month after Sharfman's decision in favor of WHDH on August 15, 1966.

"I wondered what Mr. Kessler's background had been, what he had done before becoming Wadsworth's legal assistant, so I referred to the 1965 Yearbook of Broadcasting and found Mr. Kessler identified as an attorney in the Washington office of Fly, Shuebruk, Blume and Gaguine—the law firm that represents BBI . . . I was understandably disturbed and concerned—especially so in the light of Wadsworth's performance in our case—to learn that BBI's law firm, which had instigated the delay in our oral argument so that Wadsworth could participate, had also been the source of Wadsworth's legal assistant.

"Well, why? Why would Wadsworth have accepted as his legal assistant a man so inextricably connected with an applicant in our case . . . A non-lawyer, such as Wadsworth, must have known he would need considerable legal assistance in order to understand (the case) much less decide it. So, what did he do? He accepted Kessler as his legal assistant, Kessler—a man who could not possibly give him any assistance, legal or other, in the very matter coming before him. Not, that is, without violating the ex parte rules.

"Once Wadsworth had accepted Kessler and worked for him, why didn't he abstain from the WHDH case? He wasn't needed. As it turned out, Wadsworth's participation made it possible for the chairman, Hyde, to abstain—and he took advantage of it. But no, Wadsworth went ahead and participated in a case in which he was not needed while, at the same time, knowing his legal assistant could not assist him in the case. And then Wadsworth ended up by voting for BBI—and by casting a vote that, with Hyde out, was essential to the decision against us. So there he is—with a legal assistant he has to insulate from the case and a vote which no one can reconcile with any of Wadsworth's votes on identical issues.

"Well, I asked our counsel whether the Commission had done or said anything publicly to evidence its awareness of the compro-·mising appearance resulting from Mr. Kessler's appointment as Wadsworth's assistant. All our counsel could find was a statement by Wadsworth—made after he had reached his decision in our case—to the effect that he had not availed himself of Kessler's assistance in connection with the WHDH case.

"Does Wadsworth's statement dispose of the matter? Not for me.

"All that Wadsworth's statement really establishes is this: It proves that he knew that it was necessary to insulate Kessler from the WHDH case. It doesn't tell what he did to accomplish that. It doesn't prove that he was successful.

"Compare the two situations: Choate was associated with McConnaughey on two occasions, approximately a year apart, for a total of two and a half hours. Kessler was Wadsworth's legal assistant for two and a half years or more—including the entire period when Wadsworth was deciding our case. Kessler became ill in late 1969 and died. However, Choate has been dead seven years. At all events, it is Wadsworth, not Kessler, whose qualification is being discussed. Why, if Choate's contact supports a finding of guilt, does Wadsworth's fail even to stimulate the Commission's curiosity?"

The interview had been going on for almost five hours now. These highlights serve only to illustrate the intensity of feeling behind the man. His words came slowly, but seethed with a depth of feeling that sent electric vibrations throughout the room. When the tape ran out and had to be replaced, they would shut the machine off. George Akerson, standing next to him, merely nodding now and then for emphasis, would provide tomato juice from time to time to soothe Clancy's throat. By now Clancy had answered every question thrown at him by John Griffin—and had volunteered much more "from his gut." After another few minutes spent on the Wadsworth matter, Harold Clancy took a long, reflective pause.

"If we are to be destroyed, if we are to lose our most valuable asset, if thousands of people—including our 3500 employees, stockholders and support-service personnel—are to have their jobs and savings and security jeopardized, and possibly lost, are we not at least entitled to a decent assurance that our execution, however unjust, has not also been unlawfully decreed?

"To me, the Commission's attitude in this area will someday, somehow, have to be accounted for, and the entire matter explored. Of course, by then the injury to us could be far beyond any agency's capacity to repair. We would be dead."

John Griffin concluded by asking: "Can you predict a final determination of this case?"

"Termination?"

"No, determination."

"Oh. Sorry. Yes. There is not the slighest doubt in my mind that WHDH is going to be remanded the renewal of the license which it so evidently deserves and which in justice it should have had long before now. My conviction in that respect is as strong as my faith in the judicial system of the United States—and I mean that in the broadcast terms, including administrative agencies as well. *I have complete faith in it.* It sometimes takes a long time. Problems arise. There are excursions. Things get sidetracked. Sometimes little injustices occur; sometimes even substantial ones; but it is absolutely impossible in my view for an injustice as monumental as this to be perpetuated. I do not know whether our relief will come in the appellate court of the Supreme Court, or in some way or other, from the Commission itself, but there is no question in my mind that a result as patently unjust as this will not survive."

Griffin: "Thank you, Mr. Clancy."

13

Nathan David's Problem

The *Ad East* interview created the stir that Clancy intended. The statements about Bartley, Hyde—but particularly those concerning Wadsworth.

Ed James, executive editor of *Broadcasting Magazine* talked it over with his senior correspondent, Len Zeidenberg, and they decided to find out. Len called Wadsworth in Geneseo, New York where he was retired and managing the affairs of his wealthy estate. Wadsworth gave forth with some extremely candid quotes. After admitting that the only reason he had voted was because of the "undue influence" WHDH had attempted to exercise in the past, and adding that only a few days before the consensus was reached another party had attempted to apply ex parte pressure on him. Wadsworth said, "I don't care about the concentration of control question. I don't think there is such a thing in terms of abuse. At least I never saw one." As for Joe Kessler having influenced him, Wadsworth said, forget it. "Joe came into my office and said he'd have to disqualify himself because he worked for one of the firms. He said, 'I will not advise you and will not even try.' "

On the basis of this story, Bill Dempsey immediately dispatched to the Commission a petition suggesting that Wadsworth did not really know *what* he was voting for; therefore it was a fraud on

WHDH and the court of appeals because the grounds given the court for the majority decision were not properly represented as being the product of only two of the commissioners. The decision, after all, had been based principally on the diversification and integration-of-management issues; here was Wadsworth saying that he was concerned solely with the ex parte matter; as a result, only *two* (less than a majority of the quorum) had really voted for the findings.

Benny Gaguine retorted that WHDH was "really stooping to a very low level" and eight days later filed a motion to dismiss WHDH's petition.

In April the court of appeals turned down WHDH in its request that it reconsider its November decision. Apart from conceding that five minor changes be made in the record, it gave WHDH sixty days to go to the Supreme Court so that the highest tribunal could act during its present winter term.

This, curiously, did not bother Harold Clancy for he was onto bigger things. The reporters he'd assigned to full time invesigation of BBI and its principals was beginning to pay off. (Clancy insists that only nine individuals were assigned to such task. BBI claims that Clancy virtually stripped his reportorial staff, using as many as thirty WHDH investigators who had observed the collection of BBI's daily trash thrown out by janitors who cleaned BBI offices in downtown Boston. The investigators followed the dump truck that collected the trash and identified the ultimate dumping ground in Quincy. From that point on, it was an easy matter for WHDH investigators to cart the trash away. It was mostly paper, but in that pile of thrown away carbon sheets, office memos, telephone call slips, etc., there were valuable leads that WHDH pursued.

On April 21, WHDH filed a blockbuster of a petition against BBI at the FCC. Among the charges being:

BBI officials were accused of covering up stock interests in other broadcasting organizations.

One David Freedman had sued Nathan David for "misrepresentation, fraud and violation of Federal security laws" in connection with a sale of six thousand shares of unregistered stock in a company called Synergistics, Inc.

Nate David had failed to notify the Commission of a 1970 counterclaim by Robert Brooks for $4400.

David was holding stock in Synergistics, but did not inform the Commission of this fact.

Mathew H. Brown, director and chairman of BBI, did not reveal to the Commission that he was a director of a cablevision company in Newton, Massachusetts—representing a conflict of interest.

Martin B. Hoffman, another BBI stockholder, was director of the Newton Cablevision Company, and further, was connected with a CATV applicant in Foxboro, Massachusetts, and director of a CATV company in Merrimack Valley, Massachusetts.

Richard S. Burdick, a director and stockholder of BBI, was not going to be the general manager as originally claimed in the application. Another person, Robert Bennett, formerly vice president and general manager of Metromedia's WHEW-TV, New York, had actually been hired for this job.

That BBI had failed to notify the Commission promptly of these and other matters as it should have done as soon as it became aware of them.

BBI was stung by these charges, and cried foul. This was another "sham," it said, designed to prolong the decision of 1969. "Unadultered lies . . . a desperate attempt" to cling to the franchise. Nevertheless the group was shaken up. The smiling countenance of Dr. Leo Beranek, now elevated to the job of full time president, had appeared in print showing him as he affixed his signature to a contract for three million dollars worth of equipment.

They were in trouble and they knew it. Whether Nate David was guilty or innocent of wrongdoing was not the question—that would be decided in the courts, not at the FCC; but the whole thing was messy. The sweeping charges, aired on the front page of the *Herald Traveler,* and prominently displayed elsewhere in national and trade press, struck at the very heart of BBI's credibility; at its basic character qualifications.

Ben Gaguine immediately counter filed, saying that BBI could find no precedent that would have required it to report a suit involving Nathan David—one that grew out of his efforts to obtain a fee from a client. BBI had violated no rule in failing to report interests of its principals in CATV. The stock held by David and another of their principals, C. Charles Marran, in Synergistics, Inc., was not of sufficient amount to require reporting under Commission rules. The failure to report that Matthew Brown and Martin B. Hoffman were directors of another company involved in cable television, "was due to the simple fact that neither was aware that he was a director of that company." Anyway, the company was "dormant." As for Hoffman being associated with two other cable companies, that was simply not true. A charge against another of the BBI principals, F. Stanton Deland, was labeled "manifestly ridiculous."

As for the Bennett-Burdick switch in jobs, Gaguine stated, this did not affect the integration-of-management factor because both would have equal managerial status—Bennett in overall operations; Burdick in "Creative Services"—and both would report to President Beranek.

But it had been embarrassing to Gaguine to learn that WHDH had *beaten* BBI to the Commission by a matter of hours in its filing on the Bennett hiring. At any rate, let's get on with the show, Gaguine, in effect, pleaded. The longer WHDH can prolong the final decision, the better it will be for them and the worse it will be for us. BBI was staffing up now. A transmitting tower commitment had been made with the Westinghouse station in Boston. A building at Needham had been found, ideal for studios. Payroll was increasing each week. The risk had gone much beyond that of legal expenses alone. BBI was deeply committed, along with the First National Bank of Boston which had agreed to loan the corporation some four million dollars.

Spring had come by now and still there was no word from the Supreme Court. *Variety* speculated that it was unlikely that the Supreme Court would rule favorably for WHDH since: there was no conflict between lower court rulings; no pressing constitutional issue; no new law in question; the Commission had ruled that the case was unique—*sui generis*—hence no new national standard was in question. Only eight of the nine justices would preside since

Chief Justice Warren E. Burger had previously voted on an earlier incarnation of the case when he served on the U.S. Court of Appeals. Four of eight justices would have to look favorably on WHDH's petition for review, and in the face of the solicitor general's response on behalf of the FCC, this seemed unlikely to *Variety*.

BBI petitioned for expedition. Every day's delay, it said, increased its financial risk. It asked the FCC for a termination date of September 26.

Then, suddenly, the saga of Nathan David took another turn for the worse. He was indicted in the Suffolk Superior Court on one of two charges of selling Synergistics stock while not being registered with the department of public utilities as a broker or salesman. He was fined two hundred dollars on each of five counts. Imposition of fines was stayed pending David's appeal to the state supreme court. On the second charge, David was acquitted.

Now, as the executive vice president of BBI, Nate David had definitely become an embarrassment and liability to its cause . His associates wanted to believe his vigorous protestations of innocence; they tried to accept his assessment of the situation, which was that this was what one had to expect when engaged in a "crotch fight." The whole thing was a frame, David charged, perpetrated by Clancy and his cohorts. As for Synergistics, a company that had gone sour (it now was in bankruptcy proceedings) David said, yes, he and many others had been high on the company back in 1967–1968. Yes, he had recommended the stock, and had sold some to his friends. Now his shares and those of other investors had been rendered worthless. He reminded his associates that he had been acquitted of the second charge. As to the first, even though the penalty was small, he intended to fight the verdict at the state supreme court.

Nevertheless, BBI badly needed something to bolster its corporate spirits. On June 14 that good news came.

For WHDH it was black Monday. The U.S. Supreme Court turned down the station's appeal for review of the case. The decision was unanimous, eight to one, with Chief Justice Burger not participating. *Variety* had called its shot with uncanny accuracy.

Redoubtable Harold Clancy flinched, but went on the attack harder than ever. While the decision indicated that their side was a "victim of grave injustice," he said, he was not too surprised, knowing that the overwhelming majority of petitions for certiorari are denied. Anyhow, the Commission now was going to be the battleground—again. He had given, he said, a lot of new information to the Commission and he was certain that these charges would be weighed properly with the end result being that WHDH would ultimately triumph. Meanwhile, he noted, their side was getting demonstrations of "overwhelming support and encouragment" from the Boston community.

Nate David, despite his problems, still remained spokesman for BBI. He talked about the progress their group had made. Now, with victory assured, and virtually all avenues of further delay closed to WHDH, BBI could, and would, move quickly ahead. Their transmitting tower deal had been closed with WBZ-TV. They had optioned a studio site in Needham. A starting date of September 26 was feasible if the Commission would approve. All necessary equipment had been ordered and would be delivered in the summer. Also, they now could negotiate with CBS for a network affiliation.

CBS, however, had other plans. In late June, one week after the Supreme Court action, the network announced that on a contingency basis, it was bestowing the golden gift of its affiliation upon WNAC-TV, then the ABC affiliate. CBS obviously had become disenchanted with the trend of events. It viewed with suspicion and alarm the prospect of affiliating with the likes of BBI which had promised more than 36 percent local live programing! Where would its network programs fit? One wag replied: "From midnight till three in the morning."

The move by CBS caught ABC off guard. Now, presumably, ABC would be stuck with BBI. It was a prospect that did not particularly excite that network.

BBI, however, without consulting ABC officials, assured the world that there was no problem since it would affiliate with ABC. That statement was met with stony silence. Rumors began about ABC affiliating with one of the two independent UHF stations in Boston: or maybe the network would *buy* one of the UHF's!

As summer wore on, all eyes and ears remained trained on the FCC. The court of appeals had ruled. The Supreme Court had refused to review the case. It was up to the Commission to act, and the only action it conceivably could take, according to experts, was to set a termination date for WHDH. If not the September date BBI had asked for, some date reasonably soon thereafter.

In late July the Commission made a request that had an ominous ring to it. It requested the Securities Exchange Commission in Boston for an update on its investigation into the Nathan David affair.

But at the same time (three days before, actually) the FCC did what it had no choice but do. On July 23 it ruled that the necessary period of waiting, following judicial review, had passed. Therefore, legally, BBI could go on the air at any time in the future. Yet, not quite. WHDH, it said, must be given time to wind up its affairs. Hence WHDH would *not* go off the air just yet, and no date was specified as to when it must go off the air. WHDH would continue *indefinitely,* until otherwise notified. Meanwhile, it said, there were various other pleadings before the Commission which it was looking into. However—and this became critical in terms of events to follow—it awarded BBI a construction permit, meaning that now the Commission officially sanctioned the actual construction of the station. Until now all BBI could do was take options on land and equipment. In addition it approved BBI's requested call letters: WCVB-TV.

The above good news came on Friday and Bob Bennett said, "I can't believe it." Fridays were usually bad news day for BBI. The new general manager of BBI was beginning to get jittery. He wondered if he had pulled the biggest gaffe in his career by signing on with the new group. Now he thought perhaps the tide had turned.

No such luck. One week later—again on Friday—the *Herald Traveler* blazoned spectacular headlines on its front page, as did the other Boston papers.

The Securities Exchange Commission had filed a number of serious charges against Nathan David! They were civil charges, not criminal, and they had a striking resemblance to the previous April charges filed by WHDH at the FCC. The SEC complaint was filed in U.S. District Court, Boston, and it raised "grave questions," according to the *Herald Traveler,* about BBI's qualifications on the basis of "character, because of misconduct, moral turpitude, and possibly even the commission of state and federal crimes by one or more of BBI's principals."

Harold Clancy beamed over this good news. He looked happier, more assured than he had been in months. It was about time, he told George Akerson, that BBI's chickens came home to roost. The FCC would *not* to be able to ignore these SEC charges. He wrote out a statement which he permitted his editors to use: "The complaint filed today by the SEC constitutes corroboration of the highest quality of the matters brought to the attention of the FCC (by WHDH)."

Nate David screamed "Outrage! Completely unwarranted! Thoroughly unjustified. I intend to fight and I'm confident I'll win."

Benny Gaguine wearily dashed off a letter to Ben Waple, secretary of the FCC for the purpose of keeping the Commission "fully appraised" of developments. He defended Nate as vigorously as he knew how, as though Nate were a personal client instead of merely one of the principals of BBI. Nate David, he wrote, had never been an officer or director of Synergistics. To be sure, David did, in 1968, act as a consultant to a subsidiary of Synergistics. He presently owned a small fraction of 1 percent of the company's 1,600,000 outstanding shares. There was no relation, or connection, between it and BBI. As to the David-Freedman suit, Nate David's position remained the same as expressed in previous affidavits. Anyhow, all of this had happened prior to 1968. David was confident that the suit brought against him by Mr. Freedman was without merit and would be defended at the earliest possible date in the Boston District Court. *In toto,* the allegations in the SEC complaint, he wrote, were without merit and did not appear to raise any serious questions as to Mr. David's qualifications to be a principal of BBI which was now a licensee of the FCC. Finally, the whole package of SEC complaints raised *no* questions as to BBI's qualifications.

The rumor mills ground overtime after this. Now, they went, the

Commission would have the "out" that Chairman Dean Burch had been seeking. Now all kinds of options were opened to him because the Nate David issue affected the integration-of-management factor; David was not merely a stockholder, or director; he was also the executive vice president and general counsel. The Commission would have ample grounds for asking that the U.S. Court of Appeals remand the case back to the Commission. And this time the Commission would likely *get* the remand. It could let WHDH continue to operate for months, even years. It could order another comparative hearing. It could simply disqualify BBI after a short oral hearing. Yes, the Commission had many alternatives to choose from; and for BBI they were all bleak.

Meantime, BBI got some small solace out of seeing Harold Clancy make the front pages of Boston papers. He was having a financial problem that was directly related to the decline of *Herald Traveler* stock. The *Boston Globe* and the Hearst *Record-American* gave the story prominent display: The County Bank of Cambridge was suing Clancy for breach of contract on loans totaling $575,000! Clancy had borrowed the money and pledged his stock, promising to repay the loans in ninety days. The stock had declined so much the bank called the loans, and when Clancy did not pay, the bank attached all of his properties.

Events were so topsy-turvy now, so out of hand and chaotic, one could look at them and laugh or cry depending on one's point of view. It was farce, theater of the absurd, or the closing act of a Greek tragedy—perhaps all three. Except that the lives and careers of many men and women were at stake. And the prize was still a television station worth forty to fifty million dollars.

Somewhere, in some mystic Valhalla, perhaps the ghosts of Robert Choate and George McConnaughey were still trying to digest their hundred million dollar lunch.

14

FCC
Seeks Remand

Bob Bennett, WCVB-TV's new general manager, considered himself as good a gambler as the next person; but this was getting ridiculous, he told himself, as the bad news continued coming in. In his naïveté about adjudicatory matters he thought the ball game was over when the Supreme Court had ruled. But that had been weeks ago. Now the picture looked murkier than ever. Trade papers were writing about the "new sense of buoyancy" over at WHDH. For them it was business as usual while BBI definitely was in a trap. Some insiders were offering four-to-one odds against BBI *ever* getting on the air. Bennett had been given 3.5 percent of the station—not given, actually, but the right to buy stock at the preferred price. Already he'd had an investor's call for a sizeable sum of money. He'd given up a solid future with Metromedia's broadcast group and had taken a number of colleagues with him— to the intense displeasure of John Kluge, chairman of the company and Al Krivin, chief of the Metromedia stations. If BBI went down the drain Bennett pondered how he would face his family, the friends he had brought with him. But, of course, there was no turning back. Look at the bright side, he told himself. What if it works out? Miracles sometimes *do* happen! Then he'd own 3.5

percent of a fifty-to-sixty million dollar TV station! *A piece of the action!* Something every TV manager dreamed of.

Bob Bennett had come to hate Fridays. His stomach churned on that day; he could scarcely keep his food down for on Fridays bad news always seemed to come. And, for extra laughs, there was the cheerful *Herald Traveler* to read *every* day at breakfast and it was often filled with news of the horrendous fate that would ultimately befall poor BBI. Most of all he felt sorry for Nate David. That poor guy! Trying so hard to maintain an air of confidence, assuring everyone that these tactics had to be expected from such an unscrupulous opponent. Everyone by now was getting extremely jittery. There had developed an acute sense of paranoia: Watch your phones! They're being tapped. Watch whom you talk to in bars. You're probably being tailed. Don't talk to strange women. That sort of thing. Both sides were paranoid.

Nevertheless Bennett plunged ahead. He had no other choice. He was locked in. He had to maintain a good front for the sake of others. And there was plenty of work to do; in fact the days were all too short. Hundreds of problems arose as they tried to do the impossible—build a TV station in a matter of weeks. Equipment had arrived. Programs must be bought. A rate card had to be set up. Negotiations went on secretly with dozens of WHDH staffers, particularly technicians and members of WHDH's excellent news team. Unions had to be talked to. There were labor problems in connection with installation of the antenna. Wrenches mysteriously began dropping from a thousand feet up, narrowly missing the heads of workmen of another union local.

The CBS pull-out particularly irked Bennett. Especially after Robert Wood, CBS network chief, had virtually promised him the affiliation now that CBS knew that BBI would have a "practical broadcaster" like himself.

But ABC was playing games with him as well. A recent meeting with ABC had gone rather badly. ABC, like CBS, was afraid of the heavy amount of "local live" that BBI had promised. Bob knew about the rumors that ABC was considering buying a UHF station. If true, where did that leave him? He would have to become an independent station; and that changed the ball game insofar as financial projections were concerned. It meant buying millions of dollars worth of programs. Long range, he didn't mind because an independent operation was his specialty—he had put WTTG-TV on top in Washington, and WNEW-TV on top in New York; these were independent stations—but one sure as hell did not achieve overnight success with independent stations. It took several years and meant incurring heavy losses for the first year or two.

Bennett was irritated with himself because he had violated a rule that he had formed early in his career. Called "Bennett's Law," it went: "When dealing with a corporation, approach at the highest possible level and with the greatest speed before the corporation can form a committee." He had violated "Bennett's Law" in his earlier dealings with CBS and now had done the same thing with ABC, which network had indeed formed a committee. And somewhere in that forgotten committee the matter lay buried. Irked with himself, and impatient with ABC's delays, Bennett called his friend, Elton Rule, who was the dynamic new president of the company and himself a former station manager.

"Elton," he said, "I can't wait any longer. I may have to declare my independence—like today!"

"Declare your *what*?" Rule asked.

"My independence. Like, to hell with ABC, if it doesn't want us."

"Fill me in," said Rule.

"Your guys have been procastinating. I can't get an answer out of them. I've got to know if I'm going to be an affiliate or not."

"What is it you'd like to be," asked Rule.

"You know what I want to be. I want to be an ABC affiliate. But if I can't, I'm going to announce my independence—like today."

Elton Rule did not react well to pressure, or threats; but he was also practical. He understood Bennett's problem. He needed no charts or diagrams to get the message of how tough it would be for ABC if Bob Bennett began operating an independent VHF station in Boston. "I'll call you back in an hour," said Rule.

Less than an hour he called back. "You've got a deal. Dick Beesmyer is sending you a wire."

At least that was *some* good news, Bennett thought. And it had come on a Friday! Maybe their luck was changing!

But, on Monday, it was back to the same old stand, bad news came, very bad news—from Washington.

TV Digest, an authoritative and reliable trade publication, reported in its Monday issue of August 16 that the weekly Commission meeting two days hence on a Wednesday was going to be disastrous for BBI. The Commission was going to "freeze" BBI's license because of the Nate David problem. An interim grantee might be picked with profits going to charity. Or, WHDH-TV might be allowed to continue operation. In any event it was going to be a crucial day for BBI and it appeared almost certain that the Commission would ask the court of appeals for a remand of the case so the Commission could consider what action to take. There was another rumor circulating in Washington and this one shook up Benny Gaguine even more: Not only was the Commission going to ask for remand, but it was going to take action looking toward the revocation of BBI's construction permit!

Resisting an urge to get a coronary on the spot and be done with the whole mess, Benny called for Don Ward, his extremely capable assistant, also a former Commission lawyer. Ward wasn't even in town. He was up at Cape Cod enjoying a few days' vacation—the first he'd had in a year.

"Find him!" Benny ordered. He conferred with Nate David and Leo Beranek my phone. Strategy was set. It was very simple: the fire had to be put out as quickly as possible. A letter must be sent to all the commissioners. Gaguine began drafting such a letter which would be delivered by hand the next day, Tuesday, to Chairman Burch and all of the commissioners; plus Richard Wiley, general counsel, and Leonidas P. B. Emerson, chief of the Office of Opinions and Review. There would be copies for anyone else who wanted one.

"Shall I mark it 'Confidential'?" a secretary asked.

"*Keerist* no!" hollered Benny. "We want the whole world to know!"

Don Ward finally was located. He flew back to Washington Monday afternoon. The two worked all night on a draft of the crucial letter. That letter, delivered the next morning, probably saved the skin of BBI.

What you are contemplating doing will destroy us, the letter began. You cannot prejudge Nathan David. He has not even had a hearing yet. We have the license and are proceeding. Our financial risk is already in the millions. Construction is "substantially completed . . . will be completed within the next two weeks." Forty employees are now on board, many of whom left secure positions in other cities. We are prepared for our September air date. Gaguine enclosed an affidavit from Leo Beranek stating that the studio building and transmitter building were 95 percent completed. The transmitter itself had been received and was being installed. The remainder of the equipment was scheduled to arrive by August 23 and to be installed no later than August 31. Land and the studio building had been purchased at $1,050,000. Modifications to the building were costing another $800,000. The transmitter building had cost $100,000. Equipment had been purchased at $2,600,000, most of which had been delivered. The cancellation date for undelivered equipment had already expired. To forfeit these investments on the basis of "mere allegations of wrongdoing by one BBI stockholder," and, "without any semblance of a hearing—would be arbitrary and capricious and would constitute a denial of due process."

As for Nate David's hearing, the letter stated it would be held in September, as soon as the judge got back from vacation.

Then Gaguine and Ward offered a bone to the Commission. Without in any way prejudging Nate David, and to help the Commission keep on even keel, Nate David would take a "leave of absence" until he vindicated himself of all charges. He would have nothing to do with the daily affairs of BBI and would refrain from voting his stock. These conditions would maintain until Nate David was fully cleared, not only by the courts, but in the eyes of the Commission itself.

The letter was delivered on Tuesday. The Commission held its regular meeting on Wednesday. There were rumors now that the

White House was directly interested in the outcome of the case. Chairman Dean Burch was known to have had recent meetings with Charles Colson, special counsel to the president. Was this case discussed? Had Burch been given "marching orders"? The *Herald Traveler,* after all, was the only Republican paper in overwhelmingly Democratic Boston. From a partisan standpoint President Nixon had every right to take more than passing interest in the outcome.

To say that the meeting was stormy is an understatement. The entire morning was devoted to discussion of the case. The mood of Chairman Burch and Commissioners Robert Lee, Wells and Houser was stern and unrelenting. To them, the decision certainly required a hard second look. A request for remand was eminently in order, Burch declared. Commissioner Wells, a former broadcaster, emphatically agreed. Except that a request for remand did not go far enough! We should *rescind* BBI's construction permit, he said. They should be stopped from further construction!

By lunchtime he had obtained a consensus in favor of his point of view. Wells had a speaking engagement out of town and said he must catch a plane immediately after lunch. If there was going to be any change in the consensus, he would stick around and fight for his point of view. Dean Burch said he saw no reason why Wells could not proceed with his plans.

After lunch the discussion continued and became more heated.

"We cannot take this action," argued Nick Johnson. "We haven't legal grounds to pull back the construction permit. Nathan David has not been convicted of *anything* as yet! We're not a kangaroo court—or are we? We'll be making a mockery of due process! Furthermore, David has offered to separate himself from BBI, and according to Gaguine's letter, his offer has already been accepted by BBI."

The matter became deadlocked. Johnson offered another solution, "If you want to ask for remand, that's one thing. If you want to put BBI on notice by telling them that if they continue to construct they do so at their own risk . . . well, I'll even go along with that. But you can't pull the construction permit. We have no legal right to do so at this time . . ."

Finally the chairman put the matter to a vote. Nick Johnson's eloquence carried. Remand would be requested but the construction permit would not be pulled. WCVB-TV would be permitted to continue building . . . *at its own peril!*

Was it Nick Johnson's eloquence, or the seven-page letter prepared by Ward and Gaguine, that carried the day for BBI? The answer is: both.

And Bob Wells should have stayed in town!

Another weird irony entered the case: *Broadcasting Magazine,* certainly not sympathetic to BBI's cause, now unwittingly, aided BBI immeasurably!

Rufus Crater, chief correspondent for the magazine, and one of the best in the business, had taken Ed James' suggestion that he go up to Boston and do a wrap-up on the Boston story, particularly in regard to BBI's construction activities. What Crater saw, and wrote about, appeared three days after the Commission's decision to request remand—and it gave spectacular corroboration to everything that Gaguine had told the commissioners.

The story contained six pages and nine photographs of corroboration. BBI *was* in the advanced stages of construction. Not forty but forty-five people were on board. One studio had already been completed. More than one hundred workmen were working overtime to complete the job. "A truckload of Ampex equipment rolled up to the ramp Monday."

Although *Broadcasting Magazine's* story helped, BBI remained in a state of shock over the Commission's action. There could be no question that WHDH had "bought more time." Not only was there a real danger of appeals agreeing to remand, but it might take months before the court would act. The court could elect to delay until Nate David cleared himself from his indictment by the S.E.C. And the Commission warning of proceed at your own risk sent shivers up and down their spines.

And if appeals *did* remand, what then? Would the ball game be over? Yes. It was as simple as that. Dean Burch had been waiting patiently (well, not so patiently) for this opportunity ever since he had become chairman two years ago. Now he knew he had the necessary votes. Bob Lee certainly would vote with him. Bob Wells also. He had the vote of Thomas Houser, a Republican and interim commissioner. That amounted to four votes, a majority. Bartley and Johnson no longer had Wadsworth with them. Their third Democratic colleague was H. Rex Lee who had abstained from voting back in 1969. But even if Rex Lee voted with them now, it made no difference. The final decision would be four to three in favor of WHDH.

Perhaps of all the highs and lows for BBI, this was the lowest period of all. Messrs. Beranek, Bennett, David, Brown and their other stockholders (twenty-nine at this time) read the *Herald Traveler*'s confident statements with nausea. Harold Clancy was a master at rubbing it in. He was delighted, he said, by the turn of events. "It is perfectly obvious that the Commission is concerned and wants to investigate BBI's qualifications. That is precisely what we asked . . . I am therefore encouraged to learn that the Commission is doing so and I have not the slightest doubt as to what the outcome of such an investigation will, and must, be. I think this is not merely good news for WHDH. I think it is good news as well for the community we have served for so many years."

Morale at WHDH zoomed. It was business as usual. Plans were made to kick off the new fall season. Advertising budgets were being accepted. Promotion and publicly campaigns were set. New equipment was being bought, old equipment replaced. Actually, only thirteen employees had defected during the year of 1971, and most of these were women with pregnancies. The staff believed in their resolute leader. For them, the low watermark had been in June when the Supreme Court had refused to review the case. But now, with Nate David in trouble, and the Commission asking for remand, it was, "Happy days are here again!"

"We've even decided to paint our tower," said the chief engineer. "That will cost $8500. You don't think we'd spend that money if we were worried, do you?"

The station made its annual sales presentation and outing for advertisers and agencies on August 23. The production ended with a blowup of an ad that WJZ-TV had run weeks before. A cheap shot, WHDH called it. The blowup on big screen projection read:

"With all the changes in Boston TV this fall, isn't it nice to have someone to depend on."

The battle of petitions continued. BBI talked about the ruinous economic consequences of the commission's action. WHDH, suspicious of the court of appeals and its three-judge panel of Tamm, Leventhal and MacKinnon, told the Commission it should have asked for remand from the Supreme Court. Nate David frantically tried to get the district court in Boston to hear his case so he could absolve himself from these "rigged charges." On the last day of August he got the good news: the court would hear his case on September 15.

Meanwhile, BBI asked for, and got, equipment test authority from the Commission so it could begin signal test operations. No sooner had this been granted than the two transmitters collided signals at 5 AM! *On a Friday!* The *Herald Traveler,* of course, featured the news of this "unwarranted interference" in its accelerating "print" war of nerves.

Clancy and Beranek flung statements back and forth with increasing venom. Clancy, now in the underdog position, had the advantage. "One of us is lying his head off," he stated, "and we want the Commission to decide who it is. Perjury is much more serious than cheating on stock." Leo Beranek kept silent on this, but Ben Gaguine replied: "We would like to be polite, but I don't think you could print the one word answer to that!"

Broadcasting Magazine, meanwhile, did its bit with frequent editorials. Its latest one said that if the chaotic renewal situation brought about by the Boston decision was not straightened out, then "broadcasting under the American plan can go under."

A so-called "grass roots" campaign began in Boston to save WHDH. Charles W. Grinnell of Manchester—a "concerned citizen"—circulated three thousand petitions, each with space for forty signatures, and addressed them to Dean Burch; the message being that WHDH has served the community in an exemplary manner and must be saved.

BBI retaliated by circulating petitions of its own.

Nate David gathered more data to prove his innocence and

asked for a delay of his hearing. A new date of October 12 was set by Federal Judge Anthony Julian in Boston.

It didn't help BBI's morale to read in Jack Major's column in the *Providence Journal* that Martin Levy, chief of the broadcast facilities of the FCC, had candidly expressed himself about the Commission's betting mood. The odds were, Levy implied, that the court of appeals *would* remand the case back to the FCC. How long it would stay at the Commission, or what the Commission would do, was "anyone's guess."

Suddenly there was more bad news for BBI—again on Friday. Five of the six defendants in the Synergistics case entered into a consent decree with the Securities Exchange Commission, consenting to certain conditions involving the sale of unregistered stock and other matters. Only Nate David had refused to consent to the conditions. Initially, he did agree. But, after agreeing, or making an offer to consent to certain conditions set down by the SEC, and consenting not to engage in further distribution of the stock of Synergistics, and after consenting to other conditions, Nate David changed his mind and withdrew the offer one day before the SEC was scheduled to hold a hearing. A "Washington attorney" made the withdrawal. Perhaps BBI feared that the "taint" of such "consent" might place an undue burden on BBI's position.

The situation now for BBI was growing desperate. It had a cash drain of approximately $300,000 per month. At this rate its four million loan from First National of Boston would disappear before spring. Harold Clancy's strategy was working superbly. "We'll spend them broke," he had told George Akerson long ago. That prediction now seemed ominously certain to come true. In addition, Clancy's reporter-investigators were working harder than ever. They had amassed more leads, new tips that seemed productive. These Clancy placed carefully in a folder, intending to produce them one by one at the proper time.

Meanwhile, Benny Gaguine continued his barrage of petitions. Please, he pleaded, more delays will put us out of buisness!

Nonsense! Bill Dempsey retorted. BBI's claims of economic ruin were "bloated, unsupported and dubious." Besides, he jibed, hadn't the Commission warned BBI that, if it proceeded, it did so at its own risk?

Then came the fateful day of October 2. A day of unexpected, undreamed of victory and triumph for BBI. A miracle! A bolt of salvation from out of the blue!

The U.S. Court of Appeals refused to remand the case back to the FCC!

15

FCC Concedes

The decision from appeals was clear enough. It refused to remand, but it had one unsettling feature. It wanted more information from the FCC to support the Commission's own pleas in the event that the Supreme Court turned down WHDH's inevitable appeal to the higher tribunal (for the second time).

What about Nathan David, the court of appeals asked. Did the Commission have the authority, in protecting the "public interest," to separate Nate David from any continuing role in the operations and affairs of BBI? To what extent did the Commission consider its action on BBI as having compromised the integrity of the administrative process? Get back to us in a week, appeals told the FCC, because there is an urgency here. The Supreme Court was beginning its fall term and should give its decision on October 12, its first decision day.

BBI smelled final victory at last. WHDH's automatic appeal to the Supreme Court could only be a forlorn hope. That court rarely granted hearings on a case previously turned down. Leo Beranek made a victory statement, saying that, at last, viewers in the Greater Boston area soon would be able to see the new Channel 5.

Harold Clancy retorted, Nonsense! "Beranek was wrong in July, wrong in August, wrong in September and he is equally wrong in October."

Nate David then did the obvious thing: he obtained a postponement of the hearing of his civil suit by the SEC. Now that appeals had turned down the Commission on remand there was no need to push for a quick resolution of these matters. Nate David would be separated from activities of BBI, said Benny Gaguine. In fact he was already on a temporary leave of absence. It wasn't the ideal solution for Nate, but it was the only practical one; and the only one available under the circumstances. When Nate eventually settled his problems, he could then resume full time activities; in the meantime, he still retained his 6.5 percent stock interest.

On October 12, 1971, as expected, the Supreme Court washed its hands of the Boston case. There is nothing here for us to resolve, it said in effect. The busy shuttlecock thus was again placed squarely between the U.S. Court of Appeals and the FCC.

The Commission met its one week deadline and supplied "further information" to appeals. The matter of Nathan David was quite serious, it said. His simple removal from the management structure of BBI did not wholly solve the problem. Technically, the Commission could remove him, but since he was "fully integrated in the BBI operation," and since he was an officer and director—"no individual holds more stock"—his integration into the day-to-day affairs of the corporation played a "substantial role in BBI's receiving a significant preference in the integration factor, a crucial factor in this case."

Removing David, said the Commission, may not be "sufficient to protect the public interest against the choice of less than the best qualified applicant in the comparative process."

And, if this wasn't sufficient to motivate David to look for the nearest gas pipe—not to mention others in his group—while the court of appeals was considering the FCC's further data, Nate David, a few weeks later, was indicted by a grand jury!

A second blow! The first had been a civil action by the SEC. The second was by a Suffolk County Grand Jury under the general laws of the State of Massachusetts dealing with blue sky laws in the sale of securities.

There were three indictments containing seven counts. Maximum penalty for each count was either a five thousand dollar fine, or 2½ years in jail. Prosecutor was Attorney General of Massachusetts Robert Quinn, a good friend of both Harold Clancy and George Akerson.

Judge David A. Rose released Nate David on personal recognizance, granted him thirty days to file special pleadings and announced a trial date of January 24, 1972.

Looking haggard and angry, Nate David screamed loudly. He charged politics. It was a savage, vicious attempt to discredit him, he raged. All the charges were misdemeanors and of a highly technical nature. Never to his knowledge, he said, had such charges been made a basis of criminal proceedings in the fifty years the statute had been on the books. Moreover, he declared, the case rested on very questionable factual and legal grounds. The Massachusetts Department of Public Utilities (DPU) had primary jurisdiction over sales of stock and had, he said, conducted its own investigation of his activities. A report on him to the same Attorney General Quinn had stated: "We do not consider that the public interest requires further action and recommend that no further proceedings be initiated."

The indictment, he insisted, was entirely the result of the *"Herald Traveler* combine's" effort to discredit him and thwart BBI from commencing television operations on Channel 5.

Nate David knew about crotch fights. As counsel for clients he had been in many of them in the past. But never had he known the agony and pressure of being the central figure of the most controversial case in the history of U.S. regulatory agencies. He was to know, and feel, a lot more before it was over. In fact, Nate David would never be the same again.

Every time the course swerved in one direction it could be counted on, as though by some immutable law, to swerve just as sharply in the other. Bill Dempsey filed an appeal, not at the Supreme Court, but at U.S. Court of Appeals, asking for reconsideration of the decision.

Harold Clancy, maintaining an air of pugnacious confidence said that justice was on their side. Such a travesty could not, and would not, be allowed to prevail. The Boston community was behind him. His employees were steadfast, and the industry was behind him. That was evident from the latest growls of displeasure from *Broadcasting Magazine* which stated now that Appeals was the culprit and had to be dealt with: There was, the magazine said, "a growing sentiment for a showdown . . ." in the Supreme Court, if necessary, "over the role U.S. Court of Appeals had been playing in license-renewal proceedings."

Then it dangled before its sympathetic readers the horror chamber thought of what would happen if the Democrats won the next election and elevated Nick Johnson to chairman of the FCC! That notion sent hundreds of TV and radio managers running for the Excedrin bottle!

To add spice for Boston TV viewers, some of whom were beginning to regard this as high comedy, there occurred a second signal collision between the two transmitters. Only this was not merely a collision of test patterns at five in the morning. This happened in prime time, for nine minutes, at the beginning of WHDH-TV's special on "The Plot To Murder Hitler." The Fuhrer was seen waving his arms over a superimposition of WCVB-TV's test pattern! Was this on purpose, Clancy questioned in the *Herald Traveler*. An indication of how contemptuous BBI was of the rights of viewers?

No, said Beranek the next day. It was merely an accident. Engineers were doing some work on the transmitter and someone pulled a wrong switch.

Then with dramatic suddenness the pendulum swung in the other direction. On December 29, 1971, the court of appeals *refused to remand the case to the FCC!*

"The interest of justice would not be furthered by recalling the case," said the decision. It pointed to the "finality" of the FCC's order, and to the fact that the FCC had already awarded the construction permit to BBI. It also found that the "charge of Mr. David's violation of law did not relate to BBI, or to a matter within the correct cognizance of the FCC."

As for Nate David, the Commission could take care of that, said the decision. David could be separated from BBI's management and operation and have "no meaningful relationship with BBI unless, and until, he is cleared."

But what about the importance David had played in the integration-of-management factor which, eons in the past, had helped BBI win its license?

True, said appeals. David's participation in management *did* make a contribution; but it had "lesser significance than was involved in other cases where we ordered remand."

Finally, there was no "unconscionable injustice in permitting BBI's retention of the award" so long as appeals had the "protective condition of effective separation from Mr. David."

The spokesman for the same three-judge panel that had looked at the case so many times, Harold Leventhal, added a delicious bit of irony of his own. A critical fact, he said, was the fact that the Commission had issued a construction permit to BBI in July of the previous year. One wonders what would have happened if the Commission had *rescinded* the permit on that turbulent day last summer when Commissioner Wells had to make a speech out of town? What if he had been present at that stormy session when his consensus was overturned?

Both sides now made the usual, predictable statements. Leo Beranek said he was elated. Now WCVB-TV could bring New England viewers the quality service it planned. The only question remaining, said Ben Gaguine, was: when do we start broadcasting? When is the Commission going to give us a takeover date? He earnestly hoped, in print, that it would give BBI such a date within the next three days.

"Simply preposterous!" cried Hal Clancy. The fight was not over by a long shot!

But those experts who had been trying to keep up with all the mad twists and turns now sensed that the end was near. WHDH's death rattle was at hand. Not only for the television station, but for the *Herald Traveler* as well!

"Lord Keynes," a New York stock analyst, predicted the demise of the paper after the station went off the air. The company's stock was down to twenty dollars a share from highs in the sixties. The paper could not go it alone. Fifteen hundred jobs were on the line. The only question was: should the paper liquidate, to take the major shareholders off the hook; or would it try to stay alive, hoping for a merger? Or, would the company simply lock the doors? The paper was known to have lost three-to-four million dollars the preceding year. Even the six-to-seven million profit of WHDH-TV was not believed to have been enough to prevent an overall loss for the parent company.

In that same interview in *Ad East,* Martin Levy of the FCC spoke with a bit too much candor. (Not a week went by that he did not get dozens of calls about the case.) This time he said that it was his opinion that Nathan David would be "washed out of the picture."

What if David was convicted, the reporter asked.

No particular problem, Levy replied. "He would probably just relinquish his stock interest." Years later, however, when BBI came up for renewal Levy said that then a challenger could raise the Nate David question. But not until then. And that could take three years or longer. By then, WCVB-TV could have established its own track record.

Meanwhile, he added, it was also his opinion that WHDH had done quite a bit of procrastinating in its appeals procedures during the past year.

Bill Dempsey immediately shot off another of his countless petitions based on Martin Levy's remarks. But the Commission absolved its broadcast facilities chief of any wrongdoing.

Harold Clancy suddenly, in January of 1972, admitted the truth that he had never spoken before. The time had come to tell the whole truth and nothing but the truth: *The Herald Traveler could not survive without the profits of WHDH-TV.* The newspaper definitely would have to go out of business.

To hell with that, Benny Gaguine replied in a quick filing: our payroll is far above the figure we gave last summer. We have been granted the license. All legal roads have been traversed. Thrice traveled in fact. Our station is built. Our transmitter is ready. Our programs have been bought. Our network will be ABC. How can you, the Commission, compound our already serious "financial injury" by abetting further delays? Let's go! cried Gaguine. We're running out of money!

At the FCC the anti-BBI block was frantically searching for

legal ways to save WHDH. The anti-WHDH forces were pushing for a transfer date. How long, they asked, can this comedy of delaying tactics be allowed to continue? The pro-WHDH forces were saying: how can we avert the last act of this Greek tragedy?

John W. Pettit was busy at the latter task. As new general counsel he had just taken over from Richard Wiley who had been appointed commissioner replacing Robert Wells. Pettit, on behalf of Chairman Burch, was investigating every conceivable legal angle. *Broadcasting Magazine* speculated that the showdown was near. Wednesday, January 13, 1972 would likely be the day of decision. The Commission had two alternatives: 1) It could grant BBI an air date and separate Nathan David from the operation; 2) It could seek a Supreme Court review. But the latter course was considered unlikely. Only a few of the seven commissioners thought this was a viable alternative. They doubted that the solicitor general would support such an appeal. It would be one of "judgment," not one of "law," and therefore not the kind the Supreme Court would sustain.

However, on January 13, the Commission met and there was no action.

But a week later, with the U.S. Court of Appeals watching from the wings, the Commission did act, and in a manner that produced consternation throughout the industry.

The vote was four to nothing to put WHDH off the air as of 3 AM on March 19!

And that vote, for Dean Burch, was the most traumatic, most frustrating vote he had ever cast as chairman of the FCC.

And to the utter astonishment of WHDH—and the industry— Dean Burch *cast his vote for BBI!* Or, to be more precise, for the matter at issue, which was that WCVB-TV would sign on Channel 5 in Boston at 3 AM on March 19, 1972.

16

The
Last
Day

Before one can ask why Dean Burch voted as he did, one must first look at the vote and the decision: Commissioners Rex Lee, Charlotte Reid and Richard Wiley did not vote at all. Rex Lee had been appointed to the Commission long after the Boston case had "matriculated." Charlotte Reid only recently had come on the Commission—the first woman since Frieda Hennock in 1948. Wiley, who had strong feelings about the case (in favor of WHDH) had been general counsel and therefore felt that he should not vote in the case. Commissioners Bartley and Johnson, of course, stood firm for BBI. Hence the only vote Burch could count on was that of his friend, Bob Lee.

As for the decision, the conditions were quite specific. Nathan David must be removed from the group; he could not participate in any of the affairs of the station or corporation, and he could not vote his stock until the Commission affirmatively rescinded these restrictions, and until Nathan David proved his innocence. As to the current charges against David, the Commission stated that it would consider these at the time it considered BBI's license application.

Dean Burch voted as he did because he believed he was in a helpless position. It was like that hoary joke that ends with the punch line: You can't get there from here. No matter which way he turned he could not come out with a conclusion he wanted. The court of appeals had shut the door. The Supreme Court had refused to accept the case. Our own legal position is untenable, Commission lawyers told the chairman. Even his close friend, Bob Lee (who had consistently voted for WHDH) had told him that the cause was hopeless. Appeals had stopped the Commission at every turn, Lee reminded the chairman in their private discussions. How much clearer could the message be? We've got to end this interminable case, Lee told him. It's getting to be like something out of Jules Verne, said Lee. The ball game is over. The court of appeals blew the final whistle long ago. The players are ready to go home. Only a few fans remain in the stands, and they, too, are fed up.

But Dean Burch was adamant. He was angry, damned angry. Don't you realize what we're doing, he cried, pounding the table. We're setting a terrible precedent, that's what we're doing! What the hell's the matter with you, Bob?

Unflappable Lee from Chicago, an ex-FBI agent, was a modest, unassuming sort of person, the most humanistic of all the commissioners. He would always listen to reason; but if he wasn't sold, a ten-ton truck could not make him change his mind. This time he was not sold. When the vote came it was four to zero for the March 19th takeover date. Bartley and Johnson, of course. Burch and Lee, with "concurring statements."

And what concurring statements they were! Especially Burch's. Never has there been a "yes" vote hedged with so many negatives; or written in such vitriolic language. The bottom line of Burch's statement will linger in Commission annals for years to come. "I cannot help but feel, against the background, that contrary to the holding of the opinion, an 'unconscionable injustice' has been done here."

His "concurring statement" tore the decision to shreds. It was, he said, "flawed" and represented "irrational decision making." The errors were grievous, and stood out "stark and obvious." Paragraph forty, he charged, had been thrown in almost as an afterthought. The ex parte aspect had not even been a factor in the original decision of January, 1969. Only afterwards, in the reconsideration of May, 1970, had someone thought to put it back in.

"I am puzzled how (these matters) passed muster," he wrote, "first with the Commission and later upon review, before the court."

"Process so rent with glaring error does not commend itself!"

Bob Lee's "concurring statement" was simpler, more controlled and reflective of what he had been trying to get across to the tempestuous chairman: the ball game was over. There was no place else to play extra innings. Appeals had put that fact succinctly: "What ultimately convinces us that the interest of justice would not be furthered by recalling the mandate, is the *finality* of the FCC's order and the award of the construction permit."

There was that word *"finality"* again! Another irony in the twenty-four-year saga of ironies: appeals was hanging its hat on the FCC's "finality"; just as the Commission had previously hung its hat on the "finality" of appeals' decisions.

But, no matter, the ball game was over.

For WHDH after that it was downhill all the way. Hal Clancy, sounding like a protagonist in the last act of a tragedy, made all the proper, brave statements. He agreed with Burch that the decision was "unconscionable," then wondered aloud, and in print, why Burch had voted as he had. He likened Burch's position to the "infamous proposition" of the executioner who, thinking that he may have the wrong party on the gallows, nevertheless proceeds with the hanging immediately, vowing to check into the facts later. There was, even his strongest critics agreed, a kind of greatness and nobility in Clancy's last-act behavior. He would continue the fight, he said, "with absolute confidence that our system of law is not so impotent as to be unable to right an injustice so blatant" as this one. WHDH had been a victim of, not one, but a "series of injustices." Nevertheless, "the case is a long ways from being over. It will not be over until the injustice has been righted."

There were other avenues of last resort; more petitions, charges, maneuvers for delay. But they were tinged with desperation; one got the feeling that the inevitable was also inexorable; that the end was near. March 19 was only weeks away. WHDH filed new charges against BBI alleging that Edward C. Bursk, one of its stockholders, was involved in a questionable securities deal. They filed again at appeals, this time in the Boston circuit; but that did not work. The Boston circuit said it wasn't a proper matter for it to consider; go back to Washington.

While Tamm-Leventhal-MacKinnon were "reconsidering" the case for the umpteenth time, the Greater Boston Labor Council came to life and realized that some twelve hundred of their union members were going to be out of jobs. So the council filed a petition in favor of WHDH.

On March 2 the Herald Traveler Corporation announced what everyone had suspected: yes, the parent corporation had lost money the year before. A loss of $300,000 in 1971 on revenues of 45.9 million. The loss equaled 53¢ per share compared to earnings of $3.46 per share for 1970 when it had earned a net profit of two million dollars.

None of this fazed Tamm-Leventhal-MacKinnon. They turned WHDH down again. So, on March 13, six days before WCVB-TV was to go on the air, Clancy, Dempsey and team filed its final gasp at the U.S. Supreme Court. The third time, for certiorari—review. It asked the high tribunal to stop all further legal proceedings until the Commission looked into the case once more; and to stay the March 19th switchover date. Its reasoning was blunt and simple: 2500 wage earners would lose their jobs. The U.S. Court of Appeals had usurped the jurisdiction of the FCC. An investment worth easily over fifty million dollars would be destroyed.

Enter now, one, Abe Fortas.

When Gaguine heard the news that Fortas had been hired by WHDH to aid its cause at the Supreme Court, Benny blew sky high. "My god, they're trying to pull a cute one!" he declared. When he learned of the strategy, he said: "And they just might get away with it."

WHDH knew that it had only six days to live. Only the Supreme Court could keep it alive. Chief Justice Warren Burger had long ago disqualified himself from any consideration of the case. This left eight other justices to preside. William O. Douglas was next in command. He was a longtime friend of Abe Fortas, who himself had been a justice until some unfortunate events caused him to resign. There was, it seemed, an unwritten rule that provided that, if it was inconvenient for the full court to address an emergency matter, the senior presiding judge—in this case, Douglas—could accept the matter on behalf of the court and present it in due course at his convenience. Thus, it might go on the agenda months later. Abe Fortas had the proper qualifications to discreetly present this matter to his old crony, Bill Douglas, and to persuade him to the notion that this matter was of no great moment and that it could be placed somewhere on the back burner.

What kind of a price is paid for this kind of special consulting service? No one knows for sure, but estimates indicate something like $50,000, plus a contingency fee if WHDH had retained Channel 5. A fee of, say, one million dollars.

Hearing of this gambit, BBI promptly hired its own "consultant." That knowledgeable soul, for whatever his fee, said that the matter, while ticklish, could be handled. BBI would simply request that the matter of WHDH's petition be considered at once by the *entire* court *en banc*. This request would have the effect of nullifying Abe Fortas' maneuver. Bill Douglas did not mind paying off past "due bills," but he was not so impolitic, nor impractical as to ignore the realities of the situation and put such a matter "on the back burner."

BBI's "consultant" earned his fee, and then some. Because the strategy worked. Word came from the clerk that, yes, the Boston petition would be considered by the entire court sometime during that same week at one of its informal daily conferences.

The Supreme Court contributed its bit to the last act of the drama by *not* acting. WHDH filed its petition on Monday, March 13. Switchover time for Channel 5 and 3 AM on Sunday, the 19th, leaving only five days for the court to act. Friday would be its last day for possible action.

Ben Gaguine told his group that the court certainly would not wait until the last day. Action could be expected on Tuesday or Wednesday. But those two days passed and nothing happened.

Thursday will be the day, Gaguine assured. But Thursday also passed.

"Friday morning, for sure," said Gaguine. "Before noon. You can count on it."

Knots began gathering in the stomachs of WCVB-TV executives. They gathered in Leo Beranek's office, or paced the corridor outside—called "Coronary Alley."

"Heard anything yet?" Beranek asked Gaguine in one of half a dozen phone calls that morning.

"Leo, cool it. I talked to you just ten minutes ago."

"I know. I just thought . . ."

"Don't think. Relax. It'll be all right."

"That's easy enough said."

"The clerk will call me the minute he gets any news. And I'll be on the phone immediately."

"We'll try to be patient," Leo said lamely. "You can understand how anxious we are."

Ben said, yes, he understood. He knew that BBI was in a severe cash bind. Its weekly payroll was staggering. If the court voted to reconsider, and review, and "stay" the Sunday air date, it conceivably could put BBI into bankruptcy. There was no assurance that the bank would come up with any more money, especially if it knew that a delay could go on for months.

So Benny knew, and yet he didn't know, not really, about the incredible tension that was building up minute by minute at BBI's studios in Needham. Executives like Bob Bennett, Bill Poorvu, Dick Burdick, Tom Maney, Jim Miller, Joe Ryan and others gathered in tiny groups, or strolled the halls trying to smile and instill confidence in others. Tom Maney was so worried, he had forgotten to wear green on this, St. Patrick's Day. The first time he had ever forgotten. They tried to engage in small talk in Beranek's office, or tell jokes that would break the tension. But no one paid any attention to the punch lines. If one did laugh it was at the wrong places.

By 1 PM someone remembered that no one had eaten lunch. Beranek sent out for sandwiches. 2 PM came. 3 PM. No word. Bob Bennett broke the pall by playing the game of states: who could name the fifty states in five minutes? No one could. In their condition it would have taken all day.

"What if we don't hear *anything* today?" someone had the ill grace to ask.

The others glared at him. What a gaffe! Everyone was thinking of that possibility; but no one dared put the question. Beranek, above all, was thinking about it. If no word came would they sign on as scheduled? What would be their legal position? Would WHDH-TV sign off the air?

The phone rang and everyone jumped. The voice on the other end was that of Don Ward. "No news," he said. "Court's still in session. But . . ."

"But what?" Beranek almost shouted. The world-famous acoustics expert usually was in full control of himself. But every man had his breaking point.

"The clerk," said Ward. "The clerk wants your home phone number."

"What for? What does *that* mean?"

Don Ward said he hadn't the slightest idea.

"*Please* call the clerk again. Ask him."

"I did. Been calling him every hour. He says to let him to hell alone. He's getting calls from all over the country."

Five o'clock came. Still no word. Beranek called Ward again. This time Ben Gaguine came on the line.

"Any news, Ben? Has the court adjourned?"

"I don't know a thing."

Leo Beranek fought a growing wave of hysteria. "Call him, Ben! Do something!"

"The clerk told us not to call. He knows we're waiting."

Finally at 5:30 the phone rang. Beranek had the instrument off the hook before the first ring had ended.

"The clerk just called. The court has adjourned for the day."

"So . . . what does *that* mean? What about us?"

"Adjourned, I said. You guys better go home. Apparently they're going to consider the case over the weekend."

"*Over the weekend?*" Beranek sat there in shock. He told the others. They left, silent and grim lipped. Leo remained at his desk, staring up at the ceiling. What if the court waited till Monday? What if WCVB-TV signed on, and then on Monday, had to go off the air? What about the victory party they had planned for Saturday night at the Marriott Hotel?

Five minutes later he was still trying to muster his strength to climb out of his chair and go home when the phone rang again. It was Don Ward . . .

A moment later Leo Beranek dropped the phone and ran out the door of his office and down the hall, shouting, *"We're on the air! We're on the air!!"*

Harold Clancy learned the news at the same time from Bill Dempsey. He faced his final task with typical stoicism and fortitude: the heartbreaking task of telling some four hundred employees who were on the premises that the battle was over. He was shaken, yes, but no one knew it.

Tomorrow is our last day, he told them; let us do a great job on our final day. How proud he was of them! They were all such pros, he told himself; real pros. He hadn't the heart to look at them as he spoke; when he did he saw the disbelief in their eyes, and the sadness too. He kept his remarks brief and cool knowing that, if he were to let any emotions creep in, he would fall apart. And so would they.

At 11 PM Saturday night, on WHDH-TV's news, Clancy appeared on video tape with a "few brief valedictory remarks." He thanked the viewers of Boston for their support. He expressed gratitude to the advertisers and to the station's fine staff. If there was any road left by which they could avert the 3 AM sign-off, he said, "We would, even now, be pursuing it. But there is none."

Then he did a notable thing. He expressed the hope that, in the changeover of Channel 5, there would be no inconvenience to viewers.

"I am sure WCVB-TV requires no help from us, but if it does, we stand ready to help in any way—large or small—that we can, so that the public will not be inconvenienced."

WHDH-TV then launched into its final movie, the title of which made its own point: "Fixed Bayonets."

At the Marriott that night the BBI victory party was notably restrained, as though the fight had taken too much out of everyone to give cause for celebration. The twists and turns of the incredible case would be pondered for years. WHDH had been embroiled in this fight for almost twenty-five years. BBI had been in it for ten years. Since then, five of BBI's original stockholders had died. Many careers had been besmirched or ruined. It was not the kind of victory that gave anyone a sense of unrestrained joy.

Of all the key principals in BBI, one of the most important was not there, because he was not invited. He was under a cloud of his own, separated from the affairs of the winners until he cleared himself of charges that remained against him.

Nate David was not in Boston to watch WCVB-TV sign on at 3 AM with a cheery "Hello World!" He and his wife went to California where they could be spared that tortuous ordeal. There, on the Pacific shores, where the tides have their own special rhythm, he could ponder the strange "unrhythm" of the tides of fate and man —and how those tides can turn triumph into disaster in the twinkling of an eye.

PART III

The Aftermath

17

Nathan David Today

The *Herald Traveler* died three months after WHDH-TV signed off the air. The final edition was published Sunday, June 18, 125 years after the first edition was published in 1847.

There were some efforts to keep the paper alive, at least by the owners of stock who lived in New England, or who worked for the company. The paper lost five million dollars in 1971. After the loss of Channel 5, 150 employees were laid off, but these stringent economies were not sufficient. The numbers simply did not add up to the word "survival." A merger between the Hearst *Record-American* and the *Herald Traveler* was the logical solution, but the *Herald Traveler* had now lost its bargaining power. Hearst was able to dictate the terms of the deal which were: 8.64 million for the plant, real estate, good will, circulation, etc.

Estimates say that WHDH-TV, in the years 1963–1971, produced for its parent corporation profits before taxes of 51.5 million dollars. When one adds to that figure the market value of a VHF license in the nation's fifth largest market—estimated at between fifty to sixty million dollars, one begins to understand why the "Hundred Million Dollar Lunch" really cost that, and more.

With the demise of the newspaper, 1500 jobs went down the drain. Most of the 8.64 million went toward severance payments.

What was left was put into a new "WHDH Corporation" which currently owns a moderately profitable AM radio station and a loss-operated FM station.

All the proper obeisances and regrets were paid by media, some regretted with passion, some with indifference. Others heaved a prayerful sigh that: there, but for the grace of God . . .

There was one dissenting voice among the chorus of laments; that being the *Marblehead Messenger* which said that the paper folded because "it wasn't good enough." And that was too bad, said the *Messenger,* because the paper's brass were too busy fighting to keep its TV license. Still, it was to be regretted, the *Messenger* said, because when a paper dies, "the public loses a voice . . . and even in this case, Boston readers have lost the best part of two voices, the *Herald Traveler and the Record-American*'s."

Inevitably, of course, Harold Clancy was forced to walk the plank. He had tried. No one could have fought more tenaciously, or with more guile, or more determination. Had he been able to postpone the takeover six more months, he is still convinced he would have won.

But he lost. So Clancy was paid off and given a trite accolade of praise which went into the minutes of that day's meeting. There had been bad blood between Henry Garfinkle and him prior to the sale of the assets of the newspaper to the *Record-American.* Clancy had resisted Garfinkle's attempt to place two directors on the board.

Garfinkle lost that battle. But he did not lose the next one.

On July 3, Harold Clancy's "resignation" was accepted and he was given a severance deal that he calls "adequate." George Akerson, the wily chairman of the board, and friend of Garfinkle, was permitted to remain at full salary of ninety thousand dollars per year (the same as Clancy's) until August 1, 1973. For another year after that he was to get forty-five thousand dollars, until October 16, 1974. By then, presumably, the corporation would liquidate its remaining assets and close out the corporation.

Shareholders were given a statement that is almost boilerplate in such situations. "The board is continuing to explore what steps should be taken with respect to the remaining assets and business of the corporation . . . and will operate at a modest profit which it is hoped will improve in the future as termination payments are completed and overhead expenses are reduced."

On December 18, 1972, stockholders were told that the corporation foresees no payment of dividends now or in the near future. "The task now is to operate WHDH-AM and WCOZ-FM at maximum profitability and to manage cash reserves for the best interests of stockholders, being extremely careful to preserve tax advantages due the company."

Harold Clancy for a while hung his "legal shingle" in an office in downtown Boston. He has since closed that office for no explained reason except that he has "other plans." While not bitter, (or so he claims) he also admits to not having peace of mind. The "enormity of the injustice" keeps him awake at nights, he says. The personal loss to himself and his family bothers him not nearly so much as does the sense of "sheer injustice" of it all.

There were, and are still, ruminations and fulminations about this famous case. *Boston Magazine* looked at it this way, "We knew it had to happen sooner or later, of course. It didn't take clairvoyance to see that the future lay in the past. It was like a Greek tragedy, the outcome of which can be seen in the flaws and foolish arrogance of the heroes."

The *Phoenix*, in Boston, wrote: "Throughout two decades . . . the fight has always been dirty, low and vicious—with all parties trying to do unto others as was being done unto them. Reputations have been demolished, sometimes with little or no reason."

A Boston journalism review, *More,* called it television's longest running soap opera. "It's hard to believe that what's been going on *really* has been going on. It's as if the script for this case study of the breakdown of American bureaucracy had been devised by Kurt Vonnegut." And, "WHDH-TV goes down in the books as a First: No other company has operated a station, that it didn't really own, for so long and lost it."

One of the most insightful comments was written by Louis M. Kohlmeier in the *Wall Street Journal*. ". . . perhaps the old *Herald Traveler* didn't deserve to live if it couldn't pay its way, and perhaps the subsidization of ailing newspapers by prosperous TV stations generally is unsound economics . . . but these questions never were considered by the FCC and almost nobody expected they would be. It would be unnatural and quite probably illegal for the FCC to involve itself deeply in the life and death of newspapers, except, of course, by accident."

Kohlmeier concluded; "In the final round at the Supreme Court the FCC said that the *Herald Traveler* case presented 'no question of general importance.' That seems a reasonable conclusion, so far as the government is concerned. But it also helps explain the rise of the new populism, and the growing belief that something's wrong somewhere."

In the meantime, what has happened to WCVB-TV? What about its current status at the FCC? Will it, and can it, be challenged by WHDH Corporation, and/or others? How has that station been performing? How long is its license period? And what about the charges remaining before the Commission concerning Nathan David and other matters?

Yes, what about Nate David? And *who* is he?

Nate David was born and raised in Boston. He graduated from Yale with honors in 1934. In 1937 he completed Harvard Law School with magna cum laude honors. In 1939 he joined the FCC where he stayed until 1941 when he transferred to an "office of coordination" which was a cover between the FCC and Wild Bill Donovan's O.S.S. He returned to the FCC in early 1942, stayed there a year and was assistant general counsel when he joined the Navy as an enlisted man. He rose to officer rank and was discharged 2½ years later. After that he put together a private law practice in Washington which was not successful. Neither was his first marriage. He divorced, remarried, and went to Puerto Rico to make his fortune. A farming venture there failed. Several other enterprises did not succeed. He returned to Boston in 1962 because his mother and sister were ailing, and his father, a wealthy Boston antique dealer, was aging and needed his help. He had scarcely signed on with the prestigious Boston law firm of Brown, Rudnick, Freed & Gesmar in September of 1962 when one of that firm's clients, Herbert Hoffman, called attention to the item appearing in the Boston papers announcing that the FCC was inviting other applicants to file for Channel 5. Nate David, because of his FCC experience, was assigned the task of "looking into the matter." It was an incredible coincidence for Messrs. Brown, Rudnick, Freed & Gesmar for Nate David himself, and the other lucky principals who would have the foresight to join what was to become BBI. Nathan David was certainly the right man at the right time in the right place.

On January 10, 1973, after the incredible pressures of the preceding twenty months, Nate David had a severe heart attack. Or rather, on that date, his condition was belatedly diagnosed as such, his doctor telling him that he had "walked through" a serious coronary, the first symptoms of which had occurred three days before the preceding Christmas.

The wonder is, not that he had the attack, but that it did not happen sooner. He was lucky to be alive. Permanent cardiac damage had been done. The time had come, David realized, that he must take stock; take a serious look at his life expectancy. The pressure cooker he lived in had been one of enormous strain ever since the Securities and Exchange Commission had acted against him in 1971; and ever since the Massachusetts Public Utility Commission had filed charges against him on seven counts and three indictments. Subsequently he had been acquitted of two of three of these indictments, but on one, a "blue sky law," he'd been found guilty and fined one thousand dollars for not possessing a broker's license which cost a mere ten dollars. The violation of that blue sky law (which was repealed in May of 1972) seemed to exact a rather stiff fine for a technical violation; in any event, David appealed the conviction, which appeal is still pending. Then there was a spate of civil actions by former "friends"—Messrs. Friedman, Brooks, Power, et al—who charged that Nathan David had wronged them. David filed countercharges. These matters lay backlogged in the courts for perhaps years.

The SEC matter had been scheduled to be heard when David's heart gave out. The case has been postponed ever since because the judge who was to have heard the case has since retired and the SEC seems to be in no hurry to set a new date.

And, as if these problems were not enough, there was the emotional problem concerning the relationship he now had with his former colleagues.

The fact of the matter is that there is *no* relationship. He is ignored by all but one or two. His old friend and colleague, Benny Gaguine, put out the word to his client, BBI, that, in accord with FCC instructions none of its members should have *anything* to do with Nate David until his problems are resolved.

And yet this is the man who, more than any other single individual, is responsible for putting the BBI group together. It was he who spent tireless weeks, months, even years developing the group and the case. He structured the case with the aid of Gaguine and Don Ward. He prepared witnesses for examination during the interminable Sharfman hearing. He prepared briefs and exhibits. Because his legal training, his many years of experience in FCC law, were considered by BBI to be of great value to its cause, he was slated to become executive vice president of the station. Now he was in coventry with the very group he had helped form. This hurt most of all.

There are many opinions about Nate David. Some say he is too smart for his own good. Some say it's easy to dislike him because he is so tough; so demanding; so outspoken. Others say he is a perfectionist; yes, but one who demands no more than he gives. Even his detractors admit that he is a brilliant lawyer and tactician; but a person with little patience with mediocrity.

Yet underneath the surface of this outspoken man there is a strange, contradictory sensitivity that belies him. It is almost as if he were masquerading as the toughest kid on the block because he once got caught reading a volume of Yeats or Eliot.

Considering this quality it is easy to understand why he could not continue to take the pressure indefinitely.

Since the attack, his cardiogram tests have not been reassuring. He was sixty years of age when he was struck down. How much longer does he have to go? His own hard-nosed sense of realism tells him that, if he lives ten more years, he will be fortunate. Therefore he decided that it was time to step out of the main arena.

His family breathed a sigh of relief. They, too, would like the pleasure of his company for a few more years. So, after months of protracted negotiations, Nate David has settled "out of court" so to speak. He has worked out a deal with his former colleagues which guarantees that he will never be active in the management affairs of the station. His fellow shareholders who owe him much will no longer have to be made uneasy by his relentless, driving spirit. He will receive settlement money for the next five years, until he reaches sixty-five; then he will move into a pension status, retaining, of course, his 6.5 percent of stock.

Human destiny and human behavior are a constant surprise package. Money and power are potent forces for divisiveness. Were Nate David's problems too much of a threat to his friends at BBI? Undoubtedly David made some mistakes. Just how serious they were remains to be seen. But, so far, he has been proven guilty on only one minor, technical charge on a law that was seldom, if ever, enforced, and which, less than a year later, was repealed. He insists that the only mistake he made was the mistake of being caught in the powerful pincers of Harold Clancy's well-oiled investigative machine. ("I was the logical target since I was to be EVP of the station.")

No matter. Nate David today is a sick man, another of the numerous permanent victims of the incredible Boston case. David is not sick in the ordinary sense. He looks well. He feels "fine" each day. But he knows his problem. He knows his time can come without warning, and that pushing himself is simply another form of cardiac roulette. He seems to be doing a good job of living with his condition. This is not true of his attractive wife. Violet David still seethes with outrage over this "supreme injustice" that has been done her husband. Her opinions of Harold Clancy, Benny Gaguine, most of the principals of BBI, are hardly printable.

And so, for Nate David, the days go by. He takes each one as it comes. He plans to move from Boston. Maybe he'll go to Florida, maybe California where he has two successful sons. Maybe he'll teach. Whatever he does, it seems likely that, despite his wife's hostility, the two of them will work out their fate together, for it is obvious that they are very much in love.

To some on the BBI board there will be hosannas of relief when Nate David finally gets out of Boston. Others, however, may wonder if they have not lost something. Something like a driving force, a spirit; a turning wheel; a main bearing in a motor. For it was this abrasive, dynamic, cryptic lawyer who structured the basic proposition that BBI stands for today.

In Boston, at BBI, at Channel 5, a ghost of Nathan David will linger long after he is gone. On the other hand, being the kind of fellow he is—tough, resilient, with a high survival factor—Nate David may outlive others on the board. And one gets the fleeting thought that *they* may miss Nate more than he will miss them. And that, instead of slashing away at his ghost, they might better be advised to vote him *back* on the board of directors, if and when the FCC approves, so he can continue to do his thing which, simply stated, would be to make sure that Channel 5 lives up to its promises forever and a day.

After all, the "paper-perfect" proposals of BBI, as surely as this globe is spinning, were to a preponderant extent, the product of Nathan David's skills, his experience, his drive, his dreams for the improvement of broadcasting.

18

WCVB-TV
Today

No matter what happens to Nate David one must take a look—
a separate and objective look—at how the new Channel 5 is performing in Boston today. It now has the license, and a heavy
burden of responsibility rests on its shoulders.

After twenty-two months of operation, one can make all the
standard, obvious comparisons and evaluations, plus a few non-
standard, or subjective comparisons that will be strictly those of the
author and will be so indicated where they appear. Such a study
makes for a fascinating exercise.

How about promise versus performance? Certain of BBI's
"promises" at filing time back in 1964 were so generous, so extensive, that Herb Sharfman virtually ignored them. The four voting commissioners who later overruled Sharfman and awarded the
license to BBI, assessed a demerit against BBI because some of the
promises as to the amount of live programing were considered
"unrealistic."

The station said it would "expect to devote an uncommon proportion of income to improve the quality and extend the range of
locally produced programs."

Has this been done?

At the end of 1972 the station filed with the FCC "Form 324" which is a detailed annual financial report of a licensee. Because WCVB-TV had not signed on the air until March 19, 1972, the report covers only nine months and thirteen days. The bottom line shows that station revenues totaled 10.8 million against expenses of 9.7 million. Profits for that period were $1,069,331. If one extends this to a full year it is reasonable to guess that a twelve-month profit figure would approximate 1.3 million.

Against this, one can compare FCC figures for the Boston market for 1972 which shows a net market profit total of seventeen million. If one assumes that the two independent UHF stations made no profit at all, or very little profit (a reasonable assumption, I believe) the average profit of the three VHF network affiliated stations in 1972 would be, roughly, 5.6 million each.

Thus it appears that WCVB-TV is far off the mark of the other VHF stations and does, indeed, pour 85 to 90 percent of its gross income back into its operation. The profit it took out was little more than sufficient to meet its loan requirements and put aside enough in retained earnings to insure financial viability and to build a reserve for new programs and additional equipment.

In its original filing BBI said it would have two hundred and three full-time employees and four part-time. In its 1972 financial report to the Commission the station disclosed that it had 291 full-time employees, twenty part-time, for a total of three hundred and eleven.

On the issue of integration of management, BBI said in 1964 that it would have thirty stockholders, of which six would be integrated full time into management operations with a stock percentage of 22.76 percent.

Today there are fifty-one stockholders, of which twenty-four owners are integrated into daily operations on a full-time basis, amounting to 28.5 percent of voting stock and 17.9 percent of nonvoting stock. This excludes Nathan David who was to have been a key executive in operations. Also, today, four owners are involved on a part-time basis of eight hours per week or more, while five others serve on the board or as program consultants.

In 1964 it planned seventy-three hours per week of locally produced programs (45 percent), of which 14.6 hours (9 percent) would be repeat programs. After twenty-two months of operation the station has reached a level of fifty-one hours of locally-produced programs, or 34 percent of its broadcast week. And, they say, more is planned. Just how, and when, the station can produce another twenty-two hours of local live programing is a question that is easy to ask and difficult to answer. The present plant, large as it is, already is taxed. The present staff (aided by some impracticable, and inherited, union contracts) also is taxed. But the station *will* find a way to reach seventy-three hours of weekly local live programing for the simple reason that it *must. That is the figure it promised the Commission.*

In 1964 the station proposed to operate twenty-four hours a day, five days a week, Tuesday through Saturday. In the fall of 1973 it achieved that goal. In fact it is off the air only six and one half hours per week! It is the only network affiliated station programing seven days of locally produced programs in the new prime-time access period.

In 1964 the station said, ". . . the interests of the people in the area will be reassessed continuously so that BBI will at all times be responsive to the kinds of programs the audience wants and from which it will benefit most."

Today WCVB-TV has an operative public opinion research unit under the full time direction of Ronald Sturman and designed by Dr. Gerhart D. Wiebe, dean of Boston University's school of public communications. In its first year the station conducted fifteen separate mail and phone studies with survey samples ranging from five hundred to one thousand. Survey questionnaires were mailed to more than 10,500 people with nearly one thousand follow-up telephone interviews.

The editorial department under Philip Balboni consists of an editorial board composed of six station executives and four members of the board. In 1972 it broadcast some sixty editorial topics in varying lengths from thirty seconds to five minutes. General manager of creative services, Richard Burdick, delivers most of the editorials and has had more than one altercation with viewers whom he meets in public places, which perhaps attests to the fact that WCVB-TV does not, as some stations do, editorialize solely for motherhood, public safety, fire prevention, and seldom *against* anything but the man-eating shark. Burdick claims the station broadcasts a 33 percent rate of rebuttals in order to meet its obligation under the fairness doctrine of the FCC.

It has, as it promised, a program advisory board consisting of forty-six community leaders, also a stockholders program policy advisory board consisting of station executives and stockholders.

The station said it would not accept paid political advertising, but would donate time to political candidates. It has done this.

There is another interesting comparison worth noting. In July of 1973 Commissioner Nicholas Johnson bid farewell to his turbulent seven-year term with a report that, while without Commission sanction or validity, did make interesting reading in the industry. He called this report "Broadcasting In America." Over the course of his term, Johnson dissented to most, if not all, bimonthly renewals largely on the basis of the "refusal of the Commission majority to agree to the promulgation of minimum levels of performance in areas of programing and employment." His report, he said, provided a methodology by which every viewer could evaluate the performance of stations in his own home town. A group of Georgetown Law Center seminar students, working with Johnson and his staff, spent six months gathering and analyzing the data. Using information that licensees file with the Commission at renewal time, "Broadcasting In America" ranked stations on a variety of criteria including news and public affairs, commercialization, local programing, employment of minorities and employment of women. Ten tables were shown for network-affiliated stations in the top fifty markets. Independent stations were excluded.

Neither WHDH-TV nor WCVB-TV were included in this report. A footnote in the report explained that WCVB-TV was "just barely into its second year of operation after a Commission and court battle that lasted nearly a decade . . ." Therefore, apparently, a fair comparison could not be made.

It would be interesting to see how WHDH-TV would have fared in the Johnson report.

It also would be interesting to see how the present WCVB-TV looks if it is overlayed on the Johnson report.

According to WCVB-TV, in a study which was made in mid-73, WCVB-TV comes out like this:

In the composite rating of all programing criteria, the Johnson report rates KPIX, a CBS affiliate, San Francisco, as number 1. The two other Boston stations listed show WNAC-TV as number 17, and WBZ-TV as number 31.

Overlaying WCVB-TV on this composite report, and using a 1972–1973 composite week, Channel 5 claims that it precedes KPIX as number 1 by a small margin.

How about ratings performance, that silly, but necessary game of numbers that stations must play if they are to get the highest amount of dollars in advertising revenues?

WCVB-TV claims that eight months after it began operation it was, in terms of percentage increase of viewers and TV homes in all day parts, the most improved ABC affiliate in the top ten markets of the country, which includes ABC's five owned and operated stations; also that, after eight months, it had achieved number one rating status in Boston in prime time seven nights a week.

WNAC-TV disagrees. In March of 1973 it took a full-page ad in a broadcast trade magazine to wish itself happy anniversary as a CBS affiliate, and to say that it is now "first in metro and total market ratings, share of audience, homes reached and total persons viewing."

But skipping all these numbers, claims and comparisons in the area of promise versus performance, let us examine on a subjective basis the impact of today's Channel 5 on the Boston market.

What does the man in the street think of the job it is doing? What do television critics think in the Boston market? What do community leaders think?

And what does Harold Clancy think?

To paraphrase the average viewer, based on personal interviews conducted by the author, the answer would go something like this: "Not bad. But there doesn't seem to be a great deal of difference between the two—the old WHDH-TV and the present WCVB-TV. After all the hullabaloo, Channel 5 today still remains a station that carries network programs that we like. WHDH-TV brought us CBS programs. WCVB-TV brings us ABC programs. The networks, like the stations, are pretty much the same."

This rather sums it up. No matter how zealous, how earnest, no matter how much money a major market VHF plows back into its operation, the average viewer enjoys (or suffers) the reflection of a station's network programs. That's how the system was when BBI filed its original application and it hardly can be otherwise today. BBI as much as admitted this fact in a booklet it circulated at the time it was waging its challenger's battle.

Under the heading: "How Will BBI Be Different?" it said, "Fly into any city. Check into any hotel. Turn on the television. Chances are, at any given hour of the day or night, whatever channel comes in view, in whatever city, the program will be very much the same as that on any other channel in any other city. BBI promises to make a difference. Its station will be a Boston station, transmitting not to an anonymous mass but to people it knows."

Some might call this hapless rhetoric. Nevertheless, the almost fanatical zeal with which BBI goes about its task of setting a new leadership standard in American broadcasting should not be ignored, or put down. It *does* program fifty-one hours a week of local live. It *does* use the valuable prime time access half hour of 7:30 to 8 PM for locally produced live programs. It *does* preempt a certain amount of network time for locally produced specials. It *does* suport a news staff of seventy people, probably the largest of any station in the country. It *does* have two investigative reporting units. It *does* budget $7500 per week for its award-winning children's show, "Jabberwocky," which appears thirty minutes a day, five days a week and is one of the few children's shows commended by ACT (Action For Children's Television). It *does* have the largest creative production staff of any station in the country.

But, despite all this, the man on the street, sadly perhaps, sees the station as a reflection of its network programs, just as he does the other two network-affiliated stations in Boston.

Television critics, who are expected to be more discerning, give WCVB-TV better marks.

Percy Shain, television critic for the *Boston Globe,* uses the word "dedicated" to describe his opinion of Channel 5 today. "It had a long and troublesome break-in period," he said. "But that was to be expected. It is showing constant improvement. I think it is doing more to bring local programs to the community than any other station in the country.

"Channel 5, in terms of excellence of operation, is not as adept as WBZ-TV; nor is it as promotion-oriented as WNAC-TV. But it is the most public-spirited commercial station in the community."

Tony LaCamera, critic for the *Boston Herald American,* gives the station very high marks for its "unprecedented effort in local programing" and thinks that Channel 5 today has already established itself as an industry leader. He notes that Channel 7 has already increased its local live programing in the prime time access strip. In comparing Channel 5 with predecessor, WHDH-TV, LaCamera gives credit to WHDH-TV for having had a "very balanced image, and very strong in sports." Today, he says, sports are more evenly distributed over all Boston stations including the two UHF independents.

He is pleased that Channel 5 does not do one thing that "sends me up the wall." It does not indulge in "happy talk" news.

LaCamera concludes: "WCVB-TV is probably the most community-oriented station in the U.S. today."

Community leaders vary in their opinion. Those in the academic world are ample in their praise of today's Channel 5. Others say it still has a long way to go to equal WGBH-TV, Boston's educational station, long considered to be one of the best, if not *the* best educational station in the United States. Some community leaders with Irish names were, for a time, bitter and rancorous about the loss of WHDH-TV and the *Herald Traveler* because they considered the company to be Irish in character. But these people seem less bitter today. "What the hell, business is business," they now say.

What does Harold Clancy think of Channel 5 today? He says, "For reasons I cannot divulge I prefer *not* to give my opinion of Channel 5 at this time. Do I have opinions? Yes, of course! One day the time will be right for me to give them. I assure you they will make *interesting* reading. On the technical side, I can say that, at the beginning, the station was every bit as bad as one would expect it to be. Since then it has improved, as one would expect it to improve with time and experience. Its improvement was hastened by some 125 technical veterans from WHDH-TV who were hired by WCVB-TV. This cadre, plus the fine news and sports personnel which also were hired from WHDH, constituted a real corps of professionalism for WCVB-TV. Without these people the station would have been in a hell of a fix. And, considering the many rank amateurs the WHDH pros had to work with, it must have been a harrowing initial adjustment for them.

"But as for my real opinion, creatively, conceptually, and professionally, that opinion will have to wait until some future propitious time."

This hedging reply is uncharacteristic of the outspoken Clancy, causing one to wonder if he has plans for the future, choosing now to bide his time until he can select his weapons, his arena and his time for some future bid to regain the license.

What is the author's opinion?

Well, the "look" of WCVB-TV is highly interesting. Its graphics have improved remarkably since it went on the air. Its look is neither commercial, nor educational, but something in between. Its creative work is improving steadily under the capable hands of Dick Burdick. The technique of cinema verité is used a great deal and with improving quality. There is no house genius yet in Burdick's creative stable; but one surely will show up in this kind of atmosphere. The next Billy Friedkin (who came out of WBKB nine years ago to win the Academy Award for *French Connection*) will surely come from Channel 5, if effort, determination, zeal and the law of probability prevail. WCVB-TV's news and sports personalities who switched over from the former WHDH-TV continue to be excellent, as do other additions from other stations. The station has not yet hit the bull's-eye in its investigative reporting effort; but this is not due to lack of trying. I believe they will hit that target eventually. The effort, at present, seems to be somewhat stilted and self-conscious. It seems to lack confidence. Harder hitting is probably what is needed. The investigative unit has covered the usual subjects that one would expect such as pornography, prisons, motor vehicle inspections, urban renewal, campaign spending, drugs, mentally retarded, child abuse and others including high-rise fire safety, alcoholism, homosexuality and suicides. But nowhere in its first eighteen months has the station seen fit to take on Boston's mafia. Perhaps it will.

WCVB-TV's executive staff is excellent. Highly experienced veterans run the station, like: Richard Burdick, Larry Pickard, Eunice West, Joe Ryan, Tom Maney, Jim Miller, Pete Twaddle, Bill Poorvu, Val Conti, Steve DeSatnick, Bill Mockbee, Paul La-Camera, Mike Volpe, Ed Moore, Ronald Sturman, Phil Balboni and others. Many of them come from Bob Bennett's former company, Metromedia; Metro execs, Al Krivin and John Kluge are not exactly ecstatic about that.

The chemistry between Leo Beranek, famous acoustical-science-expert-turned-broadcaster, and Bob Bennett, the affable, but hard-nosed "bottom-line" broadcaster, is surprisingly good. Beranek is not the tweedy stereotype of académician. He is warm, open and extremely astute. Bennett, who came up the hard way through the ranks of tough Metromedia, must have been somewhat horrified when he first learned about BBI's unique game plan. His Scotch-English sense of conservatism must have been offended by the prospect of all those profits going down the drain, or back into the station's operation.

Bill Greeley wrote in *Variety* in mid-72 that perhaps the situation could not last: "All foresee WCVB-TV playing the local game for a year or so, then cautiously returning to the network button and cash-register key like any other sensible men with a license to print money, as it has been called. It takes little perception to suspect that the forecasts are as much hope as prediction."

One broadcast group leader told me, "This is the worst typecasting imaginable—putting Bob Bennett into a situation like that."

"Why?" I asked.

"Because something's got to give. Bennett has, what, three points, or so, of that action? He isn't going to want to see all those profits go down the drain. He'll go along with the game plan for a while, then change it."

I am not so sure. In fact I do not believe it. Bennett happens to love this new game plan. He never had one like it. He has no financial pressures from above. No frantic urging to squeeze more profits out of the operation. And yes, he does have his three points—2.946 percent to be exact—plus an eighty-grand salary with a firm contract for five years. He calls the shots in daily management under Leo Beranek's executive direction, while Dick Burdick calls the shots in the creative area. Never has Bob Bennett had a situation so sweet!

In terms of station morale, one can only say that it is fantastically high. How could it be otherwise when ownership points are spread among twenty-two of the troops, representing 20.283 percent of the company. One gets the feeling that WCVB-TV truly is "their station"; that it does not belong solely to management. The result is they do not merely work like a family, they *are* the family.

On balance, considering all the factors one should, my own bottom line on Channel 5 today is: *the station is good. It can get better. It will get better.*

Now for the first of two "jackpot" questions that everyone asks. The first being, when will WCVB-TV get a firm license?

As of today it operates on the slimmest, most tenuous authority of all—one called a PTA (Program Test Authority). WHDH-TV at least had a four-month license for most of the years of its struggle. Channel 5 today has, in technical terms, even less security than that.

A dozen or more so-called experts claim authorship of the line. "The best FCC license is a temporary one." I don't know who is the real author of that gem—I thought I was until I learned that there are many other claimants. In any event, the line is, of course, inspired by the twenty-five-year-old Boston battle. If a station can keep its license in limbo, and avoid the three-year renewal process, why not go that route?

There is little doubt, however, that the Commission will go that route in this situation. New England stations come up for renewal in April of 1975. I am sure WCVB-TV will be asked to file its renewal forms along with other licensees. Whether it gets a firm license earlier than that date depends on the disposition of the Nathan David matter at the Securities and Exchange Commission.

The FCC said that it will *not* act on a firm license for Channel 5 until Nate David's legal problems are resolved.

Nathan David, however, has been removed from any and all possible involvement directly or indirectly, now or in the future, in the operation of WCVB-TV. With that obstacle removed, the Commission presumably can be expected to readdress itself to the station's Program Test Authority license status. The FCC can do that now, or it can wait until April of 1975 when all Boston TV stations must apply for license renewal. If the Commission is impressed with the station's record . . . if it is satisfied that WCVB-TV has performed creditably and properly under Commission rules and regulations, there is every reason to expect that the station will be given full membership in the "club"—its dues paid, its good standing assured along with other members of the broadcast establishment.

This is not to say, however, that there is not a lingering bitterness and rancor among some of the commissioners who were presiding in the fall of 1973. While there seems to be little staff resistance to the idea of giving WCVB-TV full status, Chairman Dean Burch *still* stands firmly and strongly on his record in which he excoriated the U.S. Court of Appeals for the "unconscionable injustice" it had committed in forcing the Commission to transfer the license. At least one other commissioner is known to have strong feelings akin to Chairman Burch. There may be more. Others at the Commission say that no one has the energy, the courage or the desire to pick up this "hot potato" and try to revive it as an issue—not with so many other pressing issues confronting the FCC and the broadcast industry. Only time will tell.

This leads to "jackpot" question number two. How about claim-jumping, such as a competing application at renewal time or a petition to deny at renewal time, or even before then for that matter—legal gymnastics being the flexible art that it is?

How about WHDH Corporation coming to life and trying to regain its old channel?

That hardly seems likely. What was left of the corporation, still headed by aging George Akerson, and operating only an AM and

FM station, was sold to one of its minority stockholders, John Blair & Company. Blair "represents," or sells time, for radio and TV stations throughout the country. It bought out the other stockholders (a mismatched group if ever there was one). That sale was approved by the FCC in December, 1973, at a price of 10.1 million dollars for 53 percent of the stock. The curious aspect of this matter is that John Blair & Company has a contract with George Akerson that keeps him on as chief executive officer of WHDH at a salary of $90,000! This must be the highest salary ever paid an employee to manage an AM station, or FM station, or both, causing some to wonder if this could have been a price that Blair willingly paid to ensure Akerson's cooperation in swinging other stockholder factions into a selling frame of mind. Certain of these factions were reportedly most unhappy with the Blair-Akerson transaction. The truth is, however, Blair inherited this contract which expires at the end of 1974. The odds are, now that the Commission has approved the Blair purchase of WHDH, that Akerson will quickly be retired, at which time his $180,000 severance contract will go into effect. As chairman of the board, Akerson has taken very good care of Akerson. He remains the last known survivor of the Boston case. He not only survived every palace coup, but he engineered a few of his own. The recent ninety-grand, three-year contract with Blair undoubtedly marks his last hurrah. All things considered, one must judge that during the past twenty-five years, George Akerson has been a remarkably lucky man.

Regarding WCVB-TV, however, only a miracle of events could cause John Blair & Company to put up a fight to regain the license of Channel 5. The Blair management group has reached senior citizen status. There are no young turks who would, or could, convince gentlemanly John Blair to attempt to regain Channel 5.

There remains only one other candidate to consider, Harold Clancy. The ubiquitous, bulldog-determined Harold Clancy.

That is an intriguing notion. Clancy was never directly involved in the top management of WHDH or the *Herald Traveler* during the time of the ill-advised luncheons between Choate and McConnaughey. He was an underling then. He advanced after that period, was later pressed into the main arena to fight the long, desperate, rear guard delaying action that kept WHDH and the newspaper alive longer than anyone had dared to hope. He was not Choate's "boy" as George Akerson was. So he is not personally tainted by the ex parte issue.

What will Clancy do? What is his frame of mind? Well, Clancy won't talk much about that. But one senses that, privately, he is champing at the bit, and that if he could find *any* angle, *any* crack in the door, he might indeed step up and take a healthy swing. Harold Clancy went into an expected emotional tailspin after his defeat. He had pneumonia. He fumbled around for a while, barked at his family and did all the things a strong man would be expected to do after such a bitter loss. But Clancy never once fell into a slough of self-pity. He remains a hard-nosed realist. He *is* bitter, still convinced that he should not have lost the station. He talks with burning conviction about the WHDH filings extant at the FCC—some "thirty or forty affidavits" backing up the filings by WHDH which allege "misrepresentation," "violation of reporting rules," "outside media connections by BBI principals," etc. And these briefs, he is quick to point out, involve not only Nathan David (about whom he has a very low opinion) but other BBI principals. He expresses the ardent hope and conviction that the FCC, when it looks into these matters, will be as "scrupulously consistent in its scrutiny as it was in its examination of WHDH's record."

"I am utterly convinced," he says, "that the greatest miscarriage of justice in the history of broadcasting was committed against WHDH and the *Herald Traveler,* and while it may be too late to repair the damage done to thousands of people, I believe with all my heart that true justice will ultimately prevail, and that one day the wrongs of this evil act will be righted."

Apart from this there is, of course, the chance of "petitions to deny" at renewal time by the usual assortment of public-interest groups who are always lurking behind major market transmitters these days. Some two hundred of these "petitions" have been filed since the Boston decision. About fifty "competing applications" have also been filed since that decision. So, until there is an industry-protective renewal bill, this vexing claim-jumping practice can be expected to continue. But petitions to deny, thus far, have pretty much been exercises in futility; the benefactors, for the most part, being "public-interest" lawyers who make a handsome living from their legal efforts.

But lurking ever in the background is the spectre, the presence, the shadow of one, Harold Clancy.

But Clancy won't talk about any plans that he may have about making a move.

However, the broadcast establishment would welcome . . . would be delighted to see him make such a move. Yet the road would be long and tough.

19

"What's it
all about, Alfie"?

Finally, to paraphrase the song, "What's it all about, Alfie?"

What, indeed, does this twenty-five-year-long case portend? What does it mean? What can we learn from it?

One must begin with the ex parte issue and trace its effect forward from 1963 to the fateful decision of 1969. Despite the fact that the ex parte issue, as argued by Henry Geller before the court of appeals, unquestionably won the case for BBI, that original 1969 decision was based, not on ex parte at all, but on diversification and integration of management. Both of these issues were ones which two commissioners, Bob Bartley and Nick Johnson, felt strongly about—Bartley for as long as he had been a commissioner (seventeen years at that time) and Johnson for as short a period as he had been a commissioner (three years at that time). These men were as different as two men could be. But they agreed on these two issues. Also, their ideological time had come. The political and ideological climate was ideal for their conjoining of forces. They did, they succeeded, and their results caused panic in the industry on the question of what renewal guidelines could be written that would fend off challenges by new applicants. That panic has not subsided, nor has there been a solution to the problem. There have been many proposed solutions. As of December 1, 1973 there were

760 broadcast stations (AM, FM or TV) whose renewals at the FCC were on "deferred status." Of that number, 400 had been in that status for more than two years. Currently there are 250 bills pending before Congress! Two-hundred and twenty-eight in the House and twenty-two in the Senate. The broadcast establishment was desperately trying to lobby its way into a license renewal law that would give it the kind of protection, the insurance, it believed it deserved. The results of this effort indicate a classic proof of the law of diminishing returns: the more it tries, the more problems its efforts beget. Some say the industry has a kind of myopia, that it should be happy with what it has, and that, if it persists in trying to achieve Utopia in protective licensing, it will end up with far less that what it already has.

When discussing what kind of a license renewal bill that will protect broadcasters from another Boston case, the question is asked: what guidelines should be set down? How closely must they be followed by a licensee? How closely should the Commission adjudge such guidelines when a challenger interposes? This package of "confusion" remains as the major fallout of the Boston case, and one which only the future can resolve .

Since the Boston decision there have been approximately fifty competing applications filed at the FCC and some two hundred petitions to deny filed by citizen-action groups. There is no question but that this blizzard of legal briefs was at least partially motivated or inspired by the Boston decision. Broadcasters also believe that this onslaught will continue until the industry has a "proper" license renewal bill.

But what is "proper"? The theme of five-year license renewals runs through most of the 250 bills in the hopper at Congress, not to mention the White House's own bill filed via OTP (Office of Telecommunications Policy). Some bills call for perpetual licensing. Many of them ignore, or dance around, issues of concentration of control; separation of newspapers from stations in the same markets; integration of local ownership; and integration of management. Some bills are so overly protective that they constitute a downright embarrassment to the broadcast establishment.

Torbet H. Macdonald, chairman of the House Subcommittee on

Communications and Power, said at hearings he conducted in 1973, that the problem as he saw it was: ". . . fixing precise legal standards for judging broadcast service . . . A workable definition of serving the public interest, convenience and necessity remains elusive. Every broadcaster claims he does just that and every challenger and petitioner claims the opposite." And, he warned, perhaps, they (the subcommittee) should "resist the temptation to dismantle it."

He wondered aloud why broadcasters were in such a frenzy over the need for a protective license renewal bill when they already are well protected by a motherly FCC. He cited a case subsequent to Boston, called the Moline case, which in the opinion of many legal experts, was more questionable than Boston. He asked: "If a station can promise anything, fulfill none of its promises, and still get a renewal as in the Moline case, why should Congress write something into law that the FCC might not allow anyway?

"A guy has to really try, to really *want* to lose his license," he said.

Commissioner Nick Johnson agreed. "The policy of the Commission is clear," he said. "The incumbent will win unless his behavior is so bad that we would be forced to take away the license even if there were no competing applications."

Chairman Dean Burch, at this hearing, almost agreed with Johnson. If so, it was the first time they ever agreed on anything!

Yes, admitted Burch, the industry has become a "bit insular . . . a bit self-conscious" as a result of the fears perpetrated by the "egregious error" of the Boston decision.

The Boston case also raises the question of whether or not a television station's profits should be allowed to keep a newspaper alive —or, for that matter, *any* other form of media such as an AM or FM radio station, or a cable system. Commission doctrine, until now, has considered this wrong: each media entity must stand on its own two economic feet. History, however, is ignored in such doctrine. In the early days of the establishing of a licensing grid of television stations, many had to be supported by the profits of a newspaper, radio station, theater group or other profitable enterprise. Present history also is ignored when one considers that there are *still* other media entities supporting FCC-licensed stations that operate at a loss. The *New York Times* supports a good music station in New York City. The *Boston Globe* partially supported a losing UHF-TV station in Boston. Field Enterprises, until July of 1973, supported a losing UHF station in Chicago. There are numerous other examples.

This raises the question of what is the "public interest, convenience and necessity"? That fey, imponderable, almost ephemeral term! How does one equate the public service of a daily newspaper in Boston, which also provides an editorial voice in the community, not to mention 1500 jobs—how does one equate that with a station like WCVB-TV which promises (and assuredly will) to plough much of its profit back into the community in terms of more local programs?

Of the two, which is the greater public service? Or, like the sexes themselves, are they equal, but different, with neither having the right to claim superiority over the other?

The *Herald Traveler* went down the drain. But some say, shed no crocodile tears over that fact because the *Herald Traveler* was doomed anyway. Its losses were too great. It was used as a defensive weapon to help fight its long battle. The board would not have countenanced such continuing losses had the battle been won. Robert Choate, they say, was right when he originally planned to sell the paper. At the very least, after the battle had been won (*if* it had been won!) the *Herald Traveler* would have merged with the *Record-American*. Which is precisely what was done, although strictly at Hearst's terms. The *Herald Traveler*'s bargaining position was then nil.

But back to the question: What can we learn from this incredibly complex, obtuse, expensive and lengthy case? Benny Gaguine says: If you fool around with a bull long enough you're bound to get gored. Don Ward says there is no such thing as a "free lunch." But such frivolous answers beg the question. One thing safely can be said, one learns from this case that one should *not* expect *any* kind of consistency from a government agency in a case that spans a long period of time. That is impossible. Political climate changes. Personalities change. Issues change. It becomes a wild, reckless crap game in which the odds of Las Vegas look conservative by comparison.

How about the expiation theory which both Herb Sharfman and Harold Clancy shared in differing degrees? That theory does seem to have limited application. At the staff level of the FCC throughout the long years of litigation there was little, if any, sympathy for WHDH. Not so much perhaps because of the Choate affair, as from a sense of outrage stemming from the general scandals that erupted during the FCC's Whorehouse Era. Conversely, there are those staff members who think that the Choate affair was much *worse* than it had been pictured; that Judge Stern "whitewashed" it; that much more was discussed at the Choate-McConnaughey luncheons than ever was disclosed; that the "fix" was in and the Commission finally rebelled.

Which brings one around full cycle to the 1969 decision where two commissioners took away the license from WHDH-TV, not on ex parte, but on diversification and integration of management. Bartley, a pragmatist, shrugged off ex parte as the kind of thing that one expected during those free-wheeling days. He simply disliked the idea of one medium owning another in the same community. He was joined by a much younger man, Nick Johnson, who sensed that this was his golden opportunity to put to a test—really test—the oft professed, but seldom practiced, guideline doctrine of the FCC which said that diversification and integration of management were *really* important.

What is the augury of this case? What will the future bring?

There are two camps. One believes that the Boston case was truly *sui generis* and that there never will be another major market VHF station taken away by the Commission no matter *what* future renewal guidelines purport to mean. However, this camp would feel much more secure if it could obtain a license renewal bill that *insured* against there ever being another Boston case.

The other camp says: wrong. The Boston case *will* have an effect on future renewal situations regardless of what kind of license renewal bill eventually is promulgated. These advocates are avidly and nervously watching every current renewal challenge to see how the Boston case creeps into law. This camp says that Boston *will* have a precedential effect on TV licensing for years to come. As an example, they point to the latest decision of the FCC involving another long-standing major market station challenge. The Commission recently overruled Hearing Examiner Thomas Donahue who, in 1969, recommended that the license of Channel 9, Los Angeles, be taken away from licensee, KHJ-TV, owned by RKO General, Inc., and given to challenger Fidelity Television, Inc. The Commission, in December, 1973, voted three to two (with two abstaining) to renew KHJ-TV's license. Commissioner Rex Lee wrote a strong and scholarly dissent just before he resigned. Commissioner Nick Johnson, also just before resigning, wrote the strongest dissent he has ever written. As he was packing his personal belongings to go back to his home of Iowa to run for Congress, he excoriated the decision with an opening paragraph that went: "Today's decision . . . may very well be the worst decision of this Commission during my term of seven years and five months."

The scenario that may follow could go something like this: Fidelity, of course, will appeal—has, in fact, already appealed *directly* to the U.S. Court of Appeals. If that court retains control as it did in the Boston case, and if it orders the Commission to construct a different resolution, all of the factors that maintained in the Boston case will exist once again. Five years from now, or ten, after new hearings and innumerable appeals . . . after the usual, and probably futile, appeal to the Supreme Court, the final result very well could be that a *second* major market VHF station will be taken away and granted to a challenger.

Where is the precedent in law? In 1969, when Hearing Examiner Donahue opted for Fidelity, he used the WHDH-TV decision as a precedent. He said it was "the only contemporary precedent" that could lend support and credence to his action.

Is it any wonder then that this camp declares the other camp to be wrong?

And what if this second camp *is* wrong? What if—as a result of the Boston case and the overkill of protection resulting from it—what if *no* other major station is *ever* taken away under present or future guidelines?

What then?

That, indeed, is the sixty-four thousand dollar question. No. The one hundred million dollar question! There are those who believe that if this becomes the Commission's way of the future, then one thing becomes tragically clear: The present wave of renewal challengers is the greatest ripoff in the history of communications. The culprits being 1) opportunistic law firms; 2) naive, gullible innocents who call themselves "public interest groups"; 3) and finally, a laissez-faire Commission itself which will have abandoned its regulatory mission; will have relinquished its authority to the U.S. Court of Appeals which will resolutely carry out the Commission's work.

There is an old Rumanian proverb: The dog becomes prisoner of the flea. And a more modern political maxim: Government regulatory agencies become prisoners of the industries they are supposed to regulate.

One result of this 25 year legal phantasmagoria is inescapably clear, BBI made some very "heavy" promises in its original application. So heavy, in fact, it was given a "demerit" for making promises so glowing that they were deemed excessive and impossible to fulfill, both by Examiner Sharfman and the voting commissioners. Such things as twenty-four hour per day operation five days a week; 36 percent local live; widely integrated management; much of the profits ploughed back into the operation; no paid political or religious programs; 25 percent of ownership invested in key executive personnel; and others.

Now WCVB-TV must live up to those promises.

There is no doubt that it will.

In doing so, however, it will be creating a kind of tidal wave in the industry. For, inevitably, the Commission—not to mention the public, press and advertisers—are going to join together and say to the rest of the broadcast stations in the U.S.: look at what that station in Boston is doing.

And the Commission is going to say, if it can be done in Boston, why not elsewhere—at least in the top ten markets where the profit leverage is enormous; where stations enjoy profit ratios in the 40 to 50 percent range, higher than any other business in the world!

And so the Commissioner will make some new rules on what is

considered good performance. And WCVB-TV, whether it had intended to do so or not, will find that it has been projected as the landmark station of a new and better television. Some will nervously eye its performance and hope that it fails; others will be hoping that it succeeds beyond all expectations.

The odds are that WCVB-TV will succeed and that, as a result, other major market stations will have to change, whether they like it or not—and for the better.

20

Bob Bennett
Reflects

Bob Bennett, general manager and vice president of operations at WCVB-TV, talking over a scotch after a busy day said, "I remember what TV was like in the early days, in Los Angeles where I got my start—like in the late forties, early fifties. Klaus Landsberg, remember him? Live remotes every time a building caught fire. The Kathy Fiscus tragedy. Remotes every night. No networks then. So we scrambled. God, how we scrambled! But what fun it was. We really thought we were part of a communications miracle. Sure we were on an ego trip in those days. It had to be—no one got paid very much. Then the excitement disappeared from the business. TV became "organized," systematized. efficiency intense, mass oriented. Those of us who were in the game went along because, by then, we were locked in. We had no place else to go, or else we didn't have the balls to leave. I guess that's why I took this mad gamble with WCVB-TV. I can tell you, so far, no regrets. Because it's like the old days are back. That excitement is back. The adrenalin flows each day. Most guys don't feel that way much anymore at other stations. But here, yes, it's really like the old days, the way we thought television was going to be. When you think of it, TV is still kind of a miracle. We shouldn't take it for granted . . ."